Anthony Trollope's Late Style

Edinburgh Critical Studies in Victorian Culture

Series Editor: Julian Wolfreys

Volumes available in the series:

In Lady Audley's Shadow: Mary Elizabeth Braddon and Victorian Literary Genres
Saverio Tomaiuolo

Blasted Literature: Victorian Political Fiction and the Shock of Modernism
Deaglán Ó Donghaile

William Morris and the Idea of Community: Romance, History and Propaganda, 1880–1914
Anna Vaninskaya

1895: Drama, Disaster and Disgrace in Late Victorian Britain
Nicholas Freeman

Determined Spirits: Eugenics, Heredity and Racial Regeneration in Anglo-American Spiritualist Writing, 1848–1930
Christine Ferguson

Dickens's London: Perception, Subjectivity and Phenomenal Urban Multiplicity
Julian Wolfreys

Re-Imagining the 'Dark Continent' in fin de siècle *Literature*
Robbie McLaughlan

Roomscape: Women Readers in the British Museum from George Eliot to Virginia Woolf
Susan David Bernstein

Women and the Railway, 1850–1915
Anna Despotopoulou

Walter Pater: Individualism and Aesthetic Philosophy
Kate Hext

London's Underground Spaces: Representing the Victorian City, 1840–1915
Haewon Hwang

Moving Images: Nineteenth-Century Reading and Screen Practices
Helen Groth

Jane Morris: The Burden of History
Wendy Parkins

Thomas Hardy's Legal Fictions
Trish Ferguson

Exploring Victorian Travel Literature: Disease, Race and Climate
Jessica Howell

Spirit Becomes Matter: The Brontës, George Eliot, Nietzsche
Henry Staten

Rudyard Kipling's Fiction: Mapping Psychic Spaces
Lizzy Welby

The Decadent Image: The Poetry of Wilde, Symons and Dowson
Kostas Boyiopoulos

British India and Victorian Literary Culture
Máire ní Fhlathúin

Anthony Trollope's Late Style: Victorian Liberalism and Literary Form
Frederik Van Dam

Forthcoming volumes:

Her Father's Name: Gender, Theatricality and Spiritualism in Florence Marryat's Fiction
Tatiana Kontou

The Sculptural Body in Victorian Literature: Encrypted Sexualities
Patricia Pulham

Visit the Edinburgh Critical Studies in Victorian Culture web page at
www.euppublishing.com/series/ecve

Also available:
Victoriographies – A Journal of Nineteenth-Century Writing, 1790–1914, edited by Julian Wolfreys
ISSN: 2044-2416
www.eupjournals.com/vic

Anthony Trollope's Late Style

Victorian Liberalism and Literary Form

Frederik Van Dam

EDINBURGH
University Press

For Shari

Edinburgh University Press Ltd
The Tun – Holyrood Road
12(2f) Jackson's Entry
Edinburgh EH8 8PJ

First published in hardback by Edinburgh University Press 2016

www.euppublishing.com

Typeset in 10.5/13 Sabon by
Servis Filmsetting Ltd, Stockport, Cheshire,
and printed and bound in Great Britain by
CPI Group (UK) Ltd, Croydon CR0 4YY

A CIP record for this book is available from the
British Library

ISBN 978 0 7486 9955 1 (hardback)
ISBN 978 1 4744 2605 3 (paperback)
ISBN 978 0 7486 9956 8 (webready PDF)
ISBN 978 1 4744 1077 9 (epub)

Contents

Series Editor's Preface

'Victorian' is a term, at once indicative of a strongly determined concept and an often notoriously vague notion, emptied of all meaningful content by the many journalistic misconceptions that persist about the inhabitants and cultures of the British Isles and Victoria's Empire in the nineteenth century. As such, it has become a by-word for the assumption of various, often contradictory habits of thought, belief, behaviour and perceptions. Victorian studies and studies in nineteenth-century literature and culture have, from their institutional inception, questioned narrowness of presumption, pushed at the limits of the nominal definition, and have sought to question the very grounds on which the unreflective perception of the so-called Victorian has been built; and so they continue to do. Victorian and nineteenth-century studies of literature and culture maintain a breadth and diversity of interest, of focus and inquiry, in an interrogative and intellectually open-minded and challenging manner, which are equal to the exploration and inquisitiveness of its subjects. Many of the questions asked by scholars and researchers of the innumerable productions of nineteenth-century society actively put into suspension the clichés and stereotypes of 'Victorianism', whether the approach has been sustained by historical, scientific, philosophical, empirical, ideological or theoretical concerns; indeed, it would be incorrect to assume that each of these approaches to the idea of the Victorian has been, or has remained, in the main exclusive, sealed off from the interests and engagements of other approaches. A vital interdisciplinarity has been pursued and embraced, for the most part, even as there has been contest and debate amongst Victorianists, pursued with as much fervour as the affirmative exploration between different disciplines and differing epistemologies put to work in the service of reading the nineteenth century.

Edinburgh Critical Studies in Victorian Culture aims to take up both the debates and the inventive approaches and departures from convention that studies in the nineteenth century have witnessed for the last half century at least. Aiming to maintain a 'Victorian' (in the most positive sense of that motif) spirit of inquiry, the series' purpose is to continue and augment the cross-fertilisation of interdisciplinary approaches, and to offer, in addition, a number of timely and untimely revisions of Victorian literature, culture, history and identity. At the same time, the series will ask questions concerning what has been missed or improperly received, misread, or not read at all, in order to present a multi-faceted and heterogeneous kaleidoscope of representations. Drawing on the most provocative, thoughtful and original research, the series will seek to prod at the notion of the 'Victorian', and in so doing, principally through theoretically and epistemologically sophisticated close readings of the historicity of literature and culture in the nineteenth century, to offer the reader provocative insights into a world that is at once overly familiar, and irreducibly different, other and strange. Working from original sources, primary documents and recent interdisciplinary theoretical models, Edinburgh Critical Studies in Victorian Culture seeks not simply to push at the boundaries of research in the nineteenth century, but also to inaugurate the persistent erasure and provisional, strategic redrawing of those borders.

Julian Wolfreys

Acknowledgements

I have become indebted to so many friends and colleagues that behind every thought in this book there are resonances and reverberations of their words. Ortwin de Graef has been my first reader since he introduced me to Trollope, nine years ago now. I cannot say how grateful I am for his constant intellectual, moral, and practical support. Lauren M. E. Goodlad, too, has been with this book from the beginning; her careful and observant reading of its preliminary drafts was invaluable. To Julian Wolfreys I owe a particular debt for encouraging me to undertake this project and for the enthusiasm with which he has shared his experience and expertise. Although all the faults that remain are my own, I am grateful to the following colleagues who kindly agreed to read and review particular chapters and who have saved me from errors: Rachel Baldacchino, Gert Buelens, Raphaël Ingelbien, Luca Caddia, Jan Vanvelk, Nigel Starck, and, especially, Pieter Vermeulen. My colleagues in the department of literary studies at the University of Leuven have supported my work in various ways: in particular, I must thank Jan Baetens, Sascha Bru, Brecht de Groote, Arne De Winde, Elke D'hoker, Stephanie Eggermont, Anke Gilleir, Sientje Maes, Bart Philipsen, Hedwig Schwall, and Tom Toremans. Outside of Leuven, I have had the good fortune to work with Gordon Bigelow, Silvana Colella, Simon Grennan, J. Hillis Miller, Hedwig Schwall, Julia Thomas, and Michael Williamson. Regenia Gagnier and David Skilton have kindly acted as mentors ever since we met.

This book would never have been written without the generous doctoral and postdoctoral fellowships granted by the Flemish Research Council (FWO) and the University of Leuven's Special Research Fund (BOF). My deepest thanks go to the various committees and the anonymous readers who reviewed my applications. Without the freedom that these fellowships provided, I could never have embarked upon this project. I also thank the Flemish Research Council for awarding me with a travel grant for a research stay at the University of Oxford, which was also assisted by a bursary of the Paul Druwé Fund. Helen Small's individual guidance was a formative influence; I would also like to thank Stefano Evangelista, Robert Douglas-Fairhurst, Roy Foster, and Andrew Miller for their judicious advice. I have presented the germs of this project at the University of Sheffield, the University of Exeter, Columbia University, the University of Liverpool, the University of Birmingham, Wolfson College Oxford, University College Brussels, the Hebrew University of Jerusalem, and Ca' Foscari University of Venice. I thank the organisers of these conferences for their invitations and the audience members for helping me refine my ideas. Finally, this book would never have seen the light of day without the superb support of Jackie Jones and her team at Edinburgh University Press.

Thanks are also due to the editors and anonymous reviewers of two texts written while this book was still in its infancy. Chapter seven includes material that was previously published in *Literature Compass* 9.11 (2012): 801–12 under the title 'Victorian Instincts: Anthony Trollope and the Philosophy of Law' (© 2012 Blackwell Publishing Ltd). I thank Blackwell Publishing for permission to reproduce parts of this article and I gratefully acknowledge the help I received from Kate Foster-Carter, the issue's editor. I thank the Hebrew University of Jerusalem Press and Johns Hopkins University Press for permission to reproduce sections of '"Wholesome Lessons": Love as Tact Between Matthew Arnold and Anthony Trollope', which appeared in *Partial Answers* 12.2 (2014): 287–310, and which is fleshed out more fully in chapters eight and nine. Leona Toker went beyond the call of duty in her swift and caring guidance.

My greatest debt is to my family. Nothing would seem possible or worthwhile without Shari, to whom *Anthony Trollope's Late Style* is dedicated. I completed the book after the birth of our son, Phineas: his presence has made this period the happiest of my life.

Note on Editions and Dates

With a few exceptions, I have made use of the collected works published by the Trollope Society and edited by David Skilton; details will be found in the bibliography. For ease of reference, I am here presenting an alphabetical overview of Trollope's books, which the reader may wish to consult to find the date of their first appearance in print; the publication dates of books by Trollope's contemporaries have been included in the body of the text.

The American Senator (1877)
Australia and New Zealand (1873)
An Autobiography (1883)
Ayala's Angel (1881)
Barchester Towers (1857)
The Belton Estate (1866)
The Bertrams (1859)
Can You Forgive Her? (1865)
Castle Richmond (1860)
The Claverings (1867)
Clergymen of the Church of England (1866)
The Commentaries of Caesar (1870)
Cousin Henry (1879)
Doctor Thorne (1858)
The Duke's Children (1880)
The Eustace Diamonds (1872, dated 1873)
An Eye for an Eye (1879)
The Fixed Period (1882)
Framley Parsonage (1861)
The Golden Lion of Granpère (1872)
Harry Heathcote of Gangoil (1874)
Sir Harry Hotspur of Humblethwaite (1871)

He Knew He Was Right (1869)
Hunting Sketches (1865)
Is He Popenjoy? (1878)
John Caldigate (1879)
The Kellys and the O'Kellys (1848)
Kept in the Dark (1882)
Lady Anna (1874)
The Landleaguers (1883)
The Last Chronicle of Barset (1867)
The Life of Cicero (1880)
Linda Tressel (1868)
London Tradesmen (1880)
Lord Palmerston (1882)
The Macdermots of Ballycloran (1847)
Marion Fay (1882)
Miss Mackenzie (1865)
Nina Balatka (1867)
North America (1862)
An Old Man's Love (1884)
Orley Farm (1862)
Phineas Finn (1869)
Phineas Redux (1874)
Rachel Ray (1863)
Ralph the Heir (1871)
Mr Scarborough's Family (1883)
The Small House at Allington (1864)
South Africa (1878)
The Struggles of Brown, Jones & Robinson (1862)
Thackeray (1879)
The Three Clerks (1858)
Travelling Sketches (1866)
La Vendée: An Historical Romance (1850)
The Vicar of Bullhampton (1870)
The Warden (1855)
The Way We Live Now (1875)
The West Indies and the Spanish Main (1859)
Dr Wortle's School (1881)

Chapter 1

Introduction: Trollope's Late Modernity

> For the most part, . . . he should be judged by the productions of the first half of his career; later, the strong wine was rather too copiously watered. His practice, his acquired facility, were such, that his hand went of itself, as it were, and the thing looked superficially like a fresh inspiration. But it was not fresh, it was rather stale; and though there was no appearance of effort, there was a fatal dryness of texture. Some of these ultimate compositions – *Phineas Redux* (*Phineas Finn* is much better), *The Prime Minister*, *John Caldigate*, *The American Senator*, *The Duke's Children* – have the strangest mechanical movement. (James 1883: 391)

Dismissing Anthony Trollope's late novels as artistically flawed, Henry James's obituary captures the tone of earlier and subsequent criticism. Stripped of its evaluative tenor, however, James's discernment of a 'stale' quality and 'dryness of texture' in Trollope's novels from *Phineas Redux* onward touches on the essence of Trollope's late style.[1] Two models can be discerned in thinking about late style: in the first the late work is understood as providing a serene conclusion to the artist's career, while in the second the late work is presented as a restless departure from earlier efforts. Sophocles and Shakespeare are often nominated as the masters of the resolution, Hölderlin and Beethoven of the withdrawal. James's imagery suggests that the late Trollope should be included in the fold of the latter: Theodor Adorno describes Beethoven's late compositions in similar terms, as 'wrinkled, even fissured. They are apt to lack sweetness, fending off with prickly tartness those interested merely in sampling them' (Adorno 2005: 123). In the case of Beethoven's *Spätstil*, this harsh quality is the result of the formal laws that his late works obey. Combining complex polyphonic structures with trite ornaments, their style is impersonal and artificial, rather than spontaneous and organic. The role of conventions is essential in creating this effect. Even where Beethoven's late works use a singular syntax, 'conventional formulae and phraseology are inserted. They are full of decorative trills, cadences, and fiorituras' (Adorno 2005: 124).[2] Although the intellectual and artistic differences between Beethoven and Trollope make an extensive comparison fruitless, it is remarkable that the texture of Trollope's late works, too, is both heavily patterned and shot through with flourishes. Marked by 'the strangest mechanical movement', as James puts it, their idiom is conventional to a fault: in one way or another, many of them obsessively rephrase the same idea, thought, or scene. This study sets out to disassemble and inspect the formal laws which sustain the late novels' mechanical movement. Rather than tracing their flair for formulae to Trollope's prolifigacy, however, it suggests that the centrality of conventions in Trollope's late works was part of a new aesthetic with which he sought to express his revised understanding of the world in the final decade of his life.

This temporal demarcation notwithstanding, 'late' is here used in a critical rather than a biographical sense. Although lateness tends to be associated with an artist's last works, late style and old age are not necessarily synonymous: 'though the proximity of the artist to the end of his or her life was seen to be its prompt, it is not obvious that for Adorno the connection to time of life need be more than metaphorical or analogical' (Small 2007: 183).[3] Trollope's oeuvre is a case in point: the stylistic appeal of the artificial and the conventional is also apparent in his earlier works. Instead of crafting original metaphors in the manner of Dickens, Trollope's fiction gains its power from his tendency to mix 'colloquialism, mottoes, maxims, platitudes, cliché and tag lines' (Langbauer 1999: 97), thus forging a language which seems to rest on proverbs but which is, when closely considered, idiosyncratic. Another sign of Trollope's lifelong inclination to late style is his emphasis on 'patterns of repetition' that 'push toward a sense of conceptual overdetermination, forcing a single word to bear the weight of multiple meanings and cumulative discriminations' (Sussman 2013: 885). Nevertheless, Trollope's attraction to the accoutrements of late style came to the fore especially in the final decade of his life. It is to Trollope's changed perception of modernity that this intensification must be traced.

For the purposes of this book's argument, it suffices to define modernity as the historical emergence and growth of free will and individual agency.[4] Modernity, in this view, rests on a strong belief in the inevitability of progress; it is 'an ongoing achievement of consciousness with intimate effects on character and on ethical life' (A. Anderson 2005: 200). Although the inception of this ongoing achievement is a debatable subject, one can more or less safely posit that it began in the humanism of the Renaissance and culminated in the rationalism of the Enlightenment. Late style checks this teleological movement because it questions the assumption that subjects can really penetrate the remotest corners of their inner minds.[5] As such, late style is a reaction against modernity or, more precisely, an intervention within it. If in the works of his mature period Beethoven crafts original, inventive idioms with which he shares his thoughts and feelings, for instance, in his late works he defamiliarises those idioms his listeners already know, presenting them with an enigma or contradiction that lies in a layer beyond conscious perception: Beethoven's late style 'aims not so much to purify the musical language of its empty phrases, as to liberate these phrases from the illusion of subjective control: the emancipated phrase, released from the dynamic flow, speaks for itself' (Adorno 2005: 125). By thus effacing the individual element, the late works of Beethoven challenge the concepts of autonomy and individualism that are the beating heart of modernity. Trollope achieves a similar effect through his play with repetition and with turns of phrase, which 'can work in powerfully compacted ways to convey an essential and disturbing hollowness both to linguistic exchange and subjective experience' (Bowen 2011: xxv), and through his aversion towards sympathy as it is normally understood: 'He presents his reader not with familiarly difficult cases of Victorian characterisation defined by narrow or excessive self-interest, but with examples of inadequate self-interest – more than that, examples of persistent resistance to external solicitation that there should be a *sufficient* self-interest. We are, as a result, provoked to a strong temptation to disregard character autonomy' (Small 2012: 413).[6] Trollope's late works take these elements in his art to new heights.

This challenge to individualism has ideological implications, for the emergence of modern subjectivity occurred in tandem with a number of related phenomena such as, among others, the rise of capitalism, of the bourgeoisie as the ruling political class, and of liberalism as this class's political philosophy. As Adorno and Horkheimer argue in *Dialectic of Enlightenment* and Jürgen Habermas demonstrates in his more generous assessment, *The Structural Transformation of the Public Sphere*, capitalism should be understood as a material counterpart to the epistemological idea of an ongoing achievement of consciousness (Adorno and Horkheimer 1972; Habermas 1989). Late style is therefore also a political statement: 'it is the name Adorno (in his late twenties and early thirties) gave to the "authentic" response of artistic form to late capitalism' (Small 2007: 183). For the critics of the Frankfurt School, 'late capitalism' generally refers 'to the form of capitalism that came to the fore in the modernist period and now dominates our own postmodern culture' (Felluga 2015: 161); in this late stage, there is an 'interpenetration of government and big business' and capital shows signs of being globalised (Jameson 1991: xviii). As Adorno's interest in Beethoven's late style suggests, however, responses to the form of late capitalism were already articulated or anticipated in the nineteenth century. For Trollope's novels written between his return to Britain from a visit to Australia in 1872 and his death in 1882, this hypothesis does not have to be tentative, since in the first of these novels, *The Way We Live Now*, he identifies the logic of late capitalism with unflinching candour: 'Ambitious parvenus and speculators create vicious excesses of capitalism and competitive individualism, but the ultimate responsibility for the bad new world lies with the "established" people, whose incompetence and selfishness disgust Trollope' (Polhemus 1968: 186).

Capitalism in *The Way We Live Now*

The decade in which Trollope's interest in late style intensified, the 1870s, was marked by a number of economic upheavals, such as the rise of gentlemanly capitalism under a conservative government, the onset of the Long Depression, and the emergence of a new economic paradigm, the theory of marginalism. Written in 1873 and published in 1875, *The Way We Live Now* confronts these issues explicitly and is, as such, a self-aware statement about the onset of late capitalism. As Trollope himself professes, the novel was conceived as an attack on the bourgeois belief in progress. Although he does not go as far as Thomas Carlyle and John Ruskin to claim 'that the general grand result of increased intelligence is a tendency to deterioration', he does wonder whether 'a world, retrograding from day to day in honesty [can] be considered to be in a state of progress' (Trollope 1999a: 345).

On one level of his narrative, this question takes the form of an invective against one of the precursors to the kind of state capitalism that the Frankfurt School criticised, so-called 'gentlemanly capitalism', also known as business imperialism or informal imperialism. This early form of late capitalism has been theorised most powerfully by P. J. Cain and A. G. Hopkins, who revolutionised the study of imperialism by displacing 'seizure of territory from its heretofore fundamental position, viewing it as a sometimes necessary adjunct to . . . the extension of the British service sector – which includes banking, transportation, communications, and insurance' (see Cain and Hopkins 1993; Schmitt 2009: 188).[7] In their view, the settler's work in Australia and the soldier's presence in India must be viewed alongside trade relations with Japan and China, investments in North American railways, and the bankrolling of South American republics. Trollope provides a vignette of this partnership of finance and imperialism in his description of the 'Great Financier', Augustus Melmotte:

> He was the head and front of the railway which was to regenerate Mexico. It was presumed that the contemplated line from ocean to ocean across British America would become a fact in his hands. It was he who was to enter into terms with the Emperor of China for farming the tea-fields of that vast country. He was already in treaty with Russia for a railway from Moscow to Khiva. He had a fleet – or soon would have a fleet of emigrant ships – ready to carry every discontented Irishman out of Ireland to whatever quarter of the globe the Milesian might choose for the exercise of his political principles. It was known that he had already floated a company for laying down a submarine wire from Penzance to Point de Galle, round the Cape of Good Hope – so that, in the event of general wars, England need be dependent on no other country for its communications with India. And then there was the philanthropic scheme for buying the liberty of the Arabian fellahs from the Khedive of Egypt for thirty millions sterling. (Trollope 1992: 368)

A second way in which the novel directly refers to the nature of late capitalism is evident in its representation of the stock market. Throughout the novel, ready money rarely exchanges hands: 'It was a part of the charm of all dealings with this great man that no ready money seemed ever to be necessary for anything. Great purchases were made and great transactions apparently completed without the signing even of a cheque' (1992: 376). This reflects the fact that capitalism found itself at a phase of financial expansion 'in which capital sets itself free to breed money from money' (Baucom 2005: 36).[8] More particularly, Melmotte's activities are a sign of the Long Depression, a long period of stagnation which followed the collapse of the Vienna Stock Exchange on 9 May 1873 and which for some countries only died down at the turn of the century.[9] *The Way We Live Now* was written in the wake of this catastrophe; Trollope's working plans reveal that he began the novel on 1 July and finished it on 22 December 1873 (Sutherland 1982). The novel itself does not describe the panic as it was unfolding, however, but is set on the eve of the catastrophe, tracing its origins in the portrayal of Melmotte's rise and fall. When Melmotte is first introduced, the reader is told 'that he had endeavoured to establish himself in Vienna, but had been warned away by the police; and that he had at length found that British freedom would alone allow him to enjoy, without persecution, the fruits of his industry' (Trollope 1992: 27). Moving from Vienna to Paris to London, Melmotte is slowly infecting the European centres of finance. Having successfully re-established himself in Britain, he finds that his fortunes take a turn for the worse after he undertakes to host a dinner for the Emperor of China. When word gets abroad that Melmotte has forged the title deeds to an estate he has bought, the value of the tickets for the event drops abruptly: 'The Melmotte tickets were certainly ruling very high. They had just culminated. They fell a little soon afterwards, and at ten p.m. on the night of the entertainment were hardly worth anything. At the moment which we have now in hand, there was a rush for them' (1992: 500). As metaphors for Melmotte's actual goods, shares, and scrip, these tickets reveal that the correspondence between things and their value is no longer tied to any objective standard.

The perceived lack of a stable correspondence was further heightened by the rise of a new economic paradigm. If the emergence of gentlemanly capitalism in an era of financial catastrophes provided the incentive for Trollope's turn to late style, there is a third contextual factor that explains more fully why this turn was accompanied by an interest in the effacement of individuality. In the 1870s, the publication of William Stanley Jevons's *The Theory of Political Economy* (1871) finally gave marginalism the upper hand in its struggle against the ideas of classical political economy. This struggle can be summarised as a clash between a theory of labour and a theory of utility. In the thinking of the classical economists of the Enlightenment such as John Locke and Adam Smith, value is a secondary category determined by 'the quantity of labour that one might exchange for the production of a commodity in the market' (Bigelow 2003: 51). For a neo-classical economist like Jevons, in contrast, value is determined by the utility of a commodity in a given context: it is a function of the autonomous influence of demand upon the cost of production. In this system, value is not a derivative function, but a motivating force. Gordon Bigelow argues that the shift between these two paradigms in the nineteenth century was accompanied by attendant changes in the philosophical conception of human subjectivity. Working within a Lockean empiricism and maintaining that desire is determined by experience and sensations, Smith and Ricardo believed human nature to be 'eminently pliable, subject to market forces which could be manipulated from London' (Bigelow 2003: 53). Jevons's cast of mind, in contrast, is Kantian. He presumes that desires are ingrained, fixed, 'reified, a stable point of agency that pre-exists and authors the market's "meanings"' (Bigelow 2003: 57). Instead of addressing subjects as producers, neo-classical economists address them as consumers, whose desires and wishes can be quantified within a mechanical system of curves – of supply and demand, cost and production, wages and employment, interest rates and profit – that intersect in points of equilibrium. As such, the economy is differentiated from other spheres of life: unlike political economists, marginalists argue that the economy functions 'apart from cultural or psychological or political considerations' (Bigelow 2003: 3). *The Way We Live Now* takes issue with these tenets even as it incorporates them into its form.

First of all, the novel sketches the world of the economy as distinct from everyday reality: it has become the prerogative of experts. Even though he has been invited to be a director of the English Board of the South Central Pacific and Mexican Railway, Sir Felix Carbury initially does not understand why he should not be paid. Slowly, however, it dawns on him that if he injects capital, he too 'could realise a perennial income, buying and selling' (Trollope 1992: 290). Just as Sir Felix does not understand how or why this system works, so most characters seem to have lost the power of judgement; Mr Longestaffe, for instance, reflects that he 'had been taught to believe that if he could get the necromancer even to look at his affairs everything would be made right for him' (1992: 103). Only Paul Montague, who has been drawn into Melmotte's scheme because he is bound to Melmotte's partner, Fisker, is reasonably anxious to understand what the company is doing. In *The Way We Live Now*, the economy has become a sphere disconnected from daily life, inaccessible to outsiders.

At the same time, most characters have unconsciously internalised their position as economic beings. Throughout the novel, men think of women and women think of themselves – or are told to think of themselves – as commodities, as goods whose value depends on the market, not their inherent qualities.[10] With a perverse inclination to ignore her own miserable past, Lady Carbury admonishes her daughter Henrietta to accept her cousin's proposal, thus following in her footsteps and marrying for comfort. Marie Melmotte, the heiress of the day, finds herself in worse straits: after the family's migration from Paris to London, she is 'at once thrown into the matrimonial market. No part of her life had been more disagreeable to her, more frightful, than the first months in which she had been trafficked for by the Nidderdales and Grassloughs' (1992: 96). This theme receives its most powerful elaboration in the story of Georgiana Longestaffe, who is noble but poor, which makes her mission in life to find a suitable husband well-nigh impossible. When her prospects continue to worsen, she engages herself to Mr Brehgert, a Jewish banker. Georgiana Longestaffe thinks that she is doing him a favour because of her status, manners, education, and beauty:

> Miss Longestaffe was a girl possessing considerable discrimination, and was able to weigh her own possessions in just scales. She had begun life with very high aspirations, believing in her own beauty, in her mother's fashion, and her father's fortune . . . But now she was aware that hitherto she had always fixed her price a little too high. On three things she was still determined – that

> she would not be poor, that she would not be banished from London, and that she would not be an old maid. (1992: 505)

The kind of cultural and social capital that Georgiana Longestaffe here imagines herself to possess is of little value to Brehgert, however. For Brehgert, the prospect of companionship and family life seem to be the most important thing she can offer. She, however, is horrified when Brehgert expresses his hope that her advancing years will not hinder her from bearing children. Whereas she thinks of herself as a commodity, Brehgert wants her to be a productive subject, as it were.

Not only do characters imagine themselves as commodities, they also act like consumers. Mr Broune, for instance, immediately comes to regret his marriage proposal to Lady Carbury, leaving her as her inebriated son stumbles in. His calculations had not taken into consideration the existence of an errant future stepson, and he wakes up with a hangover: 'Who does not know that sudden thoughtfulness at waking, that first matutinal retrospection, and prospection, into things as they have been and are to be . . . On this Wednesday [Mr Broune] found that he could not balance his sheet comfortably' (1992: 301). One can find a similar assumption in the work of Jevons:

> Jevons's conception of economics as 'a Calculus of Pleasure and Pain' resembles Freud's understanding of the libidinal economy as a kind of balance sheet on which individuals carefully assess avenues of pleasure, calculate potential negative consequences of pleasure-seeking activities, and attempt to manage their pleasure accounts in such a way that pluses exceed minuses. (R. T. Gray 2012: 124)

The representation of characters' subjectivity in *The Way We Live Now* is informed by these marginalist – or Freudian – principles.[11] The novel brims with scenes such as Broune's internal monologue, in which characters unconsciously use rational procedures to find a balance between their desires (the pleasure principle) and the circumstances that they find themselves in (the reality principle). There is one major exception, however. Melmotte's thoughts are not presented in detail: 'With no subjectivity to speak of, Melmotte *is* the market' (Gagnier 2000: 73).

Approaching the Late Novels

In many of his late works – *Is He Popenjoy?*, *The American Senator*, *An Autobiography*, *John Caldigate*, *The Life of Cicero*, *Ayala's Angel*, *Cousin Henry*, *Marion Fay*, *Dr Wortle's School*, *The Fixed Period*, *Mr Scarborough's Family*, *An Old Man's Love*, and *The Landleaguers* –

Trollope explores the consequences of the diagnosis of modern life that we find articulated so candidly in *The Way We Live Now* for other related manifestations of modernity, such as colonialism, nationalism, Hellenism, education, the law, and sociability.[12] His views about these phenomena are also performed in the style of his writing: Trollope's late novels experiment with a multitude of literary conventions in order to articulate a form of subjectivity in which the individual element, agency, has been erased. Shifting its focus gradually from late capitalism to the effacement of individuality, this study disentangles this late style in all its richness and diversity. It pieces together the many genres, mechanisms, textures, themes, tropes, and narrative arrangements that structure Trollope's late novels, all the while illustrating how these stylistic elements are part of his engagement with the logic of modernity.[13] Although '[n]either his admirers nor his critics', so Stefan Collini writes, 'have ever described Trollope as "an intellectual"' (1999: 59), this study contends that the depth of Trollope's late style made him an intellectual exile among the elite of his time.

As the emphasis on Adorno's conceptualisation of late style in the previous pages will have made clear, my reading is informed by the principles of Frankfurt School critical theory. This disclosure requires two annotations, however. First, this study hopes to bear this burden lightly. Its primary aim is to shed light on formal and stylistic elements in Trollope's late novels that have not been sufficiently recognised and to explore their political implications. The intention to let Trollope's works speak for themselves prevails over what would otherwise be a blinkered attempt to present the late Trollope as a Marxist *avant la lettre*. Second, Adorno's critical focus on avant-garde forms of art makes it challenging to pair his writings and theories with the 'middlebrow' form of the Victorian novel as practised by Trollope. Instead, when the analyses that follow do refer to critical theory, they often fall back on the writings of Adorno's erstwhile mentor, Walter Benjamin, whose ambivalent fascination with bourgeois life and culture makes him a more amenable interlocutor.[14] Many of Benjamin's ideas about modernity are immanent in Victorian literature, whether one wants to talk about the almost misanthropic cynicism of *The Way We Live Now* in particular or about the anxieties of the age generally. In particular, it is tempting to interpret Trollope's late novels through the lens of Benjamin's last work, the unfinished *Arcades Project*, his exploration of life in nineteenth-century Paris. But while such an approach may yield insights with regard to Dickens, whom Benjamin in fact refers to (Benjamin 2003b: 28), in the case of Trollope this attempt lacks sufficient grounding.[15] Trollope's late style has little in common with the texts that buttress Benjamin's analysis of the phantasmagoria of the big city, such as the sketches of Parisian life known as the physiologies, which present the physiognomic skill of 'mak[ing] out the profession, character, background, and lifestyle of passers-by' as 'a gift which a good fairy lays in the cradle of the big-city dweller' (Benjamin 2003b: 20). In contrast, Trollope's own attempts in this genre tend to deal with rustic life. *Hunting Sketches*, *Travelling Sketches*, and *Clergymen of the Church of England* are not the writings of a *flâneur*. When in the last years of his life Trollope does sketch the city, as in *London Tradesmen*, he focuses on a class of people whose professions dispel the light of the magic lantern: the method of the physiologies was, indeed, limited by the fact that '[p]eople knew one another as debtors and creditors, salesmen and customers, employers and employees, and above all as competitors' (Benjamin 2003b: 20).[16] Benjamin's earlier essays are more helpful in coming to terms with Trollope's late style, because they combine an attention to stylistic aspects with an interest in the Romantic reception and rejection of Kantian aesthetics, in which theory the effect of subjectivity is to produce form. It is in this Kantian side of Benjamin's work that one can find tools with which to analyse the 'formlessness' of Trollope's late style.[17] Since this book is concerned not just with the politics of Trollope's late work but also with the formal means through which these are articulated, this makes the early Benjamin often a more congenial companion. Even so, the point is not to make Trollope a Benjaminian without even knowing it, but to make Benjamin receptive to Trollope in ways Benjamin may never have imagined but that put some of his ideas to the test they invite.

This approach has certain implications for the study of Trollope's novels and of Victorian literature. Since the turn of the century, there has been a renewed interest in the liberal nature of Victorian culture. Taking issue with Foucault's genealogical framework, in which the nineteenth-century individual is likened to an inmate and analysed as the object of disciplinary power (Foucault 1977: 201), recent critics have suggested that many Victorians were invested in cultivating hitherto unrecognised forms of agency. In an age when the public use of reason seemed to be on the wane, the Victorians allegedly developed a project of 'autonomous self-authorisation' that hovers between Enlightenment rationalism and post-Victorian Aestheticism (see A. Anderson 2001; 2005: 197). David Wayne Thomas, for instance, has suggested that the ability, central to Victorian Aestheticism, to consider a situation from the perspective of its participants before acting on this consideration should be conceived of as a form of liberal agency (Thomas 2004: ix).[18] This form differs from its eighteenth-century predecessor in that it posits that the relation between our actions and our minds is not straightforward, but layered. Trollope, who famously claimed that he was 'an advanced, but still a conservative Liberal' (Trollope 1999a: 251), has often featured prominently in these recuperative efforts. Countering D. A. Miller's Foucauldian claim that the tolerant narration and providential scheme which Trollope uses in *Barchester Towers* encourage the reader to embrace disciplinary institutions (D. A. Miller 1988: 111), critics have suggested, in various ways, that Trollope's work is implicated within the historicist turn that is apparent in liberal thought from the mid-century onwards. Lauren M. E. Goodlad, for instance, has shown that Trollope unwittingly supported the covert agenda of the liberal Northcote-Trevelyan *Report on the Organisation of the Permanent Civil Service*, which seemed to promote 'a teleological definition of character implying the limitless improvability of all human beings' (Goodlad 2003: 119), whereas, in actual fact, it was invested – like Trollope's Barchester novels – in 'a comparatively limited view of individual improvement and, thus a naturalisation of relatively fixed socio-political hierarchies' (2003: 25).[19] In a more epistemological vein, Amanda Anderson has argued that Trollope's portrayal of liberal subjectivity is the product of a dialectic relationship between

> traditional individual virtue (it quintessentially defines the 'gentleman') and a kind of impersonal truth-telling or critique that is aligned both with the evaluative diagnoses of the narrative and with specific challenges by characters within the story to the doxa that defines the embedded communities that Trollope seems often to affirm. (A. Anderson 2007: 512)[20]

Expressing strong doubts about the viability of liberalism in a world increasingly marked by global capitalism, Trollope's novels from the 1870s do not easily fit into this picture. As Goodlad indicates in her more recent work, the late novels present 'a disenchanted modernity in which Hobbesian combatants struggle to wrest money and power from the all-but-substanceless flow of capital and commodities' (Goodlad 2009: 448). From a more philosophical point of view, Regenia Gagnier suggests that Trollope's late novels portray modernity as a double bind: while for a limited few, constraints on individual and collective freedom were being abolished by biological, technological, psychological, and social innovations, for many these innovations were in fact thwarting the possibility of a more just society, thus fostering the kind of resentment at the foreclosure of anticipated freedoms embodied by Ferdinand Lopez in *The Prime Minister* (Gagnier 2009). Taking its cue from observations such as these, this book questions the notion that the kind of subjectivity found in Trollope's late novels can be assimilated into the logic of liberal modernity. As Goodlad and Gagnier both show, this need not mean that we should swing back to a reading inspired by the early Foucault, or to an interpretation of Trollope's writings as quintessentially conservative. Rather, this study contends that Trollope's late writings are radical, even visionary; to use Benjamin's definition of art, they create 'a demand which could be fully satisfied only later' (Benjamin 2003a: 266). Instead of portraying the present as a stage in a teleological narrative, the fatal dryness of their texture exposes the present as inextricably discontinuous.

Notes

1. Trollope's plots and characters were certainly a source of inspiration, as Elsie Michie has shown in her comparison of Trollope's *The Prime Minister* and James's *The Portrait of a Lady* (Michie 2006), while Trollope's late novels also anticipate many of James's formal innovations such as the detailed depiction of a character's consciousness and the avoidance of overt censure. As such, James's criticism can be read as the product of a turf war; Trollope's and James's stylistic experiments are, to some extent, too close for comfort.
2. Beethoven's late style is classical as much as it is Romantic, as Michael Spitzer shows in his masterful and accessible interpretation of Adorno's thinking about Beethoven's late style (Spitzer 2006).
3. In his influential collection of essays on late style, Edward Said combines Adorno's formal analysis of late style with an insistence on the relevance of the experience of ageing (Said 2007). Other works in this area, such as Russ McDonald's study of Shakespeare's late plays, suggest that in studying an author's style it is wiser to privilege matters of language over contextual concerns (McDonald 2009).
4. Modernity can be defined in many ways; for a succinct overview, see Wolfreys et al. (2006: 67–8).
5. Trollope's own personality baffled his contemporaries. In the words of the artist W. P. Frith, who painted Trollope into his celebrated *A Private View at the Royal Academy*, Trollope's books are 'full of gentleness, grace and refinement', whereas in public Trollope was 'bluff, loud, stormy, and contentious' (Terry 1987: 142). The society poet Frederick Locker-Lampson recollects that '[h]irsute and taurine of aspect, he would glare at you from behind fierce spectacles . . . while all the time he was most amiably disposed towards you under his waistcoat' (Terry 1987: 142–3). Trollope himself seems to have been conscious of this contradiction. Whereas his photographs and *cartes de visites* show us that he 'never managed to wear his own clothes well or elegantly' (Glendinning 1994: 426–7), he himself held 'that gentleman to be the best dressed whose dress no one observes. I am not sure but that the same may be said of an author's written language' (Trollope 1879b: 200). In *The Untouchable*, John Banville's narrator picks up on this idea by suggesting not just that his father resembles a minor

character out of Trollope's fiction or that he considers Anthony Trollope a minor author, but even that Trollope contained within himself more than one minor character: 'My father sat blinking in distress. Light from the leaded window glinted on [my father's] balding pate. Trollope, I thought; he's a character out of Trollope – one of the minor ones' (Banville 1998: 70).

6. Trollope's characters often know what they ought to do but do not do it, a phenomenon which Patrick Fessenbecker has recently identified as an instance of akrasia (Fessenbecker 2014).
7. For a more recent study of business imperialism, focusing on the Spanish Main in the Victorian age, see Aguirre (2005).
8. Extrapolating from Marx's famous formula for commodity trade, MCM' (a commodity is bought for a specific price and then sold on for more), Giovanni Arrighi has suggested that commodity capital and finance capital oscillate: 'The central aspect of [historical capitalism as a world system] is the alternation of epochs of material expansion (MC phases of capital accumulation) with phases of financial rebirth and expansion (CM') phases. In phases of material expansion money capital "sets in motion" an increasing mass of commodities; and in phases of financial expansion an increasing mass of money capital "sets itself free" from its commodity form, and accumulation proceeds through financial deals (as in Marx's abridged formula MM')' (Arrighi 1994: 6; quoted in Baucom 2005: 25). Set at a hyperspeculative moment (MM'), the Vienna crisis, Trollope's novel portrays the beginning of the end of the British cycle, which began in 1750 and ended in 1925. This is due to the fact that the American cycle, which had begun in 1860, was gathering steam. Indeed, speculation in the novel comes from across the Atlantic. It is Hamilton Fisker who suggests the idea of a trans-American railway, not Melmotte. As such, Trollope is playing a curious trick: American speculation seems to be invading England, but it is actually England that needs America as a safe place for speculation. Thus Trollope can 'preserve both English culture and the speculative activity that threatens that culture' (Van 2005: 93). However, as a result he also weakens the importance of England and places the future with the Americans, 'leav[ing] the reader on the brink of a new world with a new world order and economy, a world navigated most successfully by Americans, by those who understand speculation most thoroughly and can, hence, manage its risks most competently' (Van 2005: 94).
9. For an overview of financial crises from the eighteenth century onward, see Duckenfield et al. (2006); for the panic of 1873 in particular, see Kindleberger (1990: 311–25).
10. Paul Delany maintains that Trollope's critique of the commodification of women is disingenuous. On the one hand, Trollope pays allegiance to a century-old 'system of homosocial barter' which demands that women produce 'male heirs to provide continuity of tenure and name' (Delany 2002: 32). At the same time, women also have an economic status: their dowry can revive an embarrassed estate. Trollope solves this contradiction by his 'constant recourse to Providence' (Delany 2002: 36): men should fall in love with women when they are poor and poor women should resist being loved, for which both will be rewarded with an unexpected legacy or

a similar surprise. While Delany's interpretation works to some extent for novels such as *Framley Parsonage* and *The Claverings*, it does not tally with Trollope's late novels. Delany's assumptions bring him to the conclusion that Trollope's marriageable women are either beautiful or rich and that once 'lovers have been united', Trollope 'shows little interest in their future of shared consumption' (Delany 2002: 40). The appearance of the beautiful and wealthy Lady Glencora Palliser in five novels refutes both claims (see Duguid 2002). Trollope's positive portrayal of the Jewish banker Brehgert as opposed to his negative portrayal of the Longestaffes, who spit on the hand that feeds them, heightens the impression that the values of the land fare worse than the commodity: it is 'society, the "We" of the title' that 'takes the brunt of Trollope's ire' (McGann 2008: 135).

11. Sigmund Freud's use of economic terms culminates in his 1905 treatise on *The Joke and Its Relation to the Unconscious*, in which Freud 'grounds his theory of humour in an economics of saving (*Ersparnis*) and sudden, excessive expenditure (*Abfuhr*)' (R. T. Gray 2012: 123). Although early critics such as Valentin Nikolaevich Voloshinov believed that this was mere veneer, in fact Freud proposes 'a rudimentary input-output model that strives instinctively for equilibrium' (R. T. Gray 2012: 125).
12. Other critics have chosen different novels as the beginning of Trollope's late style; James opts for *Phineas Redux*, Robert Tracy for *Sir Harry Hotspur of Humblethwaite* (Tracy 1978). In the framework of this study, *The Way We Live Now* occupies a privileged position because of its cynical portrayal of late capitalism. Since many of Trollope's final works have not received the critical attention that critics have paid to the Barchester series and the Palliser novels, I have decided to focus on these minor texts and to leave more canonical texts such as *The Prime Minister* and *The Duke's Children* outside this study's scope. A few glancing references apart, reasons of space have stopped me from fully considering a number of works written in this period: *Harry Heathcote of Gangoil*, *South Africa*, *Thackeray*, *Kept in the Dark*, *Lord Palmerston*, and Trollope's short stories. The absence of *An Eye for an Eye* can be excused on the grounds that though it was published in this period (1879), it was written much earlier (in 1870).
13. This is not the first study to claim that Trollope's realism is in fact motivated by non-mimetic concerns, such as his awareness of the ways in which one's consciousness appropriates the world (J. H. Miller 1968), his fascination with the English language (Clarke 1975), his commitment to the comedy of manners (Kincaid 1978), the dramatic and rhetorical structures of his plots (Harvey 1980; Tracy 1978), his theories about the nature of writing (Kendrick 1980), and his complex characterisation (Wall 1988).
14. Like Adorno, Benjamin suggests that contradictions within the work of art point towards a failure in historical reality: 'In the last analysis structure and detail are always historically charged. The object of philosophical criticism is to show that the function of artistic form is as follows: to make historical content, such as provides the basis of every important work of art, into a philosophical truth' (Benjamin 2009: 182). Benjamin thus makes room for a 'politicising formalism' that does not deconstruct 'the transcendent via the immanent' but 'enfolds the transcendent into the immanent' (J. Hansen 2005: 665, 69). The critic must recover a truth that has been lost, which is

why Benjamin tends to approach the artwork 'as ruin, as failed, transient form' (J. Hansen 2005: 678).

15. For Benjaminian interpretations of Dickens's novels, see Piggott (2012) and Wolfreys (2012). Historians disagree about the extent to which Benjamin's analysis of nineteenth-century Paris is applicable to Victorian London. In his recent political history of light and vision in Victorian Britain, Chris Otter agrees with Benjamin that the revival of physiognomy must be understood within the context of the changing shape of the modern city. But he reverses the causality that Benjamin reads into this correlation, showing that physiognomy was not so much a response to the conditions of urban life as one of the factors that helped these conditions come into being. Other scholars, however, suggest that the visual spectacles and exhibitions that made the *flâneur* the dominant form of visual practice in nineteenth-century Paris are relevant for our understanding of urban experience in the British colonies and at the American frontier (Brand 1991; McCann 2004).
16. Biographical elements reinforce the impression that Trollope did not feel at home in the city. By his own account, Trollope found his inspiration in a walk in the wood and his stamina in a cup of coffee in the morning (Trollope 1879a; 1999a: 271). Leaving for Australia in 1871, he did not relish the prospect of leaving Waltham Cross and the countryside. When he finally did find a new abode in Montagu Square, he couches his feelings in irony: 'not a gorgeous neighbourhood', he told Anna Steele, 'but one which will suit my declining years and modest resources' (1983: 580). If he did enjoy being near to his clubs and friends, he was less pleased with the noise: 'For myself I own that a brass band altogether incapacitates me. No sooner does the first note of the opening burst reach my ear than I start up, fling down my pen, and cast my thoughts disregarded into the abyss of some chaos which is always there to receive them' (1879a: 596). This sensitivity may have hastened his end, if the story is true that 'during the afternoon preceding his fatal stroke in 1882, Trollope had become overexcited in an altercation with the leader of a German band which played disturbingly under the window of his London hotel' (Super 1990: 389). For a consideration of physiognomy and detective fiction in Trollope's writings, see Van Dam (2015).
17. The depth of 'the unreflective Kantianism of Victorian moral commonplaces' (Collini 1993a: 98) has not yet been fully appreciated, with a few exceptions: Kevin McLaughlin argues that Matthew Arnold's concept of disinterestedness is an echo of what Kant calls 'moral fanaticism', an influence which McLaughlin establishes by means of Benjamin's essay on *The Concept of Criticism in German Romanticism* (McLaughlin 2008). On Benjamin's formalism, see Mieszkowski (2004). Benjamin's early training in Kantian aesthetics stayed with him throughout his life: although German Idealism takes a back seat in his journalistic work in the late 1920s and early 1930s and it is overruled in his more Marxist moments in the late 1930s, it never fully disappears. Benjamin's multifaceted concept of experience, for instance, is fundamentally Kantian (Gasché 1994).
18. A manifesto of sorts can be found in Amanda Anderson's 2005 article in *Victorian Studies*, where she calls for turning the tables on 'cultural studies, New Historicism, postcolonialism, and queer theory' and giving 'primacy

to political philosophy or political theory as a disciplinary partner' (2005: 196). Anderson enlists a number of other literary scholars in her ranks, including Lauren M. E. Goodlad (2003), Elaine Hadley (2005), and Irene Tucker (2000), to whom one might also add Kathleen Frederickson (2007), Nathan K. Hensley (2009), Daniel Malachuk (2005), and Bruce Robbins (2007). These critics belong to a current rather than a movement and approach liberalism in very different ways; see, for instance, Hadley (2010). For a comprehensive history of the Liberal party, see Parry (1993, 2006).

19. In 1853, growing middle-class financial pressure caused William Gladstone, then Chancellor of the Exchequer in the Peelite government of Aberdeen (1852–5), to make an official inquiry into the patronage system of government appointments (Shuman 2000: 77). The Northcote-Trevelyan *Report* included contributions and recommendations by liberal luminaries such as Sir James Fitzjames Stephen, Benjamin Jowett, Edwin Chadwick, and Rowland Hill, Trollope's detested superior at the Post Office. Most importantly, the *Report* introduced the idea of competitive examinations, which would create 'an efficient body of permanent officers, occupying a position duly subordinate to that of the Ministers who are directly responsible to the Crown and to Parliament, yet possessing sufficient independence, character, ability, and experience to be able to advise, assist, and to some extent, influence, those who are from time to time set over them' (Northcote and Trevelyan 1855: 3; quoted in Shuman 2000: 82). While the *Report* thus ostensibly met the demands for more transparency in a bureaucratic stronghold that seemed to be manned by an upper-class elite, it was actually a move to keep the elite in place, for only Oxbridge-educated gentlemen would be able to successfully complete the tests that the commissioners would set them. Trollope, who had benefited from patronage, vigorously criticised the *Report*'s apparent purpose throughout his career (1999a: 40). His most extensive critique is *The Three Clerks* (1857), a novel that lampoons Trevelyan as Sir Gregory Hardlines. Trollope may have realised that he had supported the actual ends of the *Report* without knowing it, however, as in later life he and Trevelyan became fast friends (Super 1990: 260, 81).
20. For a consideration of liberal subjectivity in *The Warden*, see Earle (2006). Other critics have emphasised the political implications of Trollope's play with literary form, such as Lynette Felber, who maintains that Trollope found an expressive equivalent for his moderate progressivism in the aesthetic form of the sequence novel or *roman fleuve*, which allows the author to stretch out the development of character over a larger canvas (Felber 2010). In a more historicist fashion, David M. Craig situates Trollope's representation of 'Liberal' politics in its contemporary context (Craig 2010). Trollope's politics have also been described as liberal in the more general sense that Trollope was socially progressive, even leftist, a line of inquiry that was initiated by Robert Polhemus and has culminated in Deborah Denenholz Morse's recent monograph, which shows that Trollope's treatment of contemporary ideologies – gender, class, and even race – became more generous as he got older (Denenholz Morse 2013; Polhemus 1968).

Chapter 2

'Getting and Spending': The Aesthetic Economist

> Of all novelists in any country, Trollope best understands the role of money. Compared with him even Balzac is too romantic. (Auden 1973: 266)

Trollope famously tailored his novels for publication as serials, priding himself 'on completing [his] work exactly within the proposed dimensions' (Trollope 1999a: 119). Although the system of serialisation had become antiquated by the time he came to write *The Way We Live Now*, Trollope still clung to the constraints he had set himself, dividing the novel into twenty parts, with each chapter being equally long (see Sutherland 1982). Trollope's reluctance to adapt to the demands of a changing market seems, at first, a sign of his unwillingness to adopt a new economic paradigm, the theory of marginalism, which posited that an object's value is determined by market forces rather than its inherent qualities.[1] As the preceding pages have suggested, this shift in economic thinking intensified Trollope's conceptualisation of a subjectivity in which free will has turned to stone. In the bleak story-world of *The Way We Live Now*, his characters' minds are presented as having become devoid of moral qualities under the influence of consumerism. *Ayala's Angel*, however, puts a more positive spin on the workings of neoclassical economics. Reading these two novels alongside one another offers an interesting contrast: in both, a financier plays an important role, even though he and his thoughts remain, to a considerable extent, in the margins. A former Governor of the Bank of England and now the director of Travers and Treason in all but name, Sir Thomas Tringle in *Ayala's Angel* is as powerful as Augustus Melmotte in *The Way We Live Now*: he 'could affect the rate of money throughout Europe, and emissaries from national treasuries would listen to his words' (Trollope 1989b: 226). Their personalities are substantially different, however. Melmotte is a conniving swindler, whereas Tringle is a respectable banker. This contrast suggests that *The Way We Live Now* and *Ayala's*

Angel respond to the machinations of marginalist economics in opposite ways. *Ayala's Angel* suggests that there is potential for joy and pleasure in this brave new world, even if there is no room for morality. This difference is also apparent in the novel's genre: as Trollope's 'one true romance', *Ayala's Angel* is modelled on 'a pattern which forces mundane experience to elevate itself to the ideal, not the reverse' (Kincaid 1978: 256).

The rise of marginalist economics in the 1870s was prepared and facilitated by the Romantic critique of classical political economy. Famously claiming that 'Getting and spending we lay waste our powers' (Wordsworth 1990: 150), writers such as William Wordsworth believed that there was need for an ethical and aesthetic sphere of life above mere buying and selling. Paradoxically, this critique allowed neo-classical economics to flourish, for it implied that the economy was to be confined to a separate domain. Because Romantic writers denied the study of economy access to – and relieved it from – truth and morality, 'Jevons's retreat into the laboratory, and out of the drawing rooms of culture and politics, in fact represents a concession to the Romantic critique of political economy in the first half of the nineteenth century' (Bigelow 2003: 3). The rise of the Aesthetic movement, *l'art pour l'art*, continued this imbricated relationship, since it provided marginalist economics with the cornerstone it needed in order to function. Marginalist theories teach that value is determined by desire; what this desire is governed by, taste, falls outside their inquiry, yet is fundamental to the workings of the process they describe:

> As the expertness of a customer declines, the importance of his taste increases proportionately – both for him and for the manufacturer. For the consumer, it serves as a more or less elaborate masking of his lack of expertness. For the manufacturer, it serves as a fresh stimulus to consumption . . . It is precisely this development which literature reflects in *l'art pour l'art* . . . In *l'art pour l'art*, the poet for the first time faces language the way the buyer faces the commodity on the open market. To an extreme extent, he has ceased to be familiar with the process of its production. (Benjamin 2003b: 65)

The aesthete, then, is a consumer *par excellence*. While neo-classical economics and the Aesthetic movement may seem at cross-purposes, 'the shift in economics actually privileged subjective psychological factors on the part of the consumer that a science of aesthetics was best placed to explain' (Gagnier 2000: 11).

The heroine of *Ayala's Angel*, Ayala Dormer, reprises the Romantic critique of political economy. When Egbert Dormer's death leaves his children burdened with debts, Ayala and Lucy Dormer are put at the mercy of their relatives, the wealthy Tringles and the poor Dosetts.

Mrs Dosett agrees to take in Lucy, while Lady Tringle chooses the more attractive Ayala. She soon comes to regret her choice, as Ayala, who 'hate[s] money' (Trollope 1989b: 70), refuses to play the part of dependent niece. On a holiday to Rome, it is she who commands the attention of the British expatriate community. The Marchesa Baldoni makes Ayala her protégé and invites her to balls and dinners, with the Tringles as an appendage, rather than the other way around. Worse things happen on the way to the forum, for Tom Tringle, the financier's son, falls in love with Ayala. Lady Tringle reprimands Ayala for having encouraged him, not counting on the fact that Ayala might dislike him precisely because of the wealth he is supposed to inherit. Bedecked with jewellery, indeed, Tom Tringle does not meet the standards of Ayala's ideal lover, the Angel of Light, with whom comparison is futile: 'the Angel of Light must have something tragic in his composition – must verge, at any rate, on tragedy. Ayala did not know that beautiful description of a "Sallow, sublime, sort of Werther-faced man", but I fear that in creating her Angel of Light she drew a picture in her imagination of a man of that kind' (1989b: 127). As Trollope's allusion to Goethe's *Die Leiden des jungen Werthers* indicates, Ayala's beliefs are Romantic, a sobriquet that is frequently applied to 'Ayala the romantic; Ayala the poetic!' (1989b: 4). Ayala's criticism of the vulgarity of money, then, is part of a Romantic disposition.

The fact that the Angel of Light is a product of Ayala's mind highlights her difference from the Tringle family, whose material prosperity is matched by an impoverished sense of the imagination.[2] Tringle's eldest daughter Augusta is an overbearing prig who becomes even more overbearing after her marriage to the Honourable Septimus Traffick, second son of Lord Boardotrade. Traffick himself is a *fainéant* parasite, unwilling to find a house for himself and his new wife despite the large settlement that he has received, and wonderfully oblivious to his father-in-law's increasingly angry demands to leave. The imagination of Tringle's other daughter, Gertrude, is governed by clichés and melodrama. Like Marie Melmotte, Gertrude Tringle huffs and puffs because she is not allowed to marry her chosen lover, Frank Houston, a flippant dandy whose intentions are unabashedly mercenary. Tringle forbids the marriage, even when Gertrude goes on a hunger strike. She then embarks on a different scheme and tries to convince Houston to elope to Ostend, a suggestion he carefully feigns not to understand. Eventually, she realises her fantasy by absconding with Captain Batsby, a fool willing to run the risk. However, just as she relieves 'herself from famine by sly visits to the larder' (1989b: 319), her elopement cannot exist without some degree of comfort: 'Of course I had to come away with very little luggage, because I was obliged to have my things mixed up with Ben's' (1989b: 389–90). Tom Tringle, finally, cannot see that his increasingly desperate and expensive attempts to win his cousin's heart are counterproductive; fantasies cannot be bought. These characters' obsession with money has entailed a loss of the imagination: although they think they believe in an idea, they cannot live up to its execution, unlike Ayala.

To be sure, this reading overlooks the fact that Trollope's allusion to Goethe's *Werther* is mediated through Thomas Moore's *The Fudge Family in Paris*, an epistolary novel in verse which, unlike Goethe's novel, is not tragic but comic. In Moore's novella, the character Biddy Fudge believes that the 'Sallow, sublime, sort of Werther-faced man' whom she has fallen in love with is the King of Prussia, only to find out that he is in fact a draper. This comparison puts Ayala's wishes in a dim light. Readers familiar with Trollope's other work would also fall back on their knowledge that, in general, Trollope has little patience for pseudo-Romantic self-aggrandisement. *Ayala's Angel*, however, is an important exception: 'Trollope seems to find [Ayala's] foolishness and perversity charming . . . In *Ayala's Angel*, Trollope reversed his usual anti-romantic attitudes to write a tongue-in-cheek defence of the romantic temperament' (Tracy 1978: 244). The novel employs irony not so much to attack 'Ayala's romanticism as her mistaken notion that others are not as romantic as she' (Kincaid 1978: 258). Ayala's Romanticism is, in fact, rewarded. When Ayala finally realises that her Angel of Light walks this earth in the shape of Colonel John Stubbs, she fears that she has lost him. As a result, 'the spirit which had haunted her' is exorcised (Trollope 1989b: 413). Yet she fails to recognise that it is this spirit that has made everybody, including Stubbs, fall in love with her: 'That the dreams had been all idle she declared to herself – not aware that the Ayala whom her lover had loved would not have been an Ayala to be loved by him, but for the dreams' (1989b: 414). As a result, Ayala does not experience the disappointment of Lizzie Eustace, Gertrude Tringle, and Biddy Fudge. Her Romanticism is not a pose, but a deeply held poetic faith; unlike other characters, she is able to willingly suspend her disbelief.[3]

Even so, Ayala Dormer's principles are not as pure as she thinks. While she finds money distasteful, she does not scorn what money can buy: 'The gaudy magnificence of the Tringles had been altogether unlike the luxurious comfort of Stalham, where everybody was at his ease, where everybody was good-natured, where everybody seemed to acknowledge that pleasure was the one object of life!' (1989b: 181). This paradox seems to have been part of her upbringing. Ayala and Lucy Dormer's father, Egbert Dormer, was a successful painter with 'the most perfect bijou of a little house at South Kensington' who, 'with every luxury around him which money could purchase, had affected to despise the heavy magnificence of the Tringles' (1989b: 3). It is therefore more accurate to talk about Ayala's Aestheticism, rather than her Romanticism. Ayala embodies the paradoxical role of the aesthetic within the theory of marginalism: her main criterion is that pre-eminently aesthetic category, taste. When her cousin proposes, 'it was the outrage to her taste rather than to her conduct which afflicted her' (1989b: 58). The reader is invited to adopt this perspective: we 'are repeatedly encouraged by a gentle sarcasm to side with the pretty, not the virtuous' (Kincaid 1978: 257).[4] As such, the novel's story-world can be said to run along marginalist principles, according to which 'consumer choice ceased to be a moral category: it did not matter whether the good desired was good or bad, just that the consumer was willing to pay for it' (Gagnier 2000: 4).

The novel extends its concern with economic theory through its play with the genre of the romance. While initially the reader may fear that Ayala Dormer will turn out to be a modern-day Don Quixote, her dreams are realised and left intact. This element tallies with the novel's unrealistic resolution: virtually every character ends up with whom or what he or she desires. Even those who are left unsatisfied, such as Tom Tringle, will not remain unhappy, or so the narrator assures us. This fairy-tale conclusion is adumbrated by means of various explicit references. To Ayala, Tom Tringle is the Beast, she the Beauty (Trollope 1989b: 83, 104, 18); following the Marchesa's lead, she calls herself Cinderella (1989b: 47, 104). Details such as these do not belong to the novel, but to the romance, a genre with which the former is historically at odds. Indeed, the rise of the English novel in the eighteenth century is often understood as a reaction against the form of the romance. The premodern romance was typically fantastic and incredible, thus meeting 'Sir Philip Sidney's criterion for "poesy": affirming "nothing", it could not lie' (Gallagher 2006: 338).[5] Whereas the romance thus demanded faith, the novel trained readers 'to take the reality of the story itself as a kind of suppositional speculation' (Gallagher 2006: 346). This attitude was essential to the development of modern subjectivity and of modern capitalism: one 'thinks immediately of merchants and insurers calculating risks, or of investors extending credit' (Gallagher 2006: 346). *Ayala's Angel*, interestingly, combines the novel with the romance, speculation with faith.

There are two ways in which the stylistic duality of Trollope's novel can be understood as a comment on economic theories about the nature of capitalism. On the one hand, capitalism 'cannot help revealing its imaginative and indeed fictive underpinnings, especially when in the throes of crisis. It is in these moments, especially, that capitalist economy might itself be grasped as a form of "magical realism"' (Beckman 2012: 146). The incorporation of romantic elements within the form of the novel makes *Ayala's Angel* an instance of such magical realism. This impression is heightened by the existence of one anomalous plotline in *Ayala's Angel*, which shows that such a crisis, or at least its after-effects, were still very much present. The Dosetts' genteel poverty is a sign that the Long Depression is not yet past. Mrs Dosett was meant to inherit a great property but 'the money, tied tight as it had been by half-a-dozen lawyers, had in some fashion vanished' (Trollope 1989b: 11). The novel does not give the cause of their savings' mysterious disappearance, but since it is described as a 'great crash' (1989b: 11), it is likely that the enduring financial crisis is to blame. Aunt Margeret's only concern is how to make ends meet; this picture of a harsher reality is in stark contrast to the pleasure that pervades the rest of the novel. At the same time, the novel's magical realism could also be a sign of the rise of neoclassical economics. One of the central presuppositions of marginalism is the scarcity of goods. The first concern that consumers are animated by is self-preservation; the possibility of indulging in desires is secondary. In the novel's narrative economy, the Dosetts represent the first position, the Dormers the second.

On the other hand, *Ayala's Angel*'s play with the form of the romance aligns it with an alternative to capitalism, the socialism of the welfare state. Its fairy-tale structure is part of a larger narrative of upward mobility. A penniless orphan, Ayala is obviously disadvantaged, both socially and economically. Yet she ends the novel in the higher echelons of society. She has thus turned her background into an advantage or, more precisely, a negative form of capital. According to Bruce Robbins, in narratives of upward mobility 'the initial state of economic deprivation represents a perverse sort of capital, capital that can only be realised by being shown off to others' (Robbins 2007: xi). As in most such narratives, Ayala is rewarded for not hiding her social origins. She holds on to the artistic beliefs that have dominated her youth and wears the badge of poverty proudly.[6] However, Ayala's rise is not something she desires, nor something she actually seeks to achieve. Ayala herself, indeed, has no agency, as the novel emphasises at every turn (Trollope 1989b: 15, 39, 57, 63, 69, 74, 239, 323). She only falls in love with Colonel Stubbs through the efforts of others, first the Marchesa Baldoni, then Lady Albury. Both are aunts to Stubbs and both are in some degree in love with him (1989b: 451). They have, as such, an important function:

> On the formal level, . . . the emotional centre of an upward mobility story lies not in its protagonist but in the protagonist's relation with a patron, mentor, or benefactor . . . [W]hatever the official ideology of individualism may say, [the story of upward mobility] has not been a story of heroic self-reliance alone. In still another sense, it says that one person's upward mobility is really someone else's story. (Robbins 2007: xv)

It is their scheming that makes Ayala's progress possible. Ayala has more scenes with Stubbs's aunts than with Stubbs himself, which highlights how it is her patrons who help her achieve success. The Marchesa and Lady Albury are, in other words, Ayala's fairy godmothers. This 'romantic' side to Trollope's story stands in contrast with the speculative realism that aligns the novel with capitalism. As a narrative of upward mobility, the novel's main plotline requires faith.

The presence of class as a hidden drive in this narrative is not an anomaly, but an essential element. *Fin-de-siècle* works, in particular, tend to align the rejection of social climbing with 'the old aristocracy, which of course did not have to climb. But this alignment also *enables* social climbing, as we see in the period's brilliant and enduringly popular array of Lecter-like sinister-but-seductive mentors, from du Maurier's Svengali to Leroux's Phantom of the Opera' (Robbins 2007: 19). *Ayala's Angel* gives us an early instance of this paradox. Like the artists that du Maurier and Leroux describe, Ayala despises the wealth of nouveaux riches such as the Tringles. She has no compunction, however, in enjoying the riches bestowed upon her by her aristocratic benefactors. This identification with the aristocracy 'is at once residual and emergent, a sense of entitlement that, like the Fabian paternalism that jump-started the welfare state, owes something both to the rentier and to the state bureaucrat' (Robbins 2007: 20).

This kind of plotline is adumbrated in *The Way We Live Now*. Paul Montague, too, is an orphan and he, too, has his mentors: Roger Carbury and Mrs Hurtle. Both initially try to discourage his love for Henrietta Carbury, but in the end both do what is necessary to make things work. Carbury and Mrs Hurtle resemble one another in at least one aspect, their 'unproductive' disposition: 'Like the homosocial bond between older and younger man, the bond between younger man and older woman' – Montague is in his mid-twenties, Mrs Hurtle, a widow, in her mid-thirties – 'stands apart from the cycle of biological reproduction that has traditionally channelled and legitimated desire' (Robbins 2007: 12). Mrs Hurtle, in particular, shows two more characteristics associated with the position of the fairy godmother. Her relationship with Montague is a case of queer tutelage, 'queer' here designating

> a narrative in which the goal of advancement has broken free from customary heterosexual bondings that refer explicitly or implicitly to marriage and the reproduction of the patriarchal family and for better or worse has come to reside increasingly in looser, half-formed relationships, neither biologically reproductive nor necessarily heterosexual. (Robbins 2007: 4)

Montague and Hurtle's relationship is heterosexual, but certainly not normative. Even though her former husband may still be alive, she envisages an exciting and enterprising life in the Wild West, which the weak and effeminate Montague is hardly cut out for. In addition, their relationship is powerfully erotic. Montague cannot resist falling into her arms, kissing her on her lips. Trollope's description of her appearance emphasises her sensuality: 'Her bust was full and beautifully shaped; but she invariably dressed as though she were oblivious, or at any rate neglectful, of her own charms' (Trollope 1992: 216). Mrs Hurtle possesses the charm that patrons usually exude because she has a particular kind of knowledge, sexual knowledge, that Montague has no access to. The bottom line is, however, that, like Ayala Dormer, Paul Montague is a homeless orphan who is made to rise in the world by the help of benefactors.

Trollope's use of narratives of upward mobility allows him to tell a story about capitalism that marginalist economics, in its resolute emphasis on the amoral working of the economy, leaves untold. The role of benefactors in his narratives of upward mobility suggests that individual self-reliance or self-help are insufficient to create social justice; upward mobility can only be achieved, it seems, through the help of friends. Trollope's inclusion of romantic and fantastic elements in his late style, such as the narrative of upward mobility, thus ultimately functions as a challenge to marginalist economics because these elements give voice to a version of the common good.

Notes

1. For examinations of the economic principles behind Trollope's writing theory as articulated in *An Autobiography*, see Colella (2006) and Byler (2009).
2. The imagination is an important point of intersection between Romanticism and economic thought (Bronk 2009).
3. This eminently Romantic phrase has had a long afterlife and is generally taken to be an expression of immersion, the experience of feeling caught up in the events of a fictional story (e.g. Wolf 2004: 328). But this is not what it was supposed to mean. Coleridge coins the expression in his *Biographia Literaria* (1817) to describe his own contributions to *The Lyrical Ballads*: 'it

was agreed, that my endeavours should be directed to persons and characters supernatural, or at least romantic, yet so as to transfer from our inward nature a human interest and a semblance of truth sufficient to procure for these shadows of imagination that willing suspension of disbelief for the moment, which constitutes poetic faith' (Coleridge 1954: 2.6). The willing suspension of disbelief, then, does not refer to aesthetic illusion, but 'more modestly to the volitional abandonment of ordinary rules for judging what may count as real within representational language' (Garratt 2012: 756). It is, importantly, an element of poetry. The popular novel, in Coleridge's view, achieves the very opposite. It impoverishes and erodes the will: 'Call [novel-reading] rather a sort of beggarly daydreaming, during which the mind of the dreamer furnishes for itself nothing but laziness and a little mawkish sensibility' (Coleridge 1954: 1.34; quoted in Garratt 2012: 756). This is the sort of reading Lizzie Eustace indulges in, whose study of Shelley and Tennyson is soon replaced by the consumption of novels. Ayala, however, is a genuine embodiment of poetic faith. She succeeds in suspending her disbelief: she knows that the shadows of her imagination should count as real.

4. An amoral point of view is not exclusive to neo-classical economics: it is also possible to read this as a sign of business cycle theory, which 'dissevers any causal relationship between individual moral agents and economic fluctuations' (McGann 2008: 138). But business cycle theory would not be able to explain as neatly as marginalism why *Ayala's Angel* balances the absence of morality with an approbation of the pretty, that is, the aesthetic.
5. The eighteenth-century novel differentiated itself from the romance by 'discovering' a new form of truth. The 'movement from romance to novel . . . is part of a larger epistemological shift from a narrow construction of truth as historical accuracy to a more capacious understanding that could include truth conceived as mimetic simulation' (Gallagher 2006: 341; see McKeon 2002). The novel made it apparent that there might be a truth in what was possible and probable. For an extensive bibliography of the novel's connection to the emergence of a speculative culture, see Rosa (2012: 142, n. 2).
6. *Ayala's Angel* represents the economy itself in the various exchanges that its characters engage in. As Jeffrey Franklin has shown (2003), it is perfectly possible to reduce the plot of Trollope's novels to relations between economic capital (in this novel, the Tringles), cultural capital (Ayala and Lucy Dormer), and social capital (Colonel Stubbs).

Chapter 3

'A Bond of Discord': Colonialism and Allegory

Benedict Anderson has famously argued that modernity relies on a sense of simultaneity that is 'transverse, cross-time, marked not by prefiguring and fulfilment, but by temporal coincidence, and measured by clock and calendar' (B. Anderson 2006: 24). According to Anderson, this form of simultaneity found its embodiment in two Enlightenment inventions, the newspaper and the novel, which by virtue of their form and structures of address connect events that have no relation other than that they happen to take place at the same time. Trollope's late novels, however, feature characters whose undisclosed activities in the past interrupt the narrative present, and who undo the teleological, progressive movement that the narrative seemed to embark upon. Trollope's late style thus revolves around states of a 'noncontemporaneous contemporaneity' (Harootunian 2007: 475), that is, 'a present that has not simply overcome the losses of the past but that remains marked and interrupted by them' (Vermeulen 2009: 104).[1] This chapter will show how Trollope creates this different kind of simultaneity by, among other things, allowing glimpses of certain characters' unknown past through selective forms of focalisation or narration. Significantly, this past is often set in the colonies. In *The Way We Live Now*, *John Caldigate*, and *An Old Man's Love* the love lives of those in the motherland are thwarted by adventurers hailing from America, Australia, and South Africa, whose return interrupts the narrative present. As such, Trollope's views about colonialism are expressed in his use of a particular form of simultaneity.

It is illuminating to consider the moments of simultaneity between past and present in Trollope's late novels as instances of allegory. In his study of the German baroque *Trauerspiel*, Benjamin conceives of allegory as 'a late manifestation', its 'most radical procedure' being 'to make events simultaneous' (Benjamin 2009: 197, 194). This allegorical form of simultaneity does not refer to the coexistence of events taking place at a different location, but of events taking place at a different time.

Allegory thus designates a precarious state in between different temporalities, as one of Benjamin's examples nicely illustrates: an emblem showing 'a rose simultaneously half in bloom and half faded, and the sun rising and setting in the same landscape' (2009: 194). This literary technique, which spells the disintegration of symbolic meaning, was born out of a particular historical conflict. The Protestant Reformation, Benjamin argues, brought with it a secular explanation of 'an empty world' 'whose importance resides solely in the stations of its decline' (2009: 139, 166). Allegory unmasks this empty world for what it is: it reveals 'the *facies hippocratica* of history as a petrified, primordial landscape', thus providing 'the dark background against which the bright world of the symbol' might stand out (2009: 166).[2]

Benjamin's account of allegory can shed some additional light on the state of 'noncontemporaneous contemporaneity' that we find in Trollope's late novels. Benjamin and Trollope share, first of all, an interest in the literature of the seventeenth century, the works of Shakespeare in particular. During his journey to Australia, Trollope began a decade-long love affair with Jacobean drama. On board the ship taking him to the Antipodes, he re-read all of Shakespeare's plays (Jenkins 1999: 161); upon his return, he became an avid collector and critic of plays by Shakespeare's forgotten contemporaries.[3] Trollope's immersion in the Jacobean theatre may explain why he, like Benjamin, was interested in allegory's dramatic prehistory.[4] Furthermore, Benjamin and Trollope both saw the nineteenth century as a repetition of the seventeenth. As Benjamin argues in the *Arcades Project*, seventeenth-century allegory was the condition of possibility for the consolidation of nineteenth-century capitalism: 'Whether allegorically construed or circulated as a commodity, things, in both systems, signify not themselves but some superordinate "value" – whether that value is understood as a meaning or an exchange value' (Baucom 2005: 18). Geoffrey Harvey has pointed out that Trollope, too, connected the economic aspects of his own moment to those of the seventeenth century, albeit in a more intuitive fashion:

> The parallels of moral and social pattern are partly due to Trollope's recognition of tensions in his own burgeoning society similar to those evident in the rapidly changing Jacobean world; and the Jacobean dramatists employ several socio-moral themes – the redemption of the prodigal, the impoverishment of the gentry by the rising merchant class, the scrutiny of aristocratic values, the newly subversive spirit of the independent wealthy woman and the testing of the response of feminine virtue to altered social conditions – which reappear in the novels. (Harvey 1980: 17)

Harvey's observation can be expanded upon and translated into Benjamin's terms. 'Under mature capitalism', according to Benjamin, allegory's transformation from a literary technique into 'the phenomenology of the entire social-material world' acquired a cosmopolitan reach; the 'commodity renders allegory obsolete by perfecting and globalising the latter's logic of representation' (Halpern 1997: 13; quoted in Baucom 2005: 21). Built on the idea of disseminating possessive individualism over the world, settler colonialism is one particular expression of this narrative; like commodification, the principles of colonialism rest on giving a phenomenological expression to the representational logic of allegory. Trollope turned to an allegorical form of simultaneity, then, because this form lends itself to a project that seeks to expose the 'transverse, cross-time' form of simultaneity on which colonialism, as an expression of modernity, relies. After briefly showing how Trollope depicts a detailed version of seventeenth-century allegory in *John Caldigate*, this chapter suggests that his views about colonialism are expressed in an allegorical aesthetic, which manifests itself not only in his manipulation of temporality, but also in his creation of perspective and in his concern with the function of seemingly insignificant details.

Set in the Cambridgeshire Fens, the heartland of Puritanism, *John Caldigate* opens – like many of Trollope's late novels, such as *The American Senator* and *The Landleaguers* – with a description of a primordial landscape, bleak and forlorn: 'The property is bisected by an immense straight dike, . . . which is so sluggish, so straight, so ugly, and so deep, as to impress the mind of a stranger with the ideas of suicide' (Trollope 1995b: 3). The character most at home in this environment is Mrs Bolton, a fanatical Puritan and 'a poor melancholy half-crazed creature' (1995b: 136), who regards all mankind as fallen and whose only interest is an unhealthy obsession with death. When her husband tells her that their daughter Hester must marry, she exclaims that she 'would sooner sit by her bedside and watch her die' (1995b: 142). All men are wicked in her opinion, and John Caldigate, her son-in-law, seems to prove her right. When an Australian woman with whom Caldigate had travelled to Australia, Euphemia Smith, arrives on the scene to claim Caldigate as her husband, Mrs Bolton derives an enigmatic satisfaction in contemplating Hester's misfortune. Having invited her daughter to her old home, 'Puritan Grange', she refuses to let her leave, which results in a coexistence that is eminently allegorical: as Trollope puts it, it is 'a bond of discord' (1995b: 251).[5] Hester herself, in contrast, continues to believe in her husband's innocence, even when all evidence points to the contrary. Trollope's description of Hester's appearance highlights how she is the only ray of light in this novel's darkness:

> When [Caldigate] had been [at Puritan Grange] before, the winter had commenced, and everything around had been dull and ugly; but now it was July, and the patch before the house was bright with flowers. The roses were in full bloom, and every morsel of available soil was bedded out with geraniums. As he stood holding his horse by the rein while he rang the bell, a side-door . . . was suddenly opened, and a lady came through with a garden hat on, and garden gloves, and a basket full of rose leaves in her hand. (1995b: 105)

This depiction of nature as fruitful and abundant is the opposite of Mrs Bolton's Puritan outlook or Euphemia Smith's description of herself as a withered flower; when John Caldigate first meets Euphemia, she hints at her fallen status by telling Caldigate that 'we burst out into full flowering early in our spring, but long before the summer is over, we are no more than huddled leaves and thick stalks' (1995b: 36). As such, Hester also embodies a different theology. The intention of Mrs Bolton and Euphemia 'does not faithfully rest in the contemplation of bones, but faithlessly leaps forward to the idea of resurrection' (Benjamin 2009: 233); this allegorical worldview is made explicit in the lines that precede Euphemia's self-description: 'You', she tells Caldigate, 'have a resurrection – I mean here upon earth. We never have' (1995b: 36).[6] Hester, in contrast, eventually delivers her husband from damnation. It is her faith that instigates a Post Office servant, Samuel Bagwax, to investigate a crucial document, the envelope of a letter which Caldigate had sent to Euphemia Smith, which Bagwax proves to be a forgery. By unconditionally insisting on her husband's innocence, Hester showcases a certain naivety that subordinates epistemology to ethics, the possible to the good. Her perspective is that of the symbol, through which 'the transfigured face of nature is fleetingly revealed in light of redemption' (Benjamin 2009: 166). *The Way We Live Now* and *An Old Man's Love* use similar symbols, though the redemptive light they should cast does not shine forth. In *The Way We Live Now*, Roger Carbury woos his niece by bringing 'a white rose from the hot-house, and plac[ing] it in a glass on the dressing table. Surely she would know who put it there' (1992: 120). As Carbury's touching self-doubt suggests, however, his suit will fail. The main location of *An Old Man's Love*, Croker's Hall, is named after the cultivator or seller of saffron, a substance derived from the crocus. Since the crocus's name originates in a myth about spurned affections, the knowing reader infers that Mr Whittlestaff, living at Croker's Hall, will lose what capacity for love and youth that he has left.

Given its theologically informed presentation of allegory, it is not surprising that *John Caldigate* also provides the most sophisticated instance of Trollope's creation of an allegorical temporality. The first twelve chapters of *John Caldigate* narrate a prototypical predicament: because of his frivolous lifestyle, the eponymous heir to Folking has run into debts which he can settle only by selling his inheritance to his father. Penniless, Caldigate decides to go hunting for gold in Australia, where he forms a romantic attachment to Euphemia Smith, a fellow passenger. Then there is a sudden gap. In the space of one chapter, all details of his gold-digging operations vanish: readers are simply told that over a five-year period Caldigate becomes a minor tycoon and reconciles with his father. In the following fifty-one chapters, the narrated time is condensed while the discourse time is extended: they take up only two years and centre on a trial that tries to uncover what happened, exactly, between Caldigate and Euphemia during the previous five years. This deceleration in narrative speed is accompanied by a rhythm that is anything but leisurely, marked as it is by the different characters' repetition of their views. This procedure creates a peculiar tension and feeling of oppression, like an orchestra that builds layer upon layer without ever bringing its chord to a resolution. The *Times* thought this to have been a mistake:

> *John Caldigate* is a good novel expanded into a dull one. The promise of the opening is excellent, and the interest rises rather than otherwise towards the close of the first volume. But then Mr. Trollope falls into that methodical and detailed narrative which we should say had been growing into a habit with him. (Smalley 1969: 455)

The novel's detailed dullness is appropriate, though. By continually keeping the past in view, the novel produces what Benjamin calls 'the irregular rhythm of the constant pause' (2009: 197). This oppressive atmosphere is heightened by the novel's lack of subplots, which, according to Cardinal Newman, normally provide room for relaxation: 'skilful novelists like Trollope have underplots. Such a contrivance obliges events to go more slowly – also it gives opportunity for variety and repose' (Newman 1961: 8; quoted in Mullen 1990: 168). But even in novels which do have multiple subplots, such as *The Way We Live Now*, Trollope's narrative tends to become jumbling and confusing:

> The two weeks between 5 July (Chapter 53), when [Melmotte] knows he must produce £50,000, to 18 July (Chapter 83), when, failing that, he commits suicide, span thirty chapters and stretch over nearly a third of a novel set over a period of six months, all while the average of almost eight pages per chapter remains steady . . . This extreme slowdown of narrative speed creates the opposite of pleasurable expectancy . . . Alfred Hitchcock famously illustrates suspense as occurring when the viewer of a film (the reader could be substituted) knows a bomb will detonate in fifteen minutes; then, the dilation of time only builds tension. (McGann 2008: 152)

Like Caldigate, Melmotte is haunted by his past abroad. His crimes, forgery and fraud, are always threatening to catch up with him: he is harried from the moment Mr Alf, his opponent for the seat of Westminster, sends reporters to Paris and Vienna and these return with unsavoury stories.

Trollope's nervous trudge in *John Caldigate* and *The Way We Live Now* does not end in closure. It continues to remain a matter of perspective whether Caldigate has been acting in good faith, or whether Melmotte's fall was unavoidable: 'Finsbury delighted for a while to talk of the great Financier, and even Chelsea thought that he had been done to death by ungenerous tongues' (Trollope 1992: 738). Melmotte's past is, like Caldigate's, a mystery, inasmuch as his origins and activities remain undisclosed. Trollope's catalogue of Melmotte's activities, in a passage that we have already examined, reveals more than just the extent of Melmotte's financial empire. It is unclear which of these ventures are real and which fictitious, an effect heightened by Trollope's use of the passive:

> It was presumed that the contemplated line from ocean to ocean across British America would become a fact in his hands . . . He had a fleet – or soon would have a fleet of emigrant ships – ready to carry every discontented Irishman out of Ireland . . . It was known that he had already floated a company for laying down a submarine wire from Penzance to Point de Galle. (1992: 368)

The narrator does not step in to separate rumour from fact. All the reader needs to know is that this smokescreen bolsters Melmotte's reputation. As such, *The Way We Live Now* is structured around a narrative enigma. Similarly, the reader knows that Caldigate fell in love with Euphemia Smith on board the *Goldfinder*, but to what extent they continued their affair afterwards remains shrouded in doubt. This formal ingenuity did not escape the notice of Edmund Sheridan Purcell, a budding biographer who, writing in *The Academy*, noted that 'in the sudden transition by which [Trollope] avoids the dubious part of the young man's story, his construction is both masterly and judicious' (Smalley 1969: 451). The urgency of Trollope's late novels, then, lies in the part that is a lie. This, too, is a sign of allegories, which 'fill out and deny the void in which they are represented' (Benjamin 2009: 233).

The fact that these novels are structured around such a void is echoed in the ghostlike aura that surrounds colonial revenants. Caldigate's confrontation with Crinkett, sleeping on a bench in a Cambridge courtyard, is distinctively eerie: 'Then it occurred to Caldigate that Crinkett's slumbers had been only a pretence' (1995b: 197). In *Dr Wortle's School*, Ferdinand Lefroy's sudden return from the dead, which makes Mrs

Peacocke a bigamist, is likewise described in ghostlike terms: it is a 'dream', a 'horrible apparition' (1989c: 23, 32). *The Way We Live Now* provides a more humorous example: 'Marylebone, which is always merciful, took [Melmotte] up quite with affection, and would have returned his ghost to Parliament could his ghost have paid for committee rooms' (1992: 738). These ghosts from the past cannot be seen directly. Trollope stresses that Bagwax's analysis depends on a photographic reproduction of the envelope rather than the envelope itself. In *Dr Wortle's School*, too, it is by means of a photograph of Ferdinand Lefroy's tombstone that Mr Peacocke can prove Mrs Peacocke's freedom (1989c: 166).

In an analogous fashion, Trollope's novels hint at the existence of another reality by drawing attention to this reality's existence but leaving its contents blank. In *The Way We Live Now*, Trollope highlights the enigma that is Melmotte by means of the dramatic mode (Friedman 1955: 1178) or external focalisation (Genette 1980: 191), in which the reader is not given insight into the inner workings of a particular character's mind, but in which the narrator simply shows what is happening.[7] At a crucial point, Trollope refuses to give us Melmotte's thoughts and secrets in great detail, and instead furnishes us with a mysterious, Hemingwayesque scene:

> Mr Melmotte on entering the room bolted the door, and then, sitting at his own table, took certain papers out of the drawers – a bundle of letters and another of small documents. From these, with very little examination, he took three or four – two or three perhaps from each. These he tore into very small fragments and burned the bits – holding them over a gas-burner and letting the ashes fall into a large china plate. Then he blew the ashes into the yard through the open window. This he did to all these documents but one. This one he put bit by bit into his mouth, chewing the paper into a pulp till he swallowed it. (1992: 527)

Why this one document is so compromising as to require actual consumption is never explained. This scene thus has a similar function to the narrative gap in *John Caldigate*: it constructs a question around which the novel weaves its constant pause. Another narrative cipher spells out the geopolitical implications of this procedure. The resolution of *The Way We Live Now* is a *deus ex machina* similar to Bagwax's discovery of the postmark: Paul Montague is able to extricate himself from Melmotte's affairs and from Mrs Hurtle's claim through the advice and counsel of one Mr Ramsbottom, whose character, curiously, is not developed and never described. Although Montague travels back and forth to Liverpool to meet him, he remains a blank. Roger Carbury enjoins Montague to trust himself completely to this man, for no apparent reason. The century's financial history, however, can dispel some of the mystery surrounding this figure. Ramsbottom represents Liverpool: just as this city was the heart of British finance in the eighteenth century (Baucom 2005), when British capitalism was still young, so he still knows what makes finance tick, unlike Londoners such as Montague, who want to play the game of finance, but have forgotten the rules.

In *John Caldigate*, the impression that readers are being denied the whole view is present from the opening sentence onward, which introduces an element of internal focalisation: 'Perhaps it was more the fault of Daniel Caldigate the father than of his son John Caldigate, that they two could not live together in comfort in the days of the young man's early youth' (1995b: 1). Trollope often creates internal focalisation through certain conjunctive adverbs; 'perhaps', 'of course', and 'certainly' are familiar signs that what follows must be considered as in some way subjective. Here, however, it is unclear through whose eyes the world is presented. This sentence is fraught with ambiguity; introducing an element of uncertainty that pervades the novel as a whole, the word 'perhaps' announces a point of view even before the story has begun. From its first word, then, the novel nudges the reader towards a point of view on the basis of information which is epistemologically unclear. In the remainder of the novel, Trollope uses free indirect discourse to present the story from Caldigate's point of view. When Caldigate returns to England, for example, he reflects that in Hester he has found 'where the gold lay at this second Ahalala' (1995b: 107), even though he resolves that 'at the very first mention of a British wife he must declare himself to be wedded to Polyeuka', his Australian mine (1995b: 116). Caldigate's perspective prevails, except when he is doing time in jail. In other words, Caldigate and the narrator seem to have struck a deal. This is not just a matter of the narrative's structural organisation. At the end of the novel, Trollope further emphasises the narrator's selective omniscience by suggesting that the narrator is actually a character: 'When last I heard from Folking, Mrs John Caldigate's second boy had just been born' (1995b: 498). This subtle use of metalepsis at the end of a novel, in which the narrator shifts his position from an extradiegetic to an intradiegetic level (Genette 1980: 234), occurs in other late novels as well, such as *Marion Fay* (1985: 422). In *John Caldigate*, however, the use of metalepsis is bewildering and makes it seem as if the narrator is a ghost-writer commissioned by Caldigate.

In another novel set in the Antipodes, *The Fixed Period*, the narrator's reliability is even more questionable, since he is not a figure on the margins of the story, but its protagonist. With the exception of *The Fixed Period*, Trollope never uses an I-protagonist (Friedman 1955: 1175) or a homodiegetic narrator (Genette 1980: 245) in his novels (although in his short stories he does experiment with this form); he considered it to be 'too egoistic' and even 'dangerous' (Trollope 1983: 429). In *The Fixed Period*, however, he uses it to good effect. Like E. T. A. Hoffmann's Kater Murr, President Neverbend is a bit too full of himself, but he cannot always maintain his pose. While he presents his case as if he had the unconditional support of the population who exiled him, there are certain inconsistencies in his account. He may initially present his subjects as 'the very cream . . . that had been skimmed from the milk-pail of . . . a wider colony' (Trollope 1997: 11), but also mentions that there 'had always been a scum of the population, the dirty, frothy, meaningless foam at the top' (1997: 97).[8] The narrator, then, is fallible, even unreliable. He presents reality, more particularly, as seen through the frame of allegory. Like Mrs Bolton, Neverbend is obsessed by death and corpses. His political programme of compulsory euthanasia at the age of sixty-seven makes him resemble the tyrant who 'provide[s] the *Trauerspiel* with [corpses]' (Benjamin 2009: 219). Looking forward to the moment of his own 'deposition', Neverbend is exiled before his scheme can be brought to fruition; the novel is written by a man who has lost his country and his family. As a result, his gaze is both contemplative and melancholic. The novel's final paragraph shows us a man and a novelist at the end of his tether: 'What shall I do with my book? Who will publish it? How shall I create an interest for it? Is there one who will believe, at any rate, that I believe in the Fixed Period?' (1997: 153–4).

In addition to his manipulation of time, plot, and perspective, Trollope infuses his late novels with allegory by resolving his plots by means of certain seemingly insignificant details. *John Caldigate* is, again, paradigmatic. Caldigate's trial revolves around an envelope which he addressed to Euphemia Smith as Mrs Caldigate but which he, so Caldigate maintains, never sent. Since this is the only material fact that supports the case against him, Caldigate's barrister declares that it is on 'this envelope . . . that the case hangs' (1995b: 325). The envelope's postmark, in particular, may have been forged. The jury and the judge, however, pay more attention to the testimonies against Caldigate. Caldigate thus finds himself in a world where, according to Benjamin, any 'person, any object, any relationship can mean absolutely anything else. With this possibility a destructive, but just verdict is passed on the profane world: it is characterised as a world in which the detail is of no great importance' (2009: 175). A lack of attention to detail, however, does not mean 'that details themselves have lost all meaning; indeed, precisely the opposite is the case' (Weber 2008: 241): it is the coexistence of the opposites of past and present that creates the dialectic of the allegorical. Paradoxically, indeed, Bagwax notices another detail, the stamp, hidden underneath the postmark, which was fabricated at a later date than that at which the letter was purportedly posted.

Embodying two divergent temporalities, the envelope encapsulates the allegorical principles that structure Trollope's late novels. Just as the envelope's authorship is unclear – it combines Caldigate's handwriting with a fabricated stamp – so Trollope's manipulation of perspective tends to make it difficult to decide through whose eyes we ought to see the world that his late novels represent. Because the late novels do not always fully detail their characters' past, the reader has to piece this past together from the various glimpses that the texts afford elsewhere. Not only do these allegorical moments of simultaneity, in which past and present coexist, subvert the modern experience of simultaneity, in which events are connected by temporal coincidence; the fact that the past is constantly kept in view but out of reach tends to bring the novels' onward movement to a halt. The allegorical aesthetic of Trollope's late novels thus suggests that possessive individualism was at odds with the Enlightenment notion of an imagined community and, concomitantly, that the liberal support for colonial capitalism was irreconcilable with the liberal belief in progress.

Notes

1. Benedict Anderson is often invoked to account for an analysis of the novel and the newspaper as 'a representational mapping of the social world of the nation' (Cheah 1999: 8), but his argument is essentially 'a formal [one] about *how* nations are imagined rather than *what* they imagine' (Cheah 1999: 6; see also Culler 1999). The sense of simultaneity had important political implications: its activation aided the rise of the nation as 'a sociological organism moving calendrically through homogeneous empty time' (B. Anderson 2006: 26). If modern nationalism relies on simultaneity, then the novel and the newspaper are technologies for '"re-presenting" the *kind* of imagined community that is the nation' (B. Anderson 2006: 25). Anderson's conflation of the form of the newspaper with the form of the novel is not as self-evident as he makes it seem, however. The newspaper's reliance on 'calendrical coincidence' (B. Anderson 2006: 35) 'binds it to the present in a way that simply does not apply to the novel' (Vermeulen 2009: 104). The novel's temporal prerogative is far more expansive: 'While the newspaper can only present the simultaneity of *today's* events, literature can present the simultaneity of any day's events' (Vermeulen 2009: 104). Trollope's negative portrayal of newspapers in *John Caldigate* – the *Isle-of-Ely-Church-Intelligencer*, the *Daily Tell-Tale*, the *Snapper* (1995b: 282, 446, 59, 47) – hints at the difference with his own mode of narration. These newspapers are not impersonal, but rumorous. Matthew Rubery has argued that, like many of his contemporaries, Trollope resented the power of the press because it could not be held

accountable: writing anonymously, journalists seemed to wield a power that was disproportionate to their concern for the truth. Trollope's portrayal of newspaper editors is accordingly consistently contemptuous (the exception being Hugh Stanbury in *He Knew He Was Right*). Quintus Slide, who reappears throughout the Palliser series, uses *The People's Banner* to further his own interests: 'Slide's editorship consists in suppressing multiple viewpoints instead of, as Trollope's authorial voice aspired to do, allowing ample room for conflicting points of view to perform the work of deliberation in the novel' (Rubery 2009: 106). Paradoxically, Trollope's characters seem to be extremely sensitive to what the papers say about them: they cannot help reading what they know to be falsehoods. Their conscience makes them susceptible to attacks from the press.

2. Benjamin's definition stands in a long history of thinking about allegory. For suggestive reflections on the voluminous literature that this subject has generated, see Copeland and Struck (2010) and Machosky (2010).
3. This is one of the few details that Nigel Starck does not document in his rich and exhaustive account of Trollope's Australasian journeys (2014).
4. The importance of this fascination is underscored in the penultimate sentences of his *Autobiography*, in which Trollope professes his intention to 'leave in [his] copies of these dramatists, down to the close of the time of James I, written criticism on every play. No one who has not looked closely into it knows how many there are' (1999a: 367). Trollope's archival inclination is not just an expression of the desire that his work, too, will stand the test of time. It is also a sign of an allegorical worldview: 'an appreciation of the transience of things, and the concern to rescue them for eternity, is one of the strongest impulses in allegory' (Benjamin 2009: 223). Trollope's editions now rest in the Folger Library, taking their part in the 'baroque ideal of knowledge, the process of storing, to which the vast libraries are a monument' (Benjamin 2009: 184).
5. This phrase is rare: it also occurs in Dora Greenwell's 'A Morning in Spring' (*Carmina Crucis*, London: Bell and Daldy, 1869). The religious fervour that characterises Greenwell's writings may have been an inspiration for Mrs Bolton.
6. According to Janet C. Myers's postcolonial study of emigration to the Antipodes, this passage shows that Mrs Smith has been forced to emigrate because she 'is no longer a "productive" citizen of the nation' (Myers 2009: 66). The surfeit of young women in England left genteel ladies with only two options: they could become a governess or an old maid, as the examples of Lucy Morris and Miss Macnulty in *The Eustace Diamonds* indicate. For women from the lower classes, emigration presented an increasingly attractive way to hedge their bets. Initiatives such as the 'Family Colonisation Loan Society' (founded in 1848 by Caroline Chisholm) and the 'Female Middle Class Emigration Society' (founded in 1862 by Maria Rye and Jane Lewin) helped women prepare for their journey and find employment on arrival, often as a governess or domestic help. Like guidebooks, these societies were manifestations of a larger disciplinary discourse that was meant to instil a belief in portable domesticity and thus to make sure that women would preserve their national identity while they were reinventing themselves. Female emigrants were made to understand that they could do as they

liked, as long as this was within the boundaries of middle-class behaviour. Portable domesticity thus harnessed 'the supposedly liberating potential of empire' by making the colony more like what home should have been (Myers 2009: 13). While many Victorian novels played a part in instilling such disciplinary images of domesticity, so Myers argues, Trollope's *John Caldigate* portrays the failure of this project. Improving her appearance and thus performing upward mobility, Euphemia Smith follows the rules laid down by portable domesticity. At the same time, she transgresses middle-class standards of behaviour by vigorously asserting her independence. Once in Australia, she takes on a variety of names, 'not to protect her identity, but to suit the requirements of a given role', and thus 'enacts the governesses' collective nightmare as she relinquishes her identity in the colony' (Myers 2009: 66). While this analysis is perfectly sound, it cannot account for the specificity of Trollope's baroque image.

7. There is a maximum of mimesis, or showing, and a minimum of diegesis, or telling. The most famous nineteenth-century example of this technique is arguably Henry James's *The Awkward Age* (1899), a tour de force in which a story is told without any comment about characters' consciousness; see Miller (2005).
8. This gaffe foreshadows the totalitarian logic that imperialism would lead to. In the words of Hannah Arendt, those 'whom the persecutor had singled out as scum of the earth – Jews, Trotskyites, etc. – actually were received as scum of the earth everywhere; those whom persecution had called undesirable became the *indésirables* of Europe' (Arendt 2004: 343).

Chapter 4

'Convivial in a Cadaverous Fashion': Satires on Sovereignty

The increasingly global dimension of capitalism in the Victorian age had a significant impact on perceptions about the nature of English sovereignty. To accommodate these changes, Lauren M. E. Goodlad has argued, English liberals created 'a nationalist discourse on the global that professed to explain Britain's place in the world and in history' (Goodlad 2009: 439–40).[1] Victorian literature contributed to the creation of this 'foreign policy'. Developing in response to imperial encounters, Victorian realism can be considered as a geopolitical aesthetic, 'the expression of "an unconscious collective effort" to "figure out" the "landscapes and forces" embedded in global processes that are at once lived and beyond conscious experience' (Goodlad 2010b: 406; Jameson 1992: 3; Stewart 2000). Authorising two interlocking conceptions of sovereignty on the basis of two different ideas of value, Trollope's works from the 1850s and 1860s are a case in point.

As a first part of his geopolitical aesthetic, Trollope depicts English sovereignty 'as the product of an organic national history' (Goodlad 2009: 443). His novels set in Barsetshire present 'in-depth portraits of England's provincial interior', thus exerting a 'centripetal force against [global] dispersion' (Goodlad 2009: 441). The Barsetshire novels accomplish this task by imagining value in symbolic terms. The value of the cathedral spire in *Barchester Towers* or the gates to the Gresham estate in *Doctor Thorne* is symbolic rather than material and resides in their history.[2] The second part of Trollope's geopolitical aesthetic authorises English sovereignty on the basis of the individual's capacity to produce economic value, thus providing an 'ideological justification for the settlement of land outside English borders' (Goodlad 2009: 441). Trollope articulates this foreign policy in his travel writings, which paradoxically intertwine the logic of cosmopolitan commerce with racial prejudice.[3] Trollope presents himself as a 'self-styled teller of hard truths' (Buzard 2010: 176): if the English did a better job at producing economic value than the colonial races, then there was nothing left for the latter but to disappear. Of 'the Australian black man', for instance, 'we may certainly say that he has to go' (Trollope 2002: 1.76). In his account of his journey to Iceland, Trollope uses the same argument for the inhabitants of St Kilda: 'Who shall say that these people ought to be deported from their homes and placed recklessly upon some point of the mainland?' (1878: 11). As a whole, then, Trollope's early novels and travel books imagine sovereignty through the productive interplay of rootedness and cosmopolitanism. This play

> articulates a basic geopolitical relation between Britain and its settler colonies which reproduces England's exceptional global status. Whereas the seemingly limitless resources of the colony enable possessive individuals to propagate, Barsetshire's limited but richly cultivated supply requires venerated establishments to conserve a shared sovereign history. (Goodlad 2009: 447)

As Gladstone stopped dominating the political scene in the 1870s, so did this liberal vision of a 'Greater Britain' disappear. It was replaced by the conservative New Imperialism, fathered by Disraeli, which used blood and race as the basis for territorial expansion. Trollope's late novels reflect this sea-change in English geopolitics; no longer do they follow the realist principles that he put into practice in his earlier work. The late novels portray a disenchanted modernity in which heirlooms can be invented and Englishness is racialised; whereas the early novels take the existence of a Greater Britain for granted, the late novels lay bare the disjunction between metropolitan experience and its colonial conditions. Lizzie Eustace's exaggerated hyper-romantic self-fashioning, for instance, 'performs the New Imperial determination to *invent* heirlooms' (Goodlad 2010a: 869), whereas in *The Prime Minister* Trollope explores what happens when colonial individualism returns to the metropole in his ambiguous portrayal of Ferdinand Lopez, a Jewish speculator who successfully poses as a gentleman. This does not imply, however, that Trollope stuck to the brand of Victorian liberalism he once supported. The present chapter shows that Trollope's late novels also criticise the foreign policy encoded in the geopolitical aesthetic of his earlier work. To this end, we must pay attention not to his use of realism, but of satire, a generic marker Trollope hints at by naming the Foreign Secretary in *Marion Fay* Lord Persiflage.

The tone of satire seems to be irreconcilable with the principles of realism. Whereas realism is supposed to evoke sympathy, satire invites scorn. Even so, the two are not necessarily antagonistic:

> Satire exists to isolate a condition or a sector of human life and hold it up for ridicule. Realism, in its nineteenth-century literary sense, is a method or

> an attitude seeking to represent experience, especially everyday experience, without implausibility. But toward the end of the Victorian period these two modes blurred into one another beyond easy division. The fiction and criticism of the era imply that to describe the world in starkly realist detail – to pursue and to represent facts and conditions without euphemism – is to expose this same world's essential folly and error. (Matz 2010: ix)

In Trollope's late work, to be sure, realism easily segues into satire. The first of his late works is a satire, having 'the fault which is to be attributed to almost all satires, whether in prose or verse. The accusations are exaggerated. The vices implied are coloured so as to make effect rather than to represent truth' (Trollope 1999a: 355). Trollope here describes *The Way We Live Now* as a form of moral or social criticism that works through exaggeration. As such, there is a certain kinship between satire and the stylistic element discussed in the previous chapter, allegory. Both modes assume that the truth is hidden by a veil of words. But whereas allegory tries to lift this veil by means of an interpretive effort, satire tries to lift it by means of a moral effort, 'an effort to see things not as they are (not as they are veiled) but as they (or we) are corrected, as when we are made aware of folly and deceit even when we can never hope to be innocent of them' (Bruns 1979: 127).[4] As critics have emphasised since the pioneering work of Mikhail Bakhtin, satires are not monologic, but dialogic: they implicate both the audience and the satirist in the very things they seem to hold up to scorn, as a result of which it becomes unclear who, exactly, is being criticised.[5] Trollope seems to have appreciated this distinction: 'The spirit which produces the satire is honest enough, but the very desire which moves the satirist to do his work energetically, makes him dishonest' (Trollope 1999a: 355). This chapter shows how in *The American Senator*, *The Fixed Period*, and *The Landleaguers*, Trollope satirises his earlier geopolitics by means of three literary techniques which, although substantially different, all serve to stage a problem or a paradox without offering a resolution: parody, irony, and poignancy. These three literary techniques are not inherently dialogical or satirical, but they become so in Trollope's hands.

Parody

In the most literal sense of the word, a parody is a song written against an ode. Changing the subject but keeping its form intact, this countersong can transform the sublime into the ridiculous; 'the imitative and critical functions of parody are always closely intertwined. We should think of parody involving a spectrum of attitudes on the part of its creators and its audiences. At one extreme of the spectrum lies critique, but at the other lies a kind of homage' (Williams 2011: xiv). To appreciate a parody, then, one must know the original. In *The American Senator*, this original is made up of the two poles of rootedness and cosmopolitanism that are the heart of Trollope's earlier geopolitics. The novel presents both as an inversion of their former selves, as a result of which their relation is not supplementary but adversative. Instead of a productive interplay, they create a negative intersection.

The American Senator represents a symbolic form of sovereign rootedness in its portrayal of the hunt. Foxhunting gives the nation unity and transforms it into a collective, for 'on hunting mornings all the lands of the county – and of the next counties if they can be reached – are the property of the hunt' (Trollope 1999b: 501). It also helps cultivate the quintessentially English virtue of manliness. It is by hunting that Lawrence Twentyman is saved from complete dejection when he is rejected by his beloved: the hunt 'did not cure poor Larry, but it helped to enable him to be a man' (1999b: 510). Trollope's emphasis on the hunt's ceremonial aspects bring to mind the '*theatrical show*' Walter Bagehot more cynically describes in *The English Constitution* (Bagehot 2001: 30).[6] In this spectacle, the fox is imagined as the personification of English sovereignty: 'There, on a clean sward of grass, laid out as carefully as though he were a royal child prepared for burial, was – a dead fox' (Trollope 1999b: 62). If the fox represents the monarch, the master of hounds functions as one of his ministers, whose position, as Trollope describes in *The Duke's Children*, is nominated under the direct control of the hunt's subscribers. Trollope thus presents the tradition of foxhunting as a symbolic form of value, a view on foxhunting that he also articulated in an earlier polemic with E. A. Freeman; as such, the hunt 'accumulates particular ethical and cultural worth in excess of abstract economic value and, in so doing binds rather than atomises' (Goodlad 2009: 443).[7] The royal fox which the hunters find has not been ritually sacrificed, however, but surreptitiously poisoned. If an animal representing the sovereign is assassinated, sovereignty must be breached. The novel's main story illustrates that this breach is due to the resurgence of barbarism.

The novel's protagonist, Lady Arabella Trefoil, strikingly personifies the barbarian aristocrat, who does not take part in the capitalist economy of exchange but 'takes possession and seizes' (Foucault 1997: 196). She abuses 'the social possibilities' that hunting offers (Hynes 1988: 53) in order to coax the wealthy but heedless Lord Rufford into marrying her, penniless as she is. She appeals to him as 'a sort of five-barred gate' (Trollope 1999b: 252) and considers him 'as much born and bred to be hunted as a fox' (1999b: 464). She is beaten, however, by a wealthy bourgeois, Miss Penge; Lady Arabella, it seems, is stuck in the discourse of the nobility of yore, feeling 'deserted and betrayed' (1999b: 299). The aristocracy as a whole, indeed, is characterised by predatory, immoral instincts. When Major Caneback is lying on his deathbed, having fallen off his horse and been kicked in the head, his friends are more worried about their ball than his soul: 'Even while drinking their wine they could not keep themselves from the subject, and were convivial in a cadaverous fashion' (1999b: 157). This is one of the many moments in the novel when realism gives way to satire: instead of representing the death of a character as it affects other characters' moral feeling (which is how the novel represents the death of another character, John Morton), the death of Major Caneback serves to expose human selfishness.

The resurgence of barbarism that the hunt is subjected to has a social cause. Trollope's novel depicts the 'political, social and moral disruption created when a country gentleman does not perform his duty by living on his estate, where he can maintain the miniature society that depends upon him' (Tracy 1978: 209). Lord Rufford may be 'much liked by all sporting men, but is not otherwise very popular with the people round Dillsborough' (Trollope 1999b: 5). 'In spite of his grace', as Ruth apRoberts remarks, Lord Rufford is 'in fact, idle, ignorant, and self-satisfied. The criticism here reminds one of Arnold on the Barbarians' (1971: 181). John Morton is even further removed from his community. As a diplomat who spends his time abroad, he 'had been an absentee since he came of age, soon after which time he inherited the property' (1999b: 5). He is an honourable figure, however, remaining faithful to Arabella Trefoil even when she leaves him to pursue Lord Rufford. He falls ill before she can realise her mistake, however, and dies prematurely.[8] This degeneracy in the English social order is reflected in the decline of the town of Dillsborough, a latter-day Barchester. The town suffers from 'decreasing business', the Bush Inn is 'fallen from its past greatness', and there is a general atmosphere of 'decadence' (1999b: 3, 4). Trollope's description of English life in *The American Senator*, then, parodies the symbolic sovereignty which the Barchester novels located in the land.

At the same time, *The American Senator* also parodies the cosmopolitanism and racism of Trollope's travel writings. Trollope began the novel while he was visiting his son in New South Wales and finished it while crossing the Pacific. On this trip, Trollope uncharacteristically did not produce a travel book, and *The American Senator* can be thought of as a substitute.[9] The novel's title character, Elias Gotobed, who has obtained leave of absence 'to study the British Constitution and to see the ways of Britons with his own eyes' (1999b: 48), exhibits many similarities with Trollope the traveller. Like Trollope, he is a self-professed teller of hard truths, both in his commendations and condemnations. Gotobed falls into the trap Trollope fell into himself: 'it is very hard to write about any country a book that does not represent the country described in a more or less ridiculous point of view' (Trollope 1951: 4). *The American Senator* can therefore be read as an attempt at redemption and rectification: it illustrates that 'an American in England behaved very much like an Englishman in America' (Stryker 1950: 148). The reception of the novel in the English press mirrors the reception of Trollope's travel books in the colonial press. Most piqued of all was the reviewer in *The Times*: 'the Senator himself is an excrescence . . . But the shrewd Mr Gotobed's outspoken criticisms prove nothing more than his incapacity for rightly understanding our "institutions"' (Smalley 1969: 431). Trollope had hit a nerve.

Like Trollope the traveller, Gotobed bases his criticisms on reason and common sense. Gotobed is a 'Rationalist' critic, bent on the destruction rather than the reformation of institutions (Nardin 1990). It 'strikes me', he says, 'that you do not know how little prone you are to admit the light of reason into either your public or private life, and how generally you allow yourselves to be guided by traditions, prejudices, and customs which should be obsolete' (1999b: 535). English rootedness, in other words, is incomprehensible to Gotobed. As such, reason in *The American Senator* functions like race in the travel writings: both function as criteria by which the traveller judges the culture in which he finds himself. This analogy is as puzzling as it is illuminating. Reason and race represent the two faces of the Enlightenment: while reason is associated with the Enlightenment's promotion of ethical agency, race is associated with the Enlightenment's embrace of hierarchies (A. Anderson 2005: 198). For Gotobed, as for Trollope the traveller, however, they share an underlying pattern. Just as Trollope the traveller defines race as a function in the game of capitalism, so is Gotobed's reliance on reason bound up with economy. Towards the end of the novel, for example, he finds out that Lord Rufford has constructed a farm to show his tenants how the work is to be done, but that this farm does not pay its way. This strikes him as folly:

> You say . . . that it is a model farm – but it's a model of ruin. If you want to teach a man any other business, you don't specially select an example in which the proprietors are spending all their capital without any return. And if you would not do this in shoemaking, why in farming? (1999b: 472)

This conclusion may seem to imply that Gotobed is an apology for Trollope's travel writings – that racism is, as it were, reasonable.

Trollope's novel suggests, however, that there is a certain perversity to the logic of reason. Reason in *The American Senator* refers more to itself than the reality which it is supposed to demystify. To say that something is unreasonable, after all, is not necessarily reasonable in itself. As the narrator puts it, Gotobed 'was angry because people were unreasonable with him, which was surely unreasonable in him who accused Englishmen generally of want of reason' (1999b: 552). The representation of Gotobed thus exposes a catch-22 in Trollope's geopolitical aesthetic: his criterion for truth is subject to itself.

The novel shows, nonetheless, that this paradox can and does in fact lead to truth. This is where Trollope's satire on his earlier foreign policy becomes more complex and layered. When a tenant, Goarly, is accused of having poisoned a fox, Gotobed sets out to correct this apparent miscarriage of justice. He believes that Goarly is targeted merely because he resists the oppression of his feudal landlord. Gotobed is wrong in his assessment of the situation and in his judgement of Goarly's character, but his oppositional stance does create the conditions of possibility for a fuller picture. Goarly turns out to be an accomplice of one Scrobby, the real murderer of the fox; were it not for Gotobed's misguided efforts, Scrobby would not have been found out. Gotobed's fundamental antagonism thus sustains the possibility of the kind of radical criticism that has its roots in the concept of the public. As Jürgen Habermas explored in detail in his influential *Strukturwandel der Öffentlichkeit* (1962), newspapers and coffeehouses created spaces in which individuals could meet on terms of equality and form a collective will outside the institutions of power. This created a relation to the state that was often antagonistic. Trollope's title character is such an antagonistic speaker. In a final attempt to expose political domination before the public use of reason, Gotobed decides to conclude his stay with a lecture in St James's Hall. This lecture is public insofar as we 'say [a thing] in a venue of indefinite address and hope that people will find themselves in it' (Warner 2002: 86) and insofar as there is no dialogical interaction with the audience: 'the agonistic interlocutor is coupled with passive interlocutors' (Warner 2002: 90). Gotobed is certainly agonistic, inveighing against most English institutions: the church, political representation, primogeniture, the army. Before he has properly begun, however, the crowd gets into an uproar and the police advise Gotobed to stop his lecture. His audience only wants to win acclaim, which reveals that Gotobed is addressing a community where the public sphere has been re-feudalised:

> Publicity once meant the exposure of political domination before the public use of reason; publicity [in the Victorian period] adds up the reactions of an uncommitted friendly disposition. In the measure that it is shaped by public

> relations, the public sphere of civil society again takes on feudal features. (Habermas 1989: 195)

Gotobed reaches insight through blindness, then, when he tells his host 'that the spirit of conservatism in this country is so strong that you cannot bear to part with a shred of the barbarism of the middle ages' (1999b: 79).[10] As the novel's portrayal of Arabella Trefoil and of the English reaction to Gotobed's criticisms suggests, barbarism of one kind or another is rife in English society, even though Gotobed reaches this conclusion through biased self-confidence rather than, as he claims, logical deduction. In short, while Gotobed is the object of the narrator's satirical gaze insofar as he represents Trollope the traveller, he at the same time functions as a mouthpiece for the novel's satire on English nationalism. As one character tells him, indeed, 'your shafts of satire pass me by without hurting me' (1999b: 191). Trollope's American reviewers perceived this. According to the *Nation*, on the one hand, 'the senator's part is the most elaborately written, and, fair or unfair in its satire, the pleasantest to read' (Smalley 1969: 433). *Harper's Magazine*, on the other hand, felt that 'the body which has given to the political world a Calhoun, a Webster, a Clay, a Sumner, and a Seward deserved some different typical man to represent it', but had to admit that 'even the caricature is clever' (Smalley 1969: 434). One might even go back a little further and see Gotobed as an echo of Benjamin Franklin, who in his late work 'becomes less an exponent of mercantile liberalism and more a satirical traducer of established power' (Giles 2008: 24).[11] This interpretation of Gotobed's voice as the voice of the satirist dovetails with Trollope's intentions. In a letter to Mary Holmes, Trollope asserted that Gotobed is 'a thoroughly honest man' who is not 'half so absurd as the things which he criticises' (Trollope 1983: 702).[12]

Trollope's emphasis on the absurdity and paradoxical discovery of truth is reinforced by the intertextual model that Gotobed brings to mind. As Ruth apRoberts has noted, the 'Senator as a device is reminiscent of a classical critical mode' (1971: 173), the foundations of which are eighteenth-century works such as Montesquieu's *Lettres persanes* (1721) and Oliver Goldsmith's *Citizen of the World* (1762). Both these works consist of a series of letters written by travellers on their visits to France and England, respectively. Trollope's novel highlights this model when Gotobed writes two long letters to his friend Josiah Scroome in Washington, in which he details his misgivings (chapters twenty-nine and fifty-one). Like them, Gotobed is a cosmopolite in that the cosmopolitanism of Montesquieu's and Goldsmith's narrators is linked to a very specific form of criticism. Their criticism rests on a paradox. It does not embody disinterestedness and worldliness, nor does it express the ethic of the tolerant and widely educated elite subject that one normally associates with the Enlightenment. In contrast, these travellers are 'necessarily and insistently foreign, trying to work through strangeness . . . rather than stressing disinterestedness and worldliness' (Goodlad and Wright 2007: 7). Gotobed, too, is startled by the strange and sometimes inhospitable practices that he has to work through. Gotobed, indeed, is an exaggeration of this paradox, since he willingly forces himself into uncomfortable positions. Trollope's allusion to these eighteenth-century models, then, serves to stress a cosmopolitan vision of truth that is subtended not by capitalism, but by the narcissism of difference.

Irony

The aura of death that surrounds nationalism in *The American Senator* returns in *The Fixed Period*, though its context is very different. *The Fixed Period* is unique in two respects: it is set in the future, around the year 1980, and it figures a first-person narrator, John Neverbend, who presents his story as a memoir of his deposition as president of the independent colony of Britannula. The reason for Neverbend's exile is his fanatical support for the law of the Fixed Period, which determines that every citizen will undergo compulsory euthanasia and cremation at the age of sixty-seven.[13] This law is the colony's founding gesture, its 'symbolic equivalent to the Declaration of Independence' (Alessio 2004: 85); as Neverbend declares, 'it was undoubtedly the strong faith which we of Britannula had in that doctrine which induced our separation' (Trollope 1997: 1). This measure, he believes, will save the colony thousands in pounds and bring relief to the aged. Neverbend is obsessed with the practical details of his doctrine, to which end he has ordered the building of a college in which the old are to be deposited and which, 'by the use of machinery . . . could almost be made self-supporting' (1997: 3). By institutionalising the demand that citizens kill themselves for the sake of an abstract ideal, the nation is thus shown to have become biopolitical: it has substituted human life for sovereignty. Neverbend's plan is not brought to fruition, however. When the date of disposal of the first victim arrives, the community rebels and calls in an international intervention. Just as Neverbend is guiding the first victim to the college in a ritual pageant, a English warship arrives that threatens to level the capital city if Neverbend does not abdicate power.

The Fixed Period's conclusion recalls Benjamin Franklin's satires, which expose 'the folly of British imperial policy by looking at it, as it were, through the wrong end of a telescope, redescribing British government policy as if its greed and cupidity were part of a deliberate, coherent plan to diminish colonial power rather than enhance it' (Giles 2008: 31).[14] Trollope may have had in mind the bombardment of Kagoshima (1863) or any other of the military interventions that the Victorian age was rife with. *The Fixed Period* thus parodies the principles of British imperialism.[15] It is also ironic, insofar as what is said is contrary to what is meant: the British say they bring peace, but are actually intent upon regaining control over lost territory. The novel's core, however, revolves around a different kind of irony. Neverbend's argument is Trollope's only 'exercise in extended Swiftian irony' (Skilton 1993: vii). Harking back to *A Modest Proposal* (1729), the novel's representation of Neverbend's speech is an instance of ironic subjectivity (see Colebrook 2004: 79–88). We are supposed to assume that what Neverbend says is the opposite of what Trollope means, but this is not always straightforward. Using rational deliberation in order to reach an unthinkable, immoral conclusion, the novel's satire is so pervasive and cynical that it becomes unclear whether the ironic speaker is not, in fact, being serious. Trollope's own comments reinforce the impression that his use of irony in this novel is far from stable:

> When an intimate friend once ventured to refer to this Utopian euthanasia as a somewhat grim jest, he stopped suddenly in his walk, and grasping the speaker's arm in his energetic fashion, exclaimed: 'It's all true – I *mean* every word of it'. (Collins 1883: 594)

The object of this Swiftian irony is not only Enlightenment reason, as in *A Modest Proposal*, but also a pre-eminent instance of one of the most important technologies of sovereignty: the cenotaph, best known in its embodiment as the tomb of the unknown soldier, and here present in the form of Neverbend's college. Trollope's narrator takes the logic of the cenotaph one step further. In the cenotaph, death is figured as 'aestheticised anonymity' (Redfield 1999: 68): it presents the citizen with the prospect that his or her own death will be 'instantly assimilated into the common death for the sake of the collective' (Vermeulen 2009: 101). The important difference from other forms of mourning is that mourning in front of the cenotaph relies on an abstraction of death. It does not cover any particular corpse, although the notion of a corpse is integral to its function: 'The corpse, then, may be read as the remainder, the excess that nationalism's official scene of mourning excludes' (Redfield 1999: 68). Through the Fixed Period, however, the work of mourning not only follows but also precedes death. To make his scheme work, Neverbend tries to turn the Fixed Period into an aesthetic project.

He consistently describes his plans in terms of the mathematical and the beautiful (Trollope 1997: 15, 19, 40). The role of language is crucial to 'imagine new truths' (1997: 43); in vain, Neverbend forbids talk of the Fixed Period in terms of death, murder, slaughter, and execution, expressions which must be replaced by euphemisms such as disposition, mode of transition, and act of grace – terms which ironically prefigure his own destiny. These abstractions are part of a nationalist strategy: the nation must be '*radically* imagined: it cannot be experienced immediately as a perception' (Redfield 1999: 61). Neverbend's cenotaph fails, however. Not only does the Fixed Period seek to inscribe its authority on the surface of the mind, it is also inscribed directly on to the body. In spite of Neverbend's efforts at cremation without smoke or smell, a trapdoor is left open during an experiment on pigs, releasing a scent which makes the populace recoil in horror but which also, so he thinks, was 'by no means disagreeable' (1997: 71). The Fixed Period thus leaves the corpses it wants to conjure away all too perceptible. This was bound to happen, for Neverbend had already introduced 'the habit of tattooing on the backs of the babies the day on which they were born' (1997: 14). These inscriptions suggest a materiality that imagined communities ought to be lacking. Neverbend cannot see, or is not willing to see, how he himself is responsible for planting the seeds of the failure of his own plan. *The Fixed Period* thus uses irony to expose the folly and fanaticism of colonial nationalism. At the same time, however, this attempt takes the novel into a zone beyond irony. As in *A Modest Proposal*, there are moments when it is difficult to decide whether *The Fixed Period*'s actual author, Trollope, is not deadly serious when he suggests that the possessive individualism that is supposed to undergird colonialist cosmopolitanism should be used as the basis for a colonial nationalism.

Poignancy

Parody and irony are absent from Trollope's last, unfinished novel, *The Landleaguers*. Michael Sadleir dismissively points out that the novel is nothing but a 'sad account of wretched actuality, in which characterisation is submerged in floods of almost literal fact' (1961: 4). This hopeless hyperrealism ultimately produces a biting satire, however. *The Landleaguers* straightforwardly attacks a particular social problem, the agrarian agitation that rocked Ireland in the late 1870s, which Gladstone had sought to address with Land Acts of 1870 and 1881. The two Land Acts amounted to a codification of Irish tenant rights, making 'sustained residency on the land, rather than ownership of the land, the basis of political claims to representation' (Small 2011: 290). To paraphrase this in the vocabulary of the present chapter, English liberals wanted to create room for the development of a form of Irish rootedness by replacing a notion of value founded on contract with a notion of value founded on custom.[16] Trollope's narrator vehemently opposes this move, arguing that in Ireland one should be free to do as one likes. The novel's actual story, however, undercuts this argument by portraying a very different political concept, freedom from want. The novel depicts this form of freedom in the boycott of an Irish estate, during which the besieged Jones family can only access basic goods through the kindness of their servants, and in Rachel O'Mahony's life as an actress on the London stage, in the course of which she falls ill. This double plot jars with the narrator's liberal propaganda, since classical liberals tend to relegate rights such as access to food and water to the workings of a healthy marketplace (Mohamed 2010: 145). Trollope may have similarly wanted to conclude the novel with a return to a healthy, liberal market society in which the wrongs that the story depicts no longer exist. In its unfinished state, however, *The Landleaguers* does not resolve the tension between its explicit defence of colonial cosmopolitanism and its implicit defence of basic human rights. As a result, as Robert Tracy observes, there

> is poignancy in this last unfinished work, as Trollope, like [his] protagonists . . . tries to show that he still has some business to perform in the world by offering an opinion on the Irish crisis, reminding his readers that he is still thinking and writing, in spite of age, illness, and approaching death. (1978: 328)

The novel's poignancy is undeniably a product of the conditions under which it was created, dictated as it was by an author who knew that his end was nearing. But it is also an expression of its political subtext. The feeling of poignancy created by descriptions of physical suffering, Feisal Mohamed proposes, is an aesthetic equivalent for the freedom from want, since it 'occurs when one feels in the marrow both the decay of the flesh and a yearning for the immortality of the soul' and as such 'prompts us to seek for our fellow subjects those conditions allowing for health and life' (2010: 149).

In his earlier novels, Trollope had voiced lukewarm support for the liberal management of Ireland. Written while the first Land Act was being drafted, *Phineas Finn* is mostly supportive of this liberal measure. Following the lead of Mr Monk, who is able to see his way to some form of tenant rights, Phineas Finn finds that he cannot reconcile his own views and opinions with his party's opposition to Irish tenant rights, and resigns. Phineas's liberal volition is thus bound up with a concern for rootedness: 'He is his most liberal when he is his most Irish' (Hadley 2010: 261). In *The Landleaguers*, however, Trollope's narrator dismisses the Land Acts directly in chapter forty-one, 'The State of Ireland': 'If the land were to be taken altogether from the present owners, and divided in perpetuity among any possible number of tenants, so as to be the property of each tenant, without payment of any rent, all England's sense of justice would be outraged' (1995a: 298). Instead, the narrator advocates a return of the principles of colonial cosmopolitanism. For the narrator, land is a source of maximisable income, rather than a symbolic form of value; to let a tenant 'have the land for ever as long as he will pay a stipulated sum, which shall be considerably less than the landlord's demand . . . I call romantic, and therefore unjust' (1995a: 304). He supports Anglicisation more than Unionism, likening the plantations of the past to the Russification of Eastern Europe:

> As far as politics are regarded, Ireland has been the vassal of England as Poland has been of those masters under which she has been made to serve. She was subjected to much ill-usage, and though she has readily accepted the language, the civilisation, and the customs of England, and has in fact grown rich by adopting them, the memories of former hardships have clung to her, and have made her ready to receive willingly the teachings of those whose only object it has been to undermine the prestige of the British Empire. (1995a: 296)

The story of Trollope's novel is told so that 'the truth of this may be seen and made apparent' (1995a: 306). Since his self-professed aim is to provide a capitalist critique of the condition of Ireland, Trollope obviously cannot portray an Anglo-Irish landlord with a past: such a past would align Jones with the Protestant Ascendancy, which was infamous for its absenteeism and mismanagement, and which was one of the forces fuelling Irish discontent. By contrast, Trollope focuses on a newly established, cosmopolitan landlord from England or, perhaps, given his surname, Wales. *The Landleaguers* opens with the misfortune that befalls Philip Jones when he refuses to give one of his tenants, Pat Carroll, abatement.[17] In retaliation, Carroll and his friends open the flood gates on the marshes which Jones had reclaimed, which is the beginning of a boycott against Jones's estate that culminates in the murder of his youngest son. It is these criminals, so Trollope seems to say, whom liberals are supporting. His representation of Philip Jones's son and heir Frank, furthermore, suggests that the liberal focus on tenant rights creates another form of nationalism in addition to the popular nationalism of revolutionary peasants. According to Benedict Anderson, the creole communities of the different American colonies developed a conception of 'nationness' because of 'the constant flow of [colonial officials] moving towards them from remote and otherwise unrelated localities' (B. Anderson 2006: 54) – figures such as the policeman Yorke Clayton, who 'had been employed as adjutant in a volunteer regiment in England, having gone over there from the police force in the north of Ireland' (Trollope 1995a: 101–2). The creole landowner's movements, in contrast, were restricted:

> the highest administrative centre to which he could be assigned was the capital of the imperial administrative unit in which he found himself. Yet on this cramped pilgrimage [the creole landowner] found travelling-companions, who came to sense that their fellowship was based not only on that pilgrimage's particular stretch, but on the shared fatality of transatlantic birth. (B. Anderson 2006: 57)

According to Anderson, then, creole nationalism was a consequence of the metropolitan reluctance to involve the colonial elite in the management of other parts of the empire. The story of Frank Jones illustrates this theory. Galway is his main port of call; occasionally the rocky road takes him to Dublin. Once Frank tries to leave his trail and heads for London in search of Rachel O'Mahony, his sweetheart, a journey which ends in rejection. Making his way back westward, however, he meets a number of anonymous characters who confide in him and with whom he can sympathise. All this strengthens Frank's Irishness: 'As Frank Jones passed through Dublin, he learned that Morony Castle had been boycotted; and he was enough of an Irishman to know immediately what was meant' (1995a: 140). Frank Jones's occupation of Irish land was a product of English capitalism, but now that liberal policy has shifted towards an idea of rootedness, he is left nowhere. It is this that nurtures his sense of nationalism: 'his curses were more deep against the Government than against the Landleague' (1995a: 233). Indeed, the liberal attempt to defuse Irish nationalism by creating tenant rights played into the hands of the Land League's president, Charles Stewart Parnell, in whose mind '[r]esolving or removing the land question . . . would enable landlord energies to flow into the national movement' (Bartlett 2010: 319).[18]

The reader is tempted to take Trollope at his word. He was one of the few observers perceptive enough to detect 'a more recognisably bourgeois Ireland than any of his Irish contemporaries' (McCormack 1994: 8).[19] His portrayal of a concerned, cosmopolitan landlord thus has the merit of correcting 'the populist anti-landlord bias of traditional historiography' (Ó Gráda 1994: 256). The novel is, indeed, painstakingly precise. *The Landleaguers* represents actual events to a degree that none of Trollope's other writings does. His deteriorating health notwithstanding, Trollope travelled to Ireland twice to research *The Landleaguers*, which lends the novel a fitting earnestness. Trollope's language has been shorn of its typical mannerisms. The 'names of the characters are . . . grounded in reality' and the specificity of locations, travel arrangements, and dates is unprecedented (Foster 2002: 141). He also makes good use of his sensitivity for Irish dialect and cadences 'to convey deviousness and insincerity, where once they had been used to show cleverness and guile' (Foster 2002: 145). Finally, the work is dense with allusions to contemporary measures (such as the Coercion Act and the Arrears Bills), events (such as the assassination of Lord Cavendish and the murder of the Joyce family), and figures (such as Gladstone and W. E. 'Buckshot' Forster).[20]

Curiously, however, many of these allusions are muted. The narrator's unsatisfactory explanation that the novelist 'can hardly venture to deal with the names and characters of those who have been concerned' (1995a: 282–3) only highlights this anomaly. A closer look at the first of these unnamed concerns suggests that the novel overshoots the mark. In its opening pages, the narrator relates how Philip Jones bought two estates under the Estates Court and proceeded to transform what must have been a mortgaged property into a thriving enterprise. By 'means of drains and sluices' and not 'without the expenditure of much capital' Jones has 'thoroughly fertilised' the Ballintubber marshes (1995a: 5). This setup assumes that the Encumbered Estates Act (1849) achieved what it set out to, that is, the creation of a class of English landlords who would be more responsible and gainful than the old absentee Ascendancy, a goal that Trollope promoted in his response to the Famine.[21] In reality, 'the new owners turned out to be overwhelmingly Irish, with the younger sons of gentry families, shopkeepers and solicitors prominent among them. Few were progressive in their methods of farming, or were zealous for improvement' (Bartlett 2010: 295). In Ireland, the post-Famine proprietor was 'hardly in the vanguard of change himself' and instead 'gave progressive tenants a fair field' (Ó Gráda 1994: 256). One of the few improving landlords was, in fact, Parnell, whose name is conspicuously absent in Trollope's novel.[22] Trollope's narrator, then, is tilting at a disguised aunt Sally. He seeks to sustain a certain fiction – a cosmopolitan landlord fixing Ireland's problems, who is thwarted by liberal efforts to give the Irish tenant rights – by submerging it into a flood of facts without footnotes. The novel has a sleight of hand as its premise.

Another anomaly in Trollope's story serves to soften the narrator's ostensibly cosmopolitan critique. Trollope's portrayal of the outside agitator is strangely gentle. Gerald O'Mahony, an American radical whose name recalls that of John O'Mahony, the founder of the Fenian Brotherhood, may have the trappings of an American demagogue, but is in fact an 'amiable and philanthropic gentleman' (1995a: 37). He eventually succeeds in entering Westminster as a member of the Irish Parliamentary Party, a decision that does not pay; the Speaker does not tolerate his deviation from parliamentary rules and O'Mahony gradually 'los[es] his self-respect' (1995a: 257). This generates pity rather than scorn: although his opinions are satirised, O'Mahony is essentially honest, like Senator Elias Gotobed. This sympathetic portrayal goes against the grain of the narrator's more explicit statements and of Trollope's own intentions, according to which the Irish Parliamentary Party would have been put at the heart of the matter: 'My own idea [is] that we ought to see the Parnell set put down' (Trollope 1983: 963). In the novel, however, the Irish Parliamentary Party escapes the whipping that Gladstone receives. The narrator may call its members 'obnoxious' (1995a: 101), but even he wonders if members of 'the Parnell set' could not have their hearts in the right place:

> But yet he was a thoroughly honest, patriotic man, desirous only of the good of his country, and wishing for nothing for himself. Is it not possible that as much may be said for others, who from day to day so violently excite our spleen? . . . Can it be possible that we are wrong in our opinions respecting the others of the set? (1995a: 257)

Rhetorical questions such as these do make one wonder whether the mask that the narrator wears is not the mask of the satirist – whether the narrator of *The Landleaguers* is not, in other words, as deluded as President Neverbend.

Trollope further qualifies the merits of the narrator's cosmopolitanism through the creation of a parallel plot. Gerald O'Mahony's career in Parliament is only a minor part of a parallel story set in London. The plot's real interest lies in Rachel O'Mahony's decision to seek her fortune as a singer when Frank Jones wants to shelve the idea of marriage. Trollope's narrative shifts back and forth between these two threads, between Galway and London. Critics have generally dismissed this part of the tale, lamenting that it is 'a disastrous error in plotting which divides the action' (Terry 1977: 193). The use of a parallel plot is hardly innovative, but it carries significant connotations, since the representation of events that are connected only because they happen to take place at the same time creates the kind of temporality that allows the nation to emerge as the 'idea of a sociological organism moving calendrically through homogeneous empty time' (B. Anderson 2006: 26). The structure of Trollope's story thus mirrors its content. Time, however, is not the only thing connecting both plots. Like the Jacobean playwrights he studied avidly, Trollope delights in creating

> a group of plots that may not be connected explicitly to one another, but whose implicit relationship gives the play its form. The separate plots are related because they provide a commentary upon one another, either through contrast or through analogy. (Tracy 1978: 10)

In the case of this novel, there are a number of significant correspondences.[23] Like the Irish scene, the London theatre world is a moral morass filled with gossip, intrigue, and violence. Rachel O'Mahony's impresario, Mahomet M. Moss, unwittingly argues that if she marries him she 'should be called the O'Mahony' (1995a: 134), a reference to Adah Isaacs Menken, notorious for her many affairs and her appearance in flesh-coloured tights in *Mazeppa* (Hamer 1993: 427). When Moss forces himself upon her, Rachel stabs him with a dagger. Trollope's double plot thus suggests that the theatre has an affinity with terror; indeed, for both it is the impact on the audience and the crowd that counts, rather than the value of the performance or action itself (Juergensmeyer 2000: 124). As Rachel reflects at one point, 'Elmira also was more pathetic than ever, as the night was supposed to be something special, because a royal duke and his young bride were in the stage box' (1995a: 195).

However, the novel also sets up a contrast between the violence of terror and the art of the theatre. While the Irish crowd is haunted by priests and revolutionary terrorists, Rachel O'Mahony enchants the metropolitan crowd on stage; Philip Jones is 'struck by the awful silence of the people' (1995a: 12) when his sluices are destroyed, whereas Rachel O'Mahony aestheticises and captivates: 'To stand on the boards of the theatre and become conscious of the intense silence of the crowd before her – so intense because the tone of her voice was the one thing desired by all the world' (1995a: 273). Rachel, indeed, manages to transcend the rules that govern the murky world of the West End.[24] This part of Trollope's plot comes close to a particular version of the *Bildungsroman*, the *Künstlerroman*, which represents the life and progress of an artist. The theatre has a privileged place in the literary history of this form. The protagonist of Goethe's *Wilhelm Meisters Lehrjahre* (1795–6), arguably the most famous instance of the *Künstlerroman*, has a mercantile career mapped out for him, but joins a travelling theatre company instead, which gives him access to a number of experiences that stimulate the development of a pure, true soul. Although this kind of narrative was challenged by the teleological model of the career, 'the model of the vocation-narrative remained theatrical – melodrama, perhaps, or even tragedy' (Dames 2003: 254). Although Rachel's decision to become an actress is born out of earthly considerations, she, like Wilhelm Meister, struggles to keep her moral character intact:

> The world ought to be perfectly innocent in regard to her because she believed herself to be innocent; and Mr Moss in expressing the opinions of others, and exposing to her the position in which she had placed herself, had simply proved himself to be the blackest of human beings.
>
> But it was necessary that she should at once do something to whitewash her own character in her own esteem. (1995a: 196)

In this, Rachel is successful. Feted by London society and courted by Lord Castlewell, she gradually becomes part of the acculturated elite and, as such, a representative of the values of Enlightenment cosmopolitanism, among which advancing the cause of civil liberties is foremost. This cause manifests a desire for freedom from the given and has as its aesthetic either the eternal beauty of art or the sublime power of nature (Mohamed 2010: 147–9). Rachel may joke that her father believes 'that Home Rule won't be passed because the people will be thinking of my singing' (1995a: 250), but this is the message that Trollope's double plot constructs. Drawing attention to the potential of a moral education, furthermore, her story highlights the imperfect nature of other forms of instruction. Frank Jones went to Queens's College Galway rather than Oxbridge, which may have helped to form his creole nationalism. Florian Jones's 'education had been much neglected' (1995a: 4; see also 170), which may have made him susceptible to the popular nationalism of priests and terrorists. The Enlightenment cosmopolitanism that Rachel's story refers to, in contrast, seems to present an alternative to the nationalism of Irish Home Rulers and, by implication, the liberal supporters of tenant rights. Both plots eventually converge: Frank would have married Rachel, had Trollope's death not intervened. Given that the allegorical marriage plot of the national tale, as Mary Jean Corbett and others have shown, cast a long shadow over nineteenth-century fictional treatments of the 1800 Act of Union (Corbett 2000), Trollope's union of a disenchanted future landlord and the artistic daughter of a Landleaguing American initially presents a bit of a puzzle. But if we see Rachel O'Mahony as a cipher for *Bildung*, she turns out to have precisely the liberal qualities that would tame Irish nationalism.

But there is a hitch. When she falls ill and loses her voice, Rachel does not act as one who has gone through the various stage of *Bildung*. She does not greet suffering with a 'brave mind, struggling against adversity' (Schiller 1861: 483), like Milton's Lucifer, one 'who brings / A mind not to be changed by place or time' (Milton 2007: 76). Instead, she is desperately unhappy:

> 'What do you want?' asked the father, when her hand for a moment ceased to scrawl.
>
> 'I want', she said, 'Frank Jones. Now you know all about it'.
>
> Then she hid her face beneath the bedclothes, and refused to write another word. (1995a: 275)

Rachel's mind *is* changed by place and time. As a result, her illness returns her to a more fundamental form of freedom, that is, the freedom from want, the freedom that is found in the mere presence of health and life. Ruefully sobbing on her pillow, Rachel begins to realise that the crowd listened to her singing not out of a desire for beauty or pathos, but because it was famished: 'And then to open her mouth and to let the music go forth and to see the ears all erect, as she fancied she could, so that not a sound should be lost – should not be harvested by the hungry hearers!' (1995a: 273). What the crowd wants, in other words, is to experience the aesthetic correlative of freedom from want, not of political independence. Rachel thus finally distances herself from the cosmopolitan elite, which does not care whether or not the crowd is fed; it takes freedom from want for granted.

This is only one of the many sad scenes that this novel is suffused with. R. H. Super similarly suggests that 'there [is] real sadness in the account of the disruption of the hunt' (1992a: vi); Philip Jones's witnessing of his son's murder is arguably even more poignant. The location of this assassination is symbolic: 'The place was one where the commencement had been made of a cutting in the road during the potato failure of 1846' (1995a: 221). This unfinished road is a reminder of the penal works that Trollope had once defended. A lifetime later, however, he writes a novel in which one such public work helps revolutionaries commit their deeds. The cosmopolitan approach to relief had not pacified the island, according to Trollope's vignette, but instead allowed ill-feeling to endure. The novel's two plotlines thus do not so much illustrate as challenge the narrator's cosmopolitanism: the actual story of *The Landleaguers* and its emotional register suggest that steadfast adherence to the rules of capitalism would not do away with calls for tenant rights, but that a focus on basic human freedoms would be more beneficial in countering the threat that Irish nationalism posed to English sovereignty.

A number of concerns recur in Trollope's satires of the nationalist discourse on the global that he had crafted in his earlier work. The assassination of the fox in *The American Senator*, the project of collective euthanasia in *The Fixed Period*, and the murder of Florian Jones and the illness of Rachel O'Mahony in *The Landleaguers* all suggest that nationalism is motivated by a barbarous drive towards death. As such, these novels subvert the organic sense of rootedness that Trollope had put forward in his Barsetshire novels. In one fell swoop, these narratives also satirise the possessive individualism that Trollope had advocated in his travel writings: Senator Elias Gotobed, President Neverbend, and the narrator of *The Landleaguers* present themselves as paragons of colonial capitalism, but beneath their apparent confidence lurks an undercurrent of narcissism and doubt. They are at once the voice and the object of satire. By alluding to the eighteenth-century models of Swift and Goldsmith and by questioning Enlightenment tenets such as the idea of a tolerant subject, the infallibility of reason, and the disregard for basic human rights, moreover, they couch their concern with British sovereignty in the grand narrative of modernity.

Notes

1. Although Trollope uses Britishness and Englishness interchangeably, like most Victorians (Parry 2006: 37–8), the two are distinguished here because of their relation to Irishness. For a thorough analysis of Englishness in the nineteenth and twentieth century, see Collini (1993a: 342–73; and 1999).
2. According to the evolutionist doctrine of survivals, such symbols, are 'not merely elements of an external decor, but . . . the junction of the collective and the person, . . . molding [the] subjectivity [of individuals] in ways bound to seem unfathomably mysterious' (Herbert 1991: 272).
3. Trollope's books *The West Indies and the Spanish Main*, *North America*, *Australia and New Zealand*, and *South Africa* depict 'all but one of the major contact zones of British imperialism' (Goodlad 2009: 439), the exception being India. Trollope was one of the most assiduous and consummate travellers of the Victorian age. His duties as a Post Office surveyor required him to look into the nooks and crannies of Ireland, south-west and eastern England, Wales, and the Channel Islands. In due course, his duties also took him to Egypt, Malta, Gibraltar, the West Indies, Central America, and the United States, where he was to negotiate treaties and inspect local offices. From 1853 onwards, he paid regular visits to the European continent for the purpose of sightseeing, often tailoring his touristic inclinations to a reunion with his brother and mother in Florence. His own son Frederic had carried the family tradition of travelling one step further by emigrating to Australia, in which colony Trollope visited him twice.
4. Trollope also hints at the literary history of satire by distinguishing between poetry and prose. The satire began, indeed, as a Latin form of poetry – and was, it is often said, the only authentic Latin contribution to classical literature. Derived from *lanx satura*, 'a full dish', it originally referred to a literary mishmash, but was increasingly marked by the use of parody, both

in content and form: in contrast to the epic, the satire does not depict the heroic but the foolish, its language is not lofty but colloquial, and its hexameters are not polished but rough.

5. In the course of the twentieth century, critics have moved from a 'structuralist' view of satire as a 'stable' attack on morally deviant behaviour (W. C. Booth 1974; Frye 1957; Elliott 1960; Kernan 1959; Paulson 1967; Rosenheim 1963) to a 'postmodern' view of satire as complex, layered, and complicit (Bakhtin 1968; Gill 1995; Griffin 1994; Snyder 1991; Test 1991).
6. For an early comparison of Trollope and Bagehot, see Briggs (1970: 87–115).
7. Freeman published his attack in the *Fortnightly*, Trollope's own brainchild, in 1869 (Freeman 1869); Trollope's reply (Trollope 1869) was published in the December issue of that same year. Trollope refers to this verbal jousting in his *Autobiography*. He denounces Freeman as a theorist who has not considered the values of pleasure and amusement: 'Mr Freeman has failed to perceive that amusement is as useful and almost as necessary as food and raiment' (1999a: 195), a sentiment the novel literally echoes with Reginald Morton as its mouthpiece (Trollope 1999b: 505). More pertinently, Freeman does not see that amusement may serve a real need. Hunting has what Trollope elsewhere calls 'a national efficacy' (1868: 71), as it is conducive 'to the preservation of that peculiar, glorious something which constitutes English national identity' (Trotter 1992: 231). Of particular relevance also are Trollope's *Hunting Sketches* and his essay 'On Hunting' (1867). For a suggestive recent eco-critical consideration, see Boddice (2008).
8. Trollope's resolution to *Is He Popenjoy?* echoes this satirical exposure of the aristocracy's immorality, to which end it uses irony. While it may seem propitious that the degenerate Marquis of Brotherton has died, thus clearing the road for a revival of the estate, this revival is actually due to the discovery of coal. Coal, however, is hardly a basis for a new sense of rootedness. As Matthew Arnold declares: 'Our coal, thousands of people were saying, is the real basis of our national greatness; if our coal runs short, there is an end of the greatness of England. But what is greatness? – culture makes us ask. Greatness is a spiritual condition worthy to excite love, interest, and admiration; and the outward proof of possessing greatness is that we excite love, interest, and admiration' (Arnold 1993b: 64).
9. Trollope began writing *The American Senator* on 4 June 1875 while he was visiting his son Frederic in Mortray (Halperin 1999: xvi). He continued the novel on his return journey from Sydney to Auckland, Honolulu to San Francisco, and Boston to New York, where he completed the manuscript on 24 September 1875. *The American Senator* appeared in *Temple Bar* from May 1876 to July 1877 and was published by Chapman and Hall in three volumes in 1877. For an examination of the manuscript and a collation with the first edition, see Taylor (1947). The name 'Dillsborough' reinforces the impression that Trollope is reflecting on his travel writings, for it is arguably an allusion to a North American town that lay on the trajectory of Trollope's 1861–2 American tour. Trollope left St Louis on 3 February 1862 and went from there to Cairo, Louisville, and Cincinnati, where he arrived on 12 February (Trollope 1951: 534). The town of Dillsboro (Indiana), which lies some 40 miles away from Cincinnati, fits right into his

track. Furthermore, Dillsborough's topography resembles the division of the United States at the time of the Civil War: 'The Dillsborough people are therefore divided, some two thousand five hundred of them belonging to Rufford, and the remaining five hundred to the neighbouring county. This accident has given rise to not a few feuds, Ufford being a large county, with pottery, and ribbons, and watches going on in the farther confines; whereas Rufford is small and thoroughly agricultural' (Trollope 1999b: 2).

10. Andrew McCann similarly argues that the comedy of the marketplace had become the only point of reference for culture in the nineteenth century: 'the public evidently finds pleasure in the revelation of its own stupidity' (McCann 2004: 74). While Trollope does not go that far, there is certainly a touch of satire in the reaction of the English public to the Senator's sermons: we may mock him for his misinterpretations, but this does not mean that the English may not also be mocked – quite the contrary. If anything, the English community has lost the ability to make independent rational choices: 'the nineteenth century increasingly saw the pathological erosion of this independence as the public sphere became increasingly administered by the mass circulation of textual objects through it' (McCann 2004: 77).
11. The twentieth-century critical consensus, however, seems to be that Gotobed is not the subject but the object of satire. Robert Tracy argues that instead 'of providing an English spokesman to defend landed gentry and tradition, Trollope refutes the Senator by the events of the story itself' (1978: 212). This is giving the English too much credit. The following scene does not 'vindicate Runce', as Trotter suggests (1992: 228): 'Words were wanting to Mr Runce, but not indignation. He collected together his plate and knife and fork and his two glasses and his lump of bread, and, looking the Senator full in the face, slowly pushed back his chair and, carrying his provisions with him, toddled off to the other end of the room. When he reached a spot where place was made for him he had hardly breath left to speak. "Well", he said, "I never – !" He sat a minute in silence shaking his head, and continued to shake his head and look round upon his neighbours as he devoured his food' (1999b: 146).
12. Like other outsiders, such as Signora Neroni in *Barchester Towers* or Marie Max Goesler in the Phineas novels, Gotobed is a character who challenges the embedded (or rooted) community's doxa (A. Anderson 2007: 512). Although at times he is wilfully oblivious to the peculiarities of the English, just as often he lacks the background necessary to enter English minds.
13. This age carries a biographical connotation, as Trollope was nearly sixty-seven when writing the book. The issue of cremation was hotly debated throughout the 1870s; Trollope was a supporter.
14. The many ways in which *The Fixed Period* parodies *Australia and New Zealand* have been documented by Helen Lucy Blythe (2014: 159–96).
15. Jonathan Parry has demonstrated that Liberals ventured upon 'the international stage to project an image of Britain as a particular kind of regime, a community upholding desirable constitutional and ethical values. Foreign tensions were frequently presented in ideological terms: between a Britain which stood for constitutionalism, law, inclusiveness, conscience and humanitarianism, and various alternative continental regimes – usually

autocratic, sometimes republican – which were threatening and "un-English"' (Parry 2006: 4).

16. This failure caused a shift in economic thinking: 'many economists came to endorse the alternative view that Irish agrarian peculiarities were the legacy of the island's separate historical development and should be recognised rather than repressed by law, and that social pacification through the acknowledgement in British legislation of Irish difference was the only viable foundation for economic progress. It is widely acknowledged that the 1860s was the key decade in this interpretative shift, as Irish economists in particular adopted a more historicist position and influenced British economic and political debates on the subject' (P. Gray 2002: 141).
17. Pat Carroll also makes an appearance in Trollope's letters to the *Examiner*, where he figures as the Irishman who must either work among the fields or languish in idleness at the poorhouse (Trollope 1987: 20).
18. This response to the Land War is characteristic of a number of liberals sympathetic to Ireland, most particularly Albert Venn Dicey. Dicey, with whose brother, Edward, Trollope was well acquainted, felt that everything should be done to appease the Irish short of recognising their sovereignty (see Ford 1973). The narrator, indeed, has no quarrel with more Irish autonomy: 'I have met gentlemen', the narrator says, 'who, as Home Rulers, have simply desired to obtain for their country an increase of power in the management of their own affairs. These men have been loyal and patriotic, and it might perhaps be well to meet their views' (Trollope 1995a: 303).
19. Trollope moved to Ireland in 1841 after having successfully volunteered for the job of clerk to one of Ireland's three postal surveyors. Not only did this supposedly suicidal move enable Trollope to resuscitate his failing career, it also brought him a soft income, a position of authority, and a sense of belonging. Trollope himself remains characteristically vague as to what exactly he owed 'the first good fortune of [his] life' (1999a: 59). For one thing, he suppresses – or takes for granted – the fact that his status as a Protestant British civil servant aligned him with elites such as the Anglo-Irish Ascendancy in general or the Masonic lodge of Banagher in particular (Hawes 1999). This affiliation of the bureaucrat with the political elite does not imply that Trollope saw Ireland only through the windows of the big house or the lodge; for eighteen years he assiduously travelled the length and breadth of the island, thus helping to bring the Irish postal system up to speed. As such, his experience in Ireland naturally provided the subject matter and inspiration for his first two novels, *The Macdermots of Ballycloran* and *The Kellys and the O'Kellys*, and for his first foray into political writing, a series of letters to the *Examiner* in which he defended the Russell administration (1846–52) against charges that the government's response to the Great Irish Famine (1845–50) was inadequate. Comprehensive accounts of Trollope's life in Ireland can be found in the biographies by Victoria Glendinning (1994: 114–40), N. John Hall (1991: 81–184), and R. H. Super (1990: 36–62). For early reconsiderations of Trollope as an Irish novelist, see John Cronin (1980), Owen Dudley Edwards (1983), and R. C. Terry (1977: 175–200). The most recent and comprehensive account of Trollope's Irishness is John McCourt's *Writing the Frontier* (2015). Curiously, the *Cambridge Companion to the Irish*

Novel mentions Trollope only once, incorrectly claiming that Trollope's early Irish novels were popular in England (Burgess 2006: 51). Roy Foster provides a rare sympathetic analysis of *The Landleaguers*, reading Trollope's Irish novels against the tradition of the national tale (2002). On Victorian economics and the Famine, see Bigelow (2003).

20. Robert Tracy's introduction to the 1981 Arno edition gives an excellent overview of this interweaving with reality (Tracy 1981). As R. H. Super indicates in his footnotes, Forster was a frequent bridge partner of Trollope's at the Athenaeum (Super 1992b: 335).
21. In dealing with the Famine, which eventually caused a quarter of the population to either starve or emigrate, the Whig government held fast to the orthodoxies of classical liberalism: free trade, laissez-faire, self-help, and anti-statism. These principles determined the approach of Charles Trevelyan, Assistant Secretary to the Treasury from 1840 to 1859, who was put in charge of the administration of government relief to the victims of the Irish Famine. Trevelyan's approach was harsh and counterproductive. In his apologia in the *Edinburgh Review* of January 1848, by which time the Famine was reaching its height, Trevelyan even argued that the potato blight was a blessing in disguise. It had laid bare the root of the social problem, the potato, which frustrated the practice of wage-labour that a flourishing market society needed: 'The relations of employer and employed, which knit together the framework of society, and establish a mutual dependence and good-will, have no existence in the potato system' (Trevelyan 1848: 5). Like many liberals who had taken the work of Thomas Robert Malthus to heart, moreover, Trevelyan goes along with the idea that Ireland could not sustain its exponentially growing population and that a catastrophe such as the Famine was divine punishment for a people who had been taking it easy for too many years. Trollope follows the so-called 'official' response (Bartlett 2010: 287) that the onset of the Famine was the work of a merciful providence putting Ireland on the road to economic progress. He does not follow Trevelyan's Evangelical moralism, but he does share his providentialism: 'Have not narratives equally true and equally fearful been written of other countries so visited by the hand of god [*sic*]' (Trollope 1987: 6). The 'severity of the circumstances' was 'ordained by providence' and the government was not incompetent 'in dealing with those circumstances' (1987: 7). Trollope even takes up the cudgels for the controversial requirement that to receive relief one had to participate in public works, such as the building or rebuilding of roads, often unnecessarily or without a useful destination. He concedes that in practice this approach had some shortcomings, but attributes this to the haphazard nature of circumstances: 'who was to calculate at a week's notice how long these works were to continue?' (1987: 7). Moreover, these works did serve a useful purpose insofar as they encouraged men of business to invest their capital and stimulated the poor to find better employment elsewhere (1987: 19–21). In his fiction, however, Trollope's judgement is less crass. In *Castle Richmond*, which is set during the Famine, Trollope attempts to argue, as R. F. Foster maintains, 'almost with himself, what should or could have been done about the Famine' (2002: 135). For recent considerations of the representation of the Famine in Trollope's fiction, see Ingelbien (2010) and Siddle (2004).

22. See Foster (1976; 2011: 40–77, 123–38). There may also have been a biographical factor: Trollope's good friend and long-standing correspondent, Anna Steele, was Katherine O'Shea's sister. She may have softened Trollope's feelings towards Parnell while he was writing his novel. Given the tensions between the sisters and the fact that the affair was at the time a well-kept secret, however, this is highly unlikely.
23. Florian Jones's sisters call his conversion from Protestantism to Catholicism 'beastly' (Trollope 1995a: 87), a word that echoes throughout Rachel O'Mahony's fight with her impresario, Mahomet M. Moss (1995a: 49–50, 58–9, 95). Roger Super wonders 'why Trollope gave [Moss] the name "Mahomet" if we are to believe that he is indeed Jewish' (1992a: xi). The point is that he is supposed to be unbelievable, illusory, fantastic. This moniker is appropriate insofar as Florian Jones and Mahomet M. Moss name contradictions: Florian between Catholicism and Protestantism, Mahomet between Islam and Judaism. Their resemblance is duplicated in the story's action: Florian Jones ends up with a bullet in his head, Mahomet M. Moss with a dagger in his guts. Although this is Florian Jones's main function in the novel's dynamic, James Pope-Hennessy's assessment that '[o]nly in one novel, and that his last, does Trollope seem to divine those treacherous depths in child psychology explored by Henry James' (1971: 129) is suggestive. On a thematic level, Rachel's story reminds the reader that there was a feminist dimension to the Land War that the Land League was, to say the least, uncomfortable with: 'It is certainly plausible to argue then that one of the contributions of the land-war novel, with its gender instabilities, was to that late nineteenth-century window of greater liberation for women, both in Britain and internationally, that comes under the new-woman rubric' (Murphy 2011: 192). Both the London stage and the Irish scene are, finally, infused with elements of phantasmagoria: a witness is shot in open court and the murderer can just walk out because 'the court was crowded in a wonderful manner' (Trollope 1995a: 226). Drawing a veil over the scene, the crowd allows the criminal to operate and to withdraw unseen in the way that the urban scene did for the *flâneur* (Benjamin 2003b: 22–34): 'the ball had entered the head just under the ear, with a slant upwards towards the brain, as though the weapon had been used by someone crouching towards the ground' (Trollope 1995a: 229). The stage similarly provides Rachel O'Mahony with a way to withdraw from the world: 'There is something in the glitter of a theatre – what people call the boards, the gaslights, the music, the mock love-making, the pretence of being somebody, the feeling of mystery which is attached to you, and the feeling you have that you are generally unlike the world at large – which has its charms' (1995a: 60).
24. The Victorian theatre was a liminal space: 'In one sense, opera and music-hall were worlds apart, at the poles of popular and élite culture; yet in fact they might both be played in the same house, at differing times' (Hamer 1993: xxi). It was the very nature of the Victorian theatre that made this concurrence possible. Tracy C. Davis (2000) has painstakingly documented how the financing and managing of the Victorian theatre paralleled trends in the economy, moving from the free-market management of the post-1843 period to the regulatory efforts of the 1880s and 1890s.

Chapter 5

'Active Citizens of a Free State': Hellenising the History of Rome

After his reviews of Charles Merivale's *History of the Romans* (1851 and 1856), Trollope's interest in classical historiography disappeared for fifteen years until, in early 1870, he published a favourable review of *Ancient Classics for English Readers*. Spurred on by John Blackwood's invitation to contribute to this series, edited by the Revd W. Lucas Collins, Trollope began *The Commentaries of Caesar*, which was the beginning of his re-education in the classics: 'Latin was not so familiar to me then as it has since become – for from that date I have almost daily spent an hour with some Latin author, and on many days many hours' (Trollope 1999a: 338). By the end of the decade, his intensive study of the classics had yielded two articles on Cicero in the *Fortnightly* in 1877 (1877b, 1877a) and a full-length biography in 1880. The rejuvenation of Trollope's interest in Latin and in Cicero's works during the autumn of his life is intrinsic to the development of his late style. In particular, Trollope's portrayal of Cicero is an attempt to articulate a political alternative to the capitalist individualism of modernity. In Trollope's dark tableau, Cicero heroically refuses to succumb to the interests of the self and instead tries to advance the common good, all the while knowing that he is fighting an uphill battle.

This claim put Trollope at odds with most of his contemporaries. Victorian writing about Rome tended to either glorify Caesar or to focus on the development of Christianity. Trollope's depiction of Cicero challenges both positions. On the one hand, Cicero's politics as depicted by Trollope are a veiled version of civic republicanism, a tradition of political thinking which emphasises participation in public life and the positive freedom to develop citizen character. On the other hand, Trollope suggests that Cicero was a Christian before the First Coming, an idea which does not tally with orthodox Christian doctrines. More generally, Trollope is also swimming against the current insofar as Victorian writing about classical history focused on the language and culture of Greece. If the classics were 'the furniture of the mind for the Victorian upper classes' (Goldhill 2011: 2), this mind-set was predominantly Hellenic: 'Greece provided familiar and idealised cultural touchstones for the classically educated Victorian gentlemen who considered themselves heirs to the Hellenic tradition' (Hurst 2010: 484). Most famously, Matthew Arnold drafts 'Hellenism' into his crusade against Nonconformism and Dissent, or 'Hebraism', borrowing these categories from Heinrich Heine (Collini 1993b: 128). Trollope does not seem to deal in Hellenism, however: when he refers to classical literature and history, his point of reference is almost exclusively Rome.[1] This may be interpreted, partly, as a sign of resentment: Victorian Hellenism was – unlike its Romantic predecessor – an academic enterprise fostered at the great universities, from which Trollope was excluded, having failed in his attempt to get a scholarship at Trinity College, Oxford (Freeman 1883: 236). Yet this chapter posits that Trollope's representation of Cicero's politics and theology is, in fact, marked by ideas more commonly associated with Victorian Hellenism.

The Roman Model

Roman history entered British public discourse with the Glorious Revolution, in the wake of which members of the Catholic and Tory country-party such as Nathaniel Hooke used the Roman republic's ideal of a mixed constitution to suggest that the Declaration of 1689 had led to a loss of liberty. In response, Whig court-party writers 'attempted to nullify the utility of the analogy between Britain and the Roman republic by offering a different interpretation of the demise of the republic' (Turner 1986: 579). Conyers Middleton's *The History of the Life of Marcus Tullius Cicero* (1741) lavishes praise on Cicero for, like Walpole, trying to save the state and its constitution by forging an alliance between nobility and commerce (Turner 1986: 580). With the advent of the French Revolution and Napoléon's coronation, however, the 'example of the Roman republic that so many associated with the British mixed constitution in the eighteenth century came to be linked not with stability, but with the insurrections first of the American revolutionaries and then subsequently with threatening events in France' (Sachs 2009: 322). Rome's function was subsumed by two different models. While reactionary intellectuals such as Edmund Burke mobilised the history of Britain and of Christianity (Turner 1986: 587), revolutionary figures such as Percy Bysshe Shelley enlisted the Hellenic past: 'When Shelley said "We are all Greeks", it was a battle cry of a philhellenic Romantic to join the revolution' (Goldhill 2011: 3). In the course of the nineteenth century, Shelley's cry was joined by more conservative voices, as a result of which Greece gradually replaced Rome as a privileged cultural touchstone: 'The democratic experience of Athens held the relevance for Victorian commentators that the quarrels among and demise of the Roman republican oligarchy had held for eighteenth-century political polemicists' (Turner 1982: 4; see also 1989).[2]

Yet, fuelled by a nascent British imperialism, the Roman model returned to the scene, although it was no longer republican Rome's mixed constitution that set the tone, but imperial Rome's authoritarianism.[3] While in Victorian public discourse 'Greece is firmly associated with liberty, democracy and popular will', as Jonathan Sachs remarks, 'Rome comes to stand for the spread of ideas and institutions through empire' (2009: 323). Traces of Burke's focus on the Christian past are still clearly visible in Thomas Arnold's essays on Roman history (1823–7), which alternate moral censure with praise for the Principate as 'a providential vehicle for the diffusion of early Christianity throughout the Mediterranean world' (Turner 1986: 589), and in Thomas De Quincey's essays on Cicero and the Caesars (1832–4), which similarly stress that 'if we figure the two worlds of Paganism and Christianity under the idea of two great continents, it is through the isthmus of Rome that the one has virtually communicated with the other' (De Quincey 2001: 160). As the nineteenth century wore on, scholars turned their attention to the success of Caesar's democratic despotism. While the propagation of this theory is most closely associated with the German historian Theodor Mommsen, it was an English clergyman, Charles Merivale, who popularised it in Britain.[4] Merivale presents his *History of the Romans under the Empire* (1850–64) as a continuation of Thomas Arnold's essays and a prelude to Gibbon's magnum opus, even though his ideological message is distinctively different. Merivale's Caesar is a thinly veiled portrait of Napoléon Bonaparte, just as Augustus's actions foreshadow those of Louis-Napoléon: 'events in France and the rhetoric of mid-century Bonapartism clearly influenced Merivale's analysis of the late Republic and early Empire' (Turner 1986: 591). Building on Merivale's suggestions, other writers began to use the fall of republican Rome to criticise the woolliness of British parliamentarianism. These writers can be divided into the opposing camps of positivism and heroism, two schools with very different political tenets.[5]

British positivists such as Richard Congreve, Frederic Harrison, and Edward Spencer Beesly believed that Caesar's despotism was the outcome of a long process and, as such, the herald of an age of progress. Beesly, in particular, showcases his distance from both Merivale and the

Great Men theory through the outrageous claim that Caesar's triumph was largely due to the forays made by 'the party of Catiline, the party which thought itself strong enough to revolutionise the state': 'This is a question which sensible men are not ashamed to answer by maundering about "dissolute youth", "insolvent debtors", and "disbanded soldiers". Any explanation must be preferable to such transparent nonsense' (Beesly 1865: 174). Beesly's real target is the Great Men theory, however, because of its unscientific assumptions: 'that most constant and calculable of forces, popular sentiment, has been treated as though it were more unreasonable, inscrutable, and fortuitous than the whims of a capricious individual' (Beesly 1866: 421). Instead, Beesly teases out the contradictions in Cicero's work so as to uncover the 'orderly evolution of political events' and, in particular, to show that 'the Roman populace, in banishing Cicero, were acting in a natural consistent way' (1866: 436, 437). More subtly, Beesly challenges Merivale's model by comparing the fall of republican Rome not to the French but to the English Revolution. Catiline should not be compared to Danton or Robespierre (Beesly 1865: 168), but to Pym and Hampden (1865: 182), just as Caesar prefigures Cromwell (1866: 436).

In contrast, Carlyle's disciples emphasised Caesar's heroic qualities. Unlike Merivale and Beesly, James Anthony Froude does not interpret the Roman fight between its two political factions – the *populares* and *optimates* – as a struggle between democracy and oligarchy. Merivale and Beesly side with the self-proclaimed leaders of the people: the Gracchi, Marius, Cinna, Caesar. Froude, in contrast, sides with any leader who could demand obedience. His book is a paean to Caesar – the most popular of the *populares* – but he also praises Sulla, arguably the most infamous of the *optimates*, who 'restored the shattered prestige of Roman authority, and he won for himself a reputation which his later cruelties might stain, but could not efface' (Froude 1879: 63). Even though Carlyle disliked Froude's *Caesar: A Sketch* (1879), this book is in many ways a postscript to *On Heroes, Hero-Worship, and the Heroic in History* (1841). In a nod towards Thomas Arnold and Burke, removed from future editions, Froude even outdoes Carlyle by suggesting that Caesar prepared the way for the coming of Christ (Froude 1879: 471).

Civic Republicanism

In his earlier historiographical works, Trollope treats Caesarism with a certain degree of scepticism. For one, he compares Roman with British, rather than French, imperialism, indicating that '[p]rolonged quiescence indeed for Rome was not possible, as in these days it is not possible for British India' (Trollope 1856: 40).[6] Trollope's doubts are more explicit when he takes aim at Merivale's favourable portrayal of Augustus, who 'was cruel as a Robespierre when goaded to madness by continual bloodshed, as reckless of humanity as a Napoléon when driven on to Moscow' (1856: 32). In his summary of Caesar's *Commentarii De Bello Gallico* and *De Bello Civili*, Trollope's tone is less serious and often bemused, as when he contrasts Caesar's conquest of Gaul with the struggles in Sebastopol: Caesar 'speaks of the difficulty often, but never with that despair which was felt as to the roasting of our coffee in the Crimea' (Trollope 1870b: 56).[7] Hints of Trollope's disagreement are also apparent in the few references to other scholars: he praises Alexander William Kinglake's *Invasion of the Crimea* (1863–87), which was severely critical of Napoléon III (1870b: 33), while he attacks both Mommsen, who 'intends to convey to us his conviction that Caesar was perfect in human capacity and intelligence', and Napoléon III, 'who claims for [Caesar] moral perfection . . . We cannot, however, quite take the facts as the Emperor of the French gives them to us' (1870b: 7).

Trollope's articles on and biography of Cicero up the ante. His criticism of Merivale's positive representation of Catiline continues: the Dean 'gives us ample proof of his sympathy with the conspirators, or rather of his strong feeling against Cicero' (Trollope 1880: 1.252, footnote). But even the defenders of the republic, Brutus and Cassius, now come in for censure, having 'all the weakness of the French Girondists, and apparently few, if any, of their virtues' (Trollope 1856: 32). Revolutionary and republican conspirators are thus given the same label. Merivale's account is redeemable when compared to Beesly's, however, since Merivale 'values too highly his own historical judgment to allow it to run on all fours with Mr Beesly's sympathies' (1880: 1.252, footnote). Trollope's feelings on first reading Beesly's articles were generous: 'I however, am myself so given to rebellion in politics that I am delighted to see and hear any Catiline defended, and any Cicero attacked' (1983: 306).[8] A decade later, his delight has evaporated. Although Beesly is not cited, Trollope bristles when he considers how Cicero has been attacked for embellishing his writings with 'mendaciuncula' (Beesly 1865: 171, footnote), little white lies, and puts this down to an Evangelical distaste for humour: 'It goes no farther than to suggest that amount of exaggeration which is used by every teller of a good story in order that the story may be good. Such "mendaciuncula" are in the mouth of every diner-out in London, and we may pity the dinner-parties at which they are not used' (Trollope 1880: 1.195–6). Furthermore, Trollope subverts Beesly's allusions to the seventeenth century by likening Catiline to a

Catholic whom Cromwell would not have wanted to be associated with, Guy Fawkes (1880: 1.318). It is Froude's brand of Caesarism, however, which bears the brunt of Trollope's ire. The opening pages of *The Life of Cicero* are directly aimed at Froude. Trollope is particularly troubled by the fact that Froude twists and turns Cicero's words to make them suit his purpose: 'it is not too much to demand that when a man's character is at stake his own words shall be thoroughly sifted before they are used against him' (1880: 1.6). The seeds of Trollope's discontent can be found in the margins of his own copy of Froude's *Sketch*, which radiate with criticism on factual errors and erroneous translations (B. A. Booth 1946).

Trollope's interest in the history of republican Rome is, as such, not an expression of Caesarism, but of a deep-seated cynicism. Trollope was not alone in taking up this stance.[9] The publication of the first volume of Napoléon III's *Histoire de Jules César* (1865) prompted Walter Bagehot to update the sardonic views he had first espoused in his eyewitness letters on the French *coup d'état*, sent to *The Inquirer* in 1851: Caesarism gives 'an admirable government for present and coarse purposes, but a detestable government for future and refined purposes' (Bagehot 1995: 443). Bagehot's concern with citizens' '*future elevation*' (1995: 443) is especially relevant. He admires the circulation of keen speculative thought in publications such as the *Revue des Deux Mondes*, but deems these ineffectual and immoral: 'there are but two instruments penetrative enough to reach [the masses'] opaque minds – the newspaper article and the popular speech; and both of these are forbidden' (1995: 444). English thought, in contrast, 'has rarely been so unfinished, so piecemeal, so *ragged* as it is now', which is the key to success: 'we beat the ideas of the few into the minds of the many' (1995: 444). Trollope's Cicero exemplifies this English way of thinking.

Cicero was not to be turned from his pursuit of an active life 'by the pseudo logic of Greek philosophers' (Trollope 1880: 1.112), which quarrelled with 'his clear common sense' (1880: 1.46). Trollope does not dismiss Cicero's philosophical treatises in their entirety, however. Instead, he introduces an unconventional distinction:

> It seems to be absurd to put forward to the world his *Tusculan Inquiries*, written with the declared object of showing that death and pain were not evils, together with a moral essay, such as that *De Officiis*, in which he tells us what it may become a man of the world to do. It is as though we bound up Lord Chesterfield's letters in a volume with Hume's essays, and called them the philosophy of the eighteenth century. (1880: 2.336)

Cicero's reflections on the nature of existence (*Academica*, *De Finibus Bonorum et Malorum*, *De Natura Deorum*, *De Divinatione*, *De Fato*,

Tusculanae Quaestiones) jar, according to Trollope, with his moral essays (*De Republica*, *De Legibus*, *De Amicitia*, *De Senectute*, *De Officiis*). While Trollope has little to say about the former, the latter are the 'most perfect of his works' (1880: 1.117). Trollope's sympathies lie with Lord Chesterfield: 'to live in accordance with the doctrine of any special school of philosophy', Cicero 'was too honest, too wise, too civilised, too modern' (1880: 2.337). As such, Cicero's moral essays would be out of place in the speculative *Revue des Deux Mondes*, but at home in the ragged newspapers of contemporary England:

> How the pages of the magazines would have run over with little essays from his pen! 'Have you seen our Cicero's paper on agriculture? That lucky fellow, Editor ——, got him to do it last month!' 'Of course you have read Cicero's article on the soul. The bishops don't know which way to turn'. 'So the political article in the *Quarterly* is Cicero's?' 'Of course you know the art-criticism in the *Times* this year is Tully's doing?' (1880: 1.38)

At the same time, there are subtle ways in which Trollope undercuts Bagehot's theory. When one is looking for an occupation as a way to find consolation in times of sorrow, '[w]riting Greek philosophy does as well as the making of shoes' (1880: 2.353). This ostensibly blunt comparison uses one of Trollope's hobby-horses; in his *Autobiography*, Trollope twice compares his own craft to that of the cobbler (1999a: 121, 323). A biographical reading of *An Old Man's Love* shows that Trollope's turn to the classics was partly inspired by such a therapeutic need:

> Then, when [Mr Whittlestaff] came to think in earnest of self-destruction, he told himself that it was a coward's refuge. He took to his classics for consolation, and read the philosophy of Cicero, and the history of Livy, and the war chronicles of Caesar. They did him good – in the same way that the making of many shoes would have done him good had he been a shoemaker. (1998a: 9–10)

Like writing novels and studying the classics, then, philosophy may have a purpose. Furthermore, Trollope challenges Bagehot's scorn for the fatuity of French thought by endorsing French critics of Bonapartism.[10] These quibbles notwithstanding, it is in Trollope's in-depth engagement with Cicero's moral essays that we find his alternative to Caesarism.

According to Trollope, Cicero's essays encourage one to live a 'full active human life, in which [the citizen] might achieve for himself all the charms of high rank, gilded by intelligence, erudition, and refined luxury, in which also he might serve his country, his order, and his friends' (1880: 1.112). This may be read as Trollope's version of civic republicanism.[11] Many such versions were at his disposal: extending back to Plato, Aristotle, and the 'Machiavellian moment' of Renaissance Florence, civic republicanism had experienced a revival in the works of Victorian poets such as Robert Browning, Elizabeth Barrett Browning, Arthur Hugh Clough, and A. C. Swinburne, and in fiction including *Romola* (1862), George Eliot's novel of Renaissance Florence. It is to John Stuart Mill's promotion of 'active and disinterested participation in public affairs' (D. E. Miller 2000: 89), however, that we should trace the kind of republicanism that shimmers through in Trollope's representation of Cicero.

Mill, like many Victorians, considered the distinction between civic virtue and individual freedom to be moot: 'To Mill the fundamental character that a democracy must possess in order to safeguard liberty, was a high degree of popular participation in public life' (Biagini 2003: 62).[12] For Trollope's Cicero, too, liberty and civic participation are mutually constitutive: liberty was 'very dear to [Cicero] – dear to him not only as enjoying it himself, but as a privilege for the enjoyment of others' (Trollope 1880: 1.81–2). Cicero therefore exerted himself on behalf of his fellow citizens to ensure that their rights were maintained: 'this liberty, though it was but of a few, was so dear to him that he spent his life in an endeavour to preserve it' (1880: 1.82). Trollope realises that the Roman idea of freedom was circumscribed, just as Mill has reservations about the nature of freedom in slave-ridden Athens: 'The love of absolute liberty as it has been cultivated among modern races did not exist in the time of Cicero. The idea never seems to have reached even his bosom, human and humanitarian as were his sympathies, that a man, as man, should be free' (1880: 1.24). Nevertheless, 'there was a something which stood in the name of liberty, and could endear itself to a real patriot' (1880: 1.25).

Furthermore, Mill argues that the civic republican should be active: although the 'most central mode of civic participation is political participation', one also 'takes part in public affairs whenever one acts in a public capacity' (D. E. Miller 2000: 90). Cicero's vigorous career as a politician and as a barrister provides Trollope with plenty of material to illustrate this aspect. In Trollope's account, the orations against Verres merit special attention. When charges were brought against Verres for his misrule of Sicily, his faction, the *optimates*, rallied to his defence, even though he had executed fellow citizens without due cause, a fact which Trollope underscores: Cicero enforced upon his audience 'the sanctity attached to the name of a Roman citizen . . . "Cives Romanus" is Cicero's cry from the beginning to the end' (Trollope 1880: 1.187).[13] Cicero thus spoke truth to power at his own personal risk, relying 'only on the public opinion which he was to create by his own words' (1880: 1.158) – a gamble that in Greek rhetoric is called parrhesia (παρρησία):

> It was in this condition of things that Cicero bethought himself that he might at one blow break through the corruption of the judgment-seat, and this he determined to do by subjecting the judges to the light of public opinion. If Verres could be tried under a bushel, as it were, in the dark, as many others had been tried, so that little or nothing should be said about the trial in the city at large, then there would be no danger for the judges. It could only be by shaming them, by making them understand that Rome would become too hot to hold them, that they could be brought to give a verdict against the accused. (1880: 1.150)

Similarly, Mill singles out 'the "feeling of duty" or conscience, shame and habituation of the will as especially serviceable' in creating fraternal sympathy between citizens (D. E. Miller 2000: 100).

Mill's civic republican is also disinterested. At certain points, Trollope may seem less exacting; Cicero, we have seen, is not immune to 'the charms of high rank, gilded by intelligence, erudition, and refined luxury' (Trollope 1880: 1.112). It is clear, however, that when push comes to shove the common good takes precedence. When Cicero was in dire straits because of Clodius's impeachment and Caesar generously offered him a legateship, for instance, Cicero refused:

> It was open to Cicero, without disloyalty, to accept the offer made to him; but with an insight into what was coming, of which he himself was hardly conscious, he could not bring himself to accept offers which in themselves were alluring, but which would seem in future times to have implied on his part an assent to the breaking up of the Republic. Αἰδέομαι Τρῶας καὶ Τρῳάδας ἑλκεσιπέπλους. What will be said of me in history by my citizens if I now do simply that which may best suit my own happiness? (1880: 1.354)[14]

In addition, Trollope suggests that Cicero's occasional consideration of his own happiness may also have been fuelled by pragmatism. Unlike Caesar, Cicero did not want to be the head of a one-man party: 'How shall a patriot do the work of his country unless he be in high place; and how shall he achieve that place except by cooperation with those whom he trusts?' (1880: 1.213). The political representative, then, must embody a paradox. He has power but must see this power as a trust. This reflects a typical conundrum in Mill's philosophy:

> In whatever way we define or understand the idea of a right, no person can have a right (except in the purely legal sense) to power over others: every such power, which he is allowed to possess is morally, in the fullest force of the term, a trust. But the exercise of any political function, either as an elector or as a representative, is power over others. (Mill 2008a: 353–4)

Trollope holds fast to similarly genteel version of the master–slave dialectic. It is not 'because [Cicero] was or was not a "real power in the State" that his memory is still worth recording', but 'because he was in truth patriotic, . . . because he was intent on doing good in public affairs' (Trollope 1880: 1.25–6). Patriotism, as these quotations indicate, is an important mediating factor in generating disinterestedness. This tallies with Mill's motivational psychology, in which public-spirited behaviour as a concern for the welfare of others can be encouraged by means of certain 'springs of action', such as 'a sense of shared nationality' (D. E. Miller 2000: 100–1). Trollope makes explicit that Cicero's epithet is meant as a sign of altruism: Cicero's 'hands were clean when those of others were dirty, and his motives patriotic while those of others were selfish' (Trollope 1880: 2.58). Mill's theory also gives Trollope an explanation for Cicero's failure insofar as another spring of action, the elimination 'of contrary influences' (D. E. Miller 2000: 102), is notably missing in Trollope's depiction of republican Rome.

Finally, Trollope's characterisation of Cicero dovetails with Mill's own admiration of the 'greatest orator, save one, of antiquity' (Mill 2008b: 42).[15] If we are to judge by Mill's enthusiastic review of Macaulay's *Lays of Ancient Rome* (1842), Cicero is surpassed only by Demosthenes: 'As for prose, we give up Cicero as compared with Demosthenes, but with no one else' (Mill 1981b: 532). Paradoxically, Demosthenes made his appearance when Athenian democracy was about to be overrun by the Macedonians, led by Philip the Great. His 'life was an incessant struggle against the fatality of the time, and the weaknesses of his countrymen' (Mill 1978: 312). This is mirrored in Trollope's depiction of republican Rome: 'Ciceronic compromises were, and must have been, equally ineffective. The patient was past cure' (Trollope 1880: 1.376, see also 2.58).

Mill's pairing of Cicero with Demosthenes suggests that Trollope's civic republicanism is ultimately an expression of Hellenism.[16] Civic republicanism is, indeed, an important substratum in Victorian Hellenism. For Mill, the institutional configuration of Athens served as a reminder that individual liberty, the freedom from external restraints, could not function without the responsibility that comes with participatory citizenship (see Biagini 1996):

> What is still more important than even this matter of feeling is the practical discipline which the character obtains from the occasional demand made upon the citizens to exercise, for a time and in their turn, some social function . . . Notwithstanding the defects of the social system and moral ideas of antiquity, the practice of the dicastery and the ecclesia raised the intellectual standard of an average Athenian citizen far beyond anything of which there is yet an example in any other mass of men, ancient or modern. The proofs of

> this are apparent in every page of our great historian of Greece. (Mill 2008a: 254)

The 'great historian of Greece' Mill refers to is George Grote, whose best-selling *History of Greece* (1846–56) Mill reviewed enthusiastically, and who can be said to be the founder of Hellenic civic republicanism.[17] Debunking William Mitford's claim that 'the lawlessness and mob rule of democratic Athens' were proof of 'the threat of liberal reform in England' (Goldhill 2011: 174), Grote believed that 'democratic freedom was the best guarantor of both stability and civic virtue' (Turner 1981: 215). Grote's Hellenism was well received in radical university circles. Edward Augustus Freeman, later Regius Professor of History at Oxford, enthusiastically endorsed Grote's work; both writers thought that the present-day Swiss cantons were closest to the Greek 'co-existence of freedom and self-imposed restraint, of obedience to authority with unmeasured censure of the persons exercising it' (Grote 1880: 154).[18] Trollope seems to have had affinities with this circle. In his obituary, Freeman mentions that he was genuinely impressed by Trollope's knowledge of Cicero when they first met, in Rome, and that Trollope was writing in the Hellenic tradition of civic republicanism initiated by Grote:

> it was because Mr Trollope had seen a good deal of men and things in England and Ireland and other parts of the world that he was able to understand men and things at Rome also. I know not how it may sound either at Balliol or at Berlin; but nothing is more certain than that Arnold and Grote, simply because they were active citizens of a free state, understood ten thousand things in Greek and Roman history which Mommsen and Curtius, with all their fresh lights in other ways, fail to understand. (Freeman 1883: 238)

Christianity

Freeman's suggestion that Trollope was also treading in the footsteps of Dr Arnold hints at a second way in which Trollope challenged the assumptions of contemporary writing on the history of ancient Rome. According to Arnold, the institutions of the Roman Empire ultimately helped further the spread of Christianity. Trollope takes up an even more radical stance by suggesting that a republican did so as well:

> But there was a humanity in Cicero, a something almost of Christianity, a stepping forward out of the dead intellectualities of Roman life into moral perceptions, into natural affections, into domesticity, philanthropy, and conscious discharge of duty. (Trollope 1880: 1.2–3)

As the final cadence of this quotation suggests, civic republicanism and Christianity are not mutually exclusive. A quick word count reveals that the distribution of 'patriotism' and 'Christianity' (and their variants) in the verbal texture of Trollope's biography is almost exactly even, which suggests that they are of equal importance. Throughout his biography, indeed, Trollope posits that Cicero's concern for the welfare and liberty of others at the expense of his own interests was guided by an innate understanding of Christian principles.

This part of Trollope's argument is a challenge to Caesarism as well. On the one hand, Trollope's emphasis on the relevance of Christianity defies positivists such as Harrison and Morley, who thought that the liberal Christianity of their time was 'a phase of soft, autumnal decay' (Willey 1969: 263).[19] Trollope's belief in the truthfulness of Cicero's account of his own life, moreover, counters the scepticism of David Friedrich Strauss's *Das Leben Jesu kritisch bearbeitet* (1835–6), Ernest Renan's *Vie de Jésus* (1863), and John Seeley's *Ecce Homo* (1865), which exposed the Gospels as the stuff of legend. Trollope does not seek to reveal the man behind the myth. On the other hand, his presentation of Cicero is a stab at the 'muscular' form of Christianity which Froude found in Caesar, and which was promoted even more vigorously by Charles Kingsley. In *Hypatia* (1853), a historical novel, Kingsley proselytises against the Christians of fifth-century Alexandria, depicting its Catholic monks as fanatic and degenerate, and suggesting that Christianity will be saved by means of healthy northern blood, 'infusing into Christian life Kingsley's necessary Protestant values of hardiness, rigour, muscularity' (Goldhill 2011: 205). Trollope does not set store by these values. He does not believe that Caesar sided with the cause of democracy 'from any philanthropic desire for equality; not from any far-seeing view of fraternal citizenship under one great paternal lord' (Trollope 1880: 1.334). Caesar is not a rewarding subject, moreover, because 'the character of the man is unpleasant to contemplate, unimpressionable, very far from divine. There is none of the human softness necessary for love; none of the human weakness needed for sympathy' (1880: 2.212–13). A similar idea was already present at the beginning of Trollope's career. The character of Augustus 'was odious to humanity and unworthy of sympathy. But what Roman ever required the sympathy of any one?' (Trollope 1856: 33). Cicero, by contrast, is aware of his own limitations, being one of those 'whose intellects are set on so fine a pivot that a variation in the breeze of the moment, which coarser minds shall not feel, will carry them round with a rapidity which baffles the common eye' (Trollope 1880: 1.19). Like Phineas Finn or Plantagenet Palliser, Cicero is prone to vacillation. In exile, for instance, Cicero contemplated suicide but decided against it. Trollope remarks that, ironically, this token of Christianity has been held against Cicero because he thus did not conform to practices of his time: 'It is because he dared to live on that we are taught to think so little of him – because he had antedated Christianity so far as to feel when the moment came that such an escape was, in truth, unmanly. He doubted, and when the deed had not been done he expressed regret that he had allowed himself to live' (1880: 1.367). This weakness is a token of 'that superiority of inward being which makes Cicero the most fit to be loved of all the Romans' (1880: 1.16).

Trollope's rejection of positivist scepticism and of muscular Christianity does not mean that he embraces the views of Froude's and Kingsley's main opponent, Cardinal Newman, whose *The Arians of the Fourth Century* (1833) and *The Church of the Fathers* (1840) had 'helped make the early church a fiercely contested arena for Christians' (Goldhill 2011: 203). Like Kingsley's novel, which it is a response to, Newman's *Callista* (1855) depicts the Church in its infancy, set as it is in the third century AD. Newman's protagonists are virtuous and brave, however. Believing in the promise of eternal life, they are willing to sacrifice themselves for what they believe to be the greater good. Newman and Trollope may have been friends – Newman sent him a 'specific' for his asthma and his compliments for his novels when he heard that Trollope was seriously ill (Trollope 1983: 991–4) – but Newman would have found much to disagree with in Trollope's biography of Cicero. Cicero is certainly not given to sacrifice: had he 'adhered to truth at the cost of being a martyr, his conduct would have been high though we might have known less of it; but, looking at all the circumstances of the period, have we a right to think that he could have done so?' (Trollope 1880: 2.134). Trollope's judgement of the Church fathers, in addition, is ambiguous. Cicero's description of the Eleusinian mysteries, on which his belief in some Eternal being rests, is 'very different from that which was attributed to them by early Christian writers. They were to those pious but somewhat prejudiced theologists mysterious and pagan, and therefore horrible' (1880: 1.65–6). This points to fundamental issue: Cicero was a pagan and thus, for Christians, beyond redemption. Trollope's biography, however, rests on the assumption that one can be a virtuous Christian even without having read the Gospel; that, as Freeman puts it, 'there may be some place in the economy of things where Tully may welcome the Anthony who has been his zealous champion' (Freeman 1883: 240).

It is Freeman's Hellenist kind of Christianity that Trollope's *Life* defers to. This may seem counterintuitive, given the conflict between

Hellenism and Christianity as captured by, for instance, Virginia Woolf: 'Entirely aware of their own standing in the shadow, and yet alive to every tremor and gleam of existence, there they endure, and it is to the Greeks that we turn when we are sick of the vagueness, of the confusion, of the Christianity and its consolations, of our own age' (Woolf 1966a: 13). As Simon Goldhill has shown, however, this is 'only one, oversimplified strand of how the love of Greek antiquity threatened, exposed, or supported Christianity' (Goldhill 2010: 475). Trollope's biography is an expression of Hellenism insofar as he is fascinated by the tension between Cicero's pagan beliefs and his quasi-Christian identity. He never fully accounts for his feeling that there 'is such a touch of humanity in [Cicero's words], such a feeling of latter-day civilisation and almost of Christianity, that we are apt to condemn what remains in them of paganism' (Trollope 1880: 1.178–9). Trollope thus challenges his contemporaries' views about the development of Christianity, a recurring concern in writing about ancient Rome, by focusing on a figure who predated this period. He was not alone in thus being caught between two worlds: 'Many serious Christians – Frederic William Farrar would be a paradigm – combined Anglican sermons, liberal educational reform, and a love of things Greek' (Goldhill 2010: 476). Trollope's thesis that Cicero's pagan beliefs foreshadow Christ's teaching dovetails with *Eternal Hope*, a series of sermons delivered in 1877 and published in 1878, in which Farrar attacked the idea of eternal torment and dismissed the doctrine of purgatory.[20] Furthermore, the *Life of Cicero* is similar in its conception to Farrar's *Life of Christ* (1874), a romantic and conservative biography which 'encouraged belief, comfort, and joy in Christian tradition' (Goldhill 2011: 155). It is telling that Trollope chose to tell Cicero's life through a biography rather than through his form of choice, the novel, and that he should do so like a believer, not a sceptic.[21]

The way in which Trollope makes the study of the Roman past an integral part of his religious beliefs thus presents a parallel to his investment in civic republicanism, insofar as both lines are part of his attempt to Hellenise the history of Rome. The theological dimension of Trollope's biography reinforces the political: like the Messiah whom he prefigures, Trollope's Cicero's hopeless advocacy of a return to the republican forms of the past interrupts the present – the Roman as well as the Victorian present – and points the way to a radically different future.

Notes

1. Two of Trollope's characters are thoroughly imbued with the Greek classics, Grace Crawley and her father in *The Last Chronicle of Barset*. But their knowledge only serves to emphasise their distance (both in terms of intellect and poverty) from their community. Perhaps Trollope was prompted to further explore the character of Mr Crawley after having come across the following satirical line in his good friend Lord Houghton's contribution to Frederic Farrar's influential *Essays on a Liberal Education*: 'Outside the Universities it is rare to find a clergyman, not engaged in tuition, whose intimacy with his previous studies goes much beyond his Greek Testament, and indeed it would hardly tend to his professional credit if it was known that he spent any considerable portion of his time in company with a literature not akin in thought and principle to his present duties' (Milnes 1867: 371).
2. The two most extensive accounts of the Victorian engagement with Greece are Jenkyns (1980) and Turner (1981).
3. Many Liberals approached the question of Greater Britain through the history of the Roman Empire, as the works of Sir Charles Dilke and John Seeley attest. These writers' comparisons show that 'arguments about the Roman Empire are inseparable from their claims about the British Empire, and in fact reveal more about the latter than the former' (Vasunia 2005: 39). For overviews of the many intersections between the classics and Victorian imperialism, see Bell (2006) and Vance (1977 and 2011). Hellenism could also be turned against imperialism, as recent postcolonial criticism attests (Vasunia 2003).
4. Merivale's younger brother, John Lewis, was one of Trollope's closest friends from his days at Harrow. Merivale was also under-secretary for the colonies and may, as such, have been a model for Phineas Finn.
5. This political difference becomes apparent in the reaction to the Governor Eyre controversy, 'one of those great moral earthquakes of Victorian public life whose fault-lines are so revealing of those subterranean affinities and antipathies of the educated classes' (Collini 1993a: 144). While colonial governor of Jamaica, Edward Eyre brutally suppressed a violent uprising among the native population of Morant Bay under the cover of martial law. In October 1865, leading Evangelical activists and philanthropists of Exeter Hall organised a committee to coordinate remonstration against Eyre's atrocities, which in turn prompted the establishment of a defence committee. The Jamaica Committee and the Jamaica Defence Committee both harboured enthusiasts of Caesar: Beesly helped found the former, Froude the latter.
6. Trollope's interest in India as a colony is deliberately nebulous (see Goodlad 2010a).
7. For other comparisons of Caesar's conquests with the first moves in the Great Game, see Trollope (1870b: 28–9, 68).
8. Beesly's essays on Catiline, Clodius, and Tiberius were published in the first issues of the *Fortnightly* (1865–8), flanking Trollope's many reviews, and were collected in 1878, while Trollope was preparing his biography of Cicero.
9. According to Frank Turner, the resistance to Caesarism was small:

'Those dissenters included Anthony Trollope, the novelist, and J. L. Strachan-Davidson, successor to Jowett as Master of Balliol, as well as the Ciceronian scholars William Forsyth and R. Y. Tyrrell' (Turner 1986: 595). This is not the whole picture, however. There was a whole array of popular histories of the Roman republic that lacked both Merivale's erudition and his political commitment, such as W. Lucas Collins's volume on Cicero for *Ancient Classics for English Readers* (1873) and J. C. Hollins's *Life of Marcus Tullius Cicero* (1839). Furthermore, Cicero's presence in the public's mind was ensured by means of other publications. Cardinal Mai's discovery of new works ensured Cicero's visibility in the press. So did Albert Watson's new edition of selected letters (1870), which were soon translated by George Edward Jeans (1880). Cicero's other works, too, were reprinted many times: 'Even Aristotle received less publishing attention' (Rosner 1986: 160). These books have been forgotten or become invisible because, perhaps, Conyers Middleton's eighteenth-century *Life* remained in print and was used as both a foil and an authority. By presenting Cicero's words without the suspicion characteristic of Caesarism, these writings implicitly resisted the negative image of Cicero created by Merivale, Beesly, and Froude.

10. Trollope finds support in the works of Morabin (1880: 1.359), Guéroult (1.304), du Rozoir (1.212), Gaston Boissier (2.35), Le Clerc (2.47), and Montesquieu (2.18). He also compares Crassus to 'M. Poirier in the play – a man who, having become rich, then allowed himself the luxury of an ambition' (1.260). The Frenchman referred to here is Émile Augier, whose plays dominated the French stage during the Second Empire. *Le Gendre de Monsieur Poirier* (1854), Augier's best-known work, illustrates his unbending moralism and advocacy of the dispossessed nobility.
11. For an engaging overview of civic republicanism, see Olsen (2006).
12. As Dale Miller notes, most previous accounts of Mill's liberalism (such as Gertrude Himmelfarb's) tend to explain elements that do not fit his image as a liberal as inconsistencies. Lauren M. E. Goodlad, in contrast, argues that 'Mill can be described as a committed humanist, determined to combat modern tendencies toward homogenisation, bureaucratisation, and embourgeoisement by fortifying the social and political foundations of positive liberty. Throughout his works he endorsed the empowering potential of education and citizenship, and expressed still more enthusiasm for the progressive aims of domestic equality, gender equity, and cooperative socialism' (Goodlad 2008: 27). According to Dale Miller, Mill 'classes the common interest in liberty among the most vital of the common interests which constitute the public good' (2000: 100). Daniel Malachuk (2005) polemically suggests that Mill even exceeds the limits of liberalism in his quest for a robust perfectionism. Since Isaiah Berlin's famous essay on positive and negative liberty it has, of course, become difficult to think outside the opposition between republicanism and liberalism. Quentin Skinner, for instance, has suggested that the early modern legacy of civic republicanism had disappeared by the beginning of the nineteenth century with the 'ideological triumph' of classical liberalism (Skinner 1998: x). On the interplay between freedom and security in contemporary neoliberalism, see Foucault (2008: 65).

13. These words' significance was rekindled in the nineteenth century during the so-called Don Pacifico affair, when Lord Palmerston justified sending a gunboat to Athens as protection for a British Jew by referring to Cicero's words. In the twentieth century, it was John F. Kennedy who revived the phrase: 'Two thousand years ago the proudest boast was *civis Romanus sum*. Today, in the world of freedom, the proudest boast is *ich bin ein Berliner*'.
14. This is one of the few instances where Trollope quotes Greek. The words are from the *Iliad* (6.442) and are spoken by Hector. It is a line that Cicero himself uses quite frequently (hence, probably, Trollope's quotation) as an element in his self-representation and self-fashioning: 'I have shame on the Trojans and the Trojans' wives with their trailing robes'.
15. Like Burke, Mill was influenced by the way in which Cicero envisages his ideal orator-statesman as a representative of the Roman people (Remer 2010). Cicero's writings were an integral part of Mill's upbringing – in 1820, for instance, he translated Cicero's *Pro Milone*. References to Cicero are scattered throughout his work. The final sentence of his *Considerations on Representative Government* begins with an invocation from Cicero's *De Senectute*: 'Di meliora' (2008a: 467). Mill furnishes one of his first published works, a pugnacious review of Thomas Malthus's essay on political economy – which is 'as bad as might naturally be expected, considering the quarter from which it comes' although 'there are peculiarities in its badness, which take it out of the ordinary run of *Quarterly Review* articles' (Mill 1967a: 25) – with a paraphrase of a sentence in Cicero's *De Divinatione*: 'There is nothing, says Cicero, so absurd as not to have been maintained by some philosophers' (1967a: 41). He also employs this paraphrase in a later essay (1967b: 344).
16. Matthew Arnold, too, sees Cicero as part of this tradition, and even dares chide the great Mommsen in a letter to John Morley (16 August 1883): 'I still think there will be murmurs, and that I shall lose something of the "benevolentia civium", of which I have not too large a stock to begin with. "Magnum telum ad res gerendas existemare oportet benevolentiam civium", says Cicero, and how true it is, and what a pedant is Mommsen, who runs this charming personage down!' (Arnold 1996–2001: 5.290–1). Arnold's authority is lessened, however, by a small inaccuracy. He tones down Cicero's litotes '*non minore telum*' to the less forceful '*magnum telum*', thus immediately furnishing his aversion to pedantry with an illustration. Arnold also makes a tiny mistake in an earlier quotation, turning Cicero's active '*probare*' into the passive (and ungrammatical) '*probari*' (to W. E. Forster, 19 May 1879, Arnold 1996–2001: 5.30). This carelessness seems to have seeped into a few of Cecil W. Lang's admirable footnotes. Lang remarks that Arnold is here referring to Cicero's *Philippics* (2.112), while Arnold in fact quotes *Laelius de Amicitia* (17.61). Accordingly, Lang's translation does not match Arnold's words, which should be translated as follows: 'a man ought not to consider the goodwill of his countrymen a poor weapon in the management of his affairs'. Strangely, Lang does cite *De Amicitia* as a source for this phrase '*benevolentia civium*' in an earlier letter in which Arnold congratulates John Campbell Shairp on his election as Oxford Professor of Poetry.

17. In his *Autobiography*, Mill notes that the 'two friends of my father from whom I derived most, and with whom I most associated, were Mr Grote and Mr John Austin' (1981a: 75).
18. This line of thinking was continued in a more ethical vein by T. H. Green, Balliol Professor of Moral Philosophy and militant prohibitionist, who sought to nurture the 'public service ethic' that first showed itself in classical Athens (Biagini 2003: 61–2).
19. Trollope did tackle the crisis of faith in an earlier novel, *The Bertrams*, which in some ways anticipates Renan's *Vie de Jésus*, partly because, like Renan's story, a good deal of the action is set in the Holy Land. This novel did not endear Trollope to Newman, who confided that it 'is decidedly the most powerful thing of his that I have read – tragic, instructive, humiliating – but there is a touch of scepticism which I have never seen in him before. I fear it is one of his last; if so he is progressing uncomfortably' (Newman 1961: 20.281). On Trollope's religious views, see chapter 8, n. 24.
20. Farrar and Trollope did not exchange letters, but there is one contextual indication that they shared a similar worldview: they both defended Colenso, bishop of Natal, when he was charged with heresy in 1853 for his biblical criticism and his advocacy for native Africans (Super 1990: 371–2; Trollope 1865c; Vance 2004).
21. The historical novel was not Trollope's forte, as he knew. After the failure of his only attempt in the genre, *La Vendée* (1850), the secretary of the publishers Hurst & Blackett told Trollope, when he was trying to sell *The Three Clerks*, 'Whatever you do, don't be historical. Your historical novel is not worth a damn' (Trollope 1999a: 110–11).

Chapter 6

'The Tone of Today': Pedagogical Paraphrases

> '*Caelum non animum mutant qui trans mare currunt*', Lucy might have said, had she known the passage. As it was she put the same feeling into simpler words, 'I should like one as well as the other, Uncle Tom, if things went comfortably'. (Trollope 1989b: 240)

Trollope's interest in the Latin classics was intensified by his search for an alternative political model, but grew out of his concern with ethics. Ruth apRoberts and Jane Nardin, among others, have suggested that Trollope's focus on moral problems in his late novels owes much to his reading of Cicero's *De Officiis*. In *Cousin Henry*, for instance, Trollope harks back to Cicero's presentation of the philosopher Diogenes' claim that in moral reasoning one ought to consider the role of expediency (apRoberts 1969: 95): 'it is one thing to conceal, another to be silent' (*De Officiis* 3.52). Cicero's adage neatly encapsulates the novel's anti-hero's conundrum. Believing himself to be the heir to the Llanfeare estate, Henry Jones discovers a second testament, hidden in a volume of sermons, according to which the vast bulk of the property is transferred to his niece, Isabel Brodrick. Jones cannot bring himself to disclose his discovery, and his mind echoes Diogenes' words: 'Was it his duty to produce the evidence of a gross injustice against himself?' (Trollope 1993b: 47; *De Officiis* 3.57).[1] ApRoberts thus suggests that *Cousin Henry* embroiders on Cicero's ideas, actualising them and providing them with a narrative elaboration. Although she does not use the term, her observation indicates that Trollope's novel is a paraphrase, that is, in an extension of the sense in which the term is used in rhetoric, a free rendering of something written or spoken 'using different words, especially to achieve greater clarity' (Stevenson 2010: 1289).

Paraphrases are essential ingredients in Trollope's late style and add a number of specific flavours: the principles of paraphrasis are at work in his creation of certain allusions and certain motifs, in his development of the form of the novella (*Cousin Henry*, *An Old Man's Love*, and *Dr*

Wortle's School), and in the methodology of his literary criticism (*The Life of Cicero* and *The Commentaries of Caesar*). These different manifestations, which span the range from a single passage to a whole text, reveal that Trollope's use of the paraphrase is part and parcel of his critique of Enlightenment modernity and its contemporary manifestation, Victorian liberalism. This chapter will first explore how the paraphrase can be considered as a post-Romantic form, both intrinsically and historically, before examining how the various guises that paraphrases in Trollope's late works take put this theory into practice and how, in its Victorian context, Trollope's take on the paraphrase is distinctively pedagogical. Trollope's paraphrases, that is, are part of an attempt to rectify the imbalance in the distribution of knowledge by making the public-school domain of classical literature accessible to all. At the same time, his paraphrases pose a challenge to a hermeneutical way of reading that privileges individuality and citationality. These two purposes are intertwined. On both counts, the paraphrase preserves the original while withdrawing its appearance, thus creating a desire for a lost or denied sense of commonality.

Salvation

The paraphrase has a long history and an eclectic tradition (Fuchs 1982: 10–13). Although παραφράζειν ('to speak alongside') originally covered a variety of meanings, the term quickly came to denote an exercise in the rewording of a passage, often with a change in genre or style. Classical rhetoricians such as Quintilian argued that a paraphrase ought to rival the original in the expression of the same thought (*Institutio Oratoria* 10.5.4–5). In the late Middle Ages, this technique was put to the service of the controversies surrounding the exegesis of sacred texts. Writers found that the paraphrase allowed them to retell the Psalms and the Gospels, to give two of the most popular examples, in accordance with a particular set of theological doctrines; the form thus acquired a polemical function. From the early modern period onwards, as the principles of *imitatio* and *aemulatio* were replaced by the concept of originality, the paraphrase began to decline in popularity. In a world of too many books, practices of citation seemed to provide the conditions of modernity with a more suitable way of relating to literary texts (Piper 2010: 181). Citationality first gained prominence through commonplacing, the excerpting of quotations. By the end of the eighteenth century, this method had developed into a 'new way of reading that fell under the heading of hermeneutics, one that moved from the memorisation of a citation to its interpretation', as a result of which it 'was the individuality, not commonality of the citation that mattered' (Piper 2010: 186). Relating to texts through citations thus gradually occasioned a sense of crisis about the possibility of literary sociability: 'The more the literary came to be inscribed within a commercial modernity, the more its value was a function of innovation, the *less* it seemed that literature was something that could be mutually shared among readers' (Piper 2010: 181). A return to the model of the paraphrase was one way in which this new crisis was met. In his post-classical novel *Wilhelm Meisters Wanderjahre* (1821), for instance, Goethe uses paraphrasis as 'a new way of having literature in common, one that was based not on a model of possession, of having originals, and thus originality, in common, but instead on the commonality of a shared transformative grammar' (Piper 2010: 181). This use of paraphrasis was different from its polemical predecessor, as this chapter will show: it substituted for the model of the polemic a model of redemption and nostalgia, what Benjamin calls *Rettung*, salvation.[2]

Both in its polemical and redemptive manifestations, the paraphrase's intrinsic qualities differ substantially from the citation's. Cleanth Brooks famously condemned the paraphrase as a heresy because, at least when used without full awareness of its supposedly temporary nature, it disarticulates the original work's unity of form and content. Citations do not come in for such condemnation, presumably because they do keep the bond between form and content alive even while breaking the original up into parts. Walter Benjamin's essay on 'The Task of the Translator', the preface to his own translation of Baudelaire's *Tableaux parisiens*, shows that there may be a creative side to the paraphrase that Brooks ignores. Benjamin's idiosyncratic definition of translation is the opposite of Brooks's definition of poetry. Whereas the poet, according to Brooks, 'must return to us the unity of the experience itself as man knows it in his own experience' (Brooks 1947: 212–13), the translator, according to Benjamin, should discompose the original's unity and break it into parts, thus piercing through the veil of its semblance and giving an intimation of the pure language that is to come: 'The task of the translator consists in finding that intended effect upon the language into which he is translating which produces in it the echo of the original' (Benjamin 2004c: 258). The translator, in other words, should not focus on the transmission of historical experience, but on the way in which the original transmits its material content, on the way in which it means. Paraphrases, as used by Goethe, relate to the original in an analogous fashion. At once enfolding and unfolding their source, paraphrases give birth to 'something new that could at some point in the future be held in common' (Piper 2010: 188).

Allusion

Trollope's work may, at first sight, seem an inhospitable environment for this literary technique. As David Skilton and Hugh Osborne have shown, Trollope's novels make frequent use of a particular, out-dated form of citation, the tag. Tags had a clear ideological function in Victorian Britain, serving to exclude those who had not had the benefit of public-school education: 'Tags as social signals differentiate between characters within the fiction, and, by establishing within the novel an image of what competences the reader should possess, divide the sheep from the goats among the actual readers outside the novel's literal sway' (Skilton 1988: 48). In Thackeray's last novel, *The Adventures of Philip* (1862), for instance, Dr Firmin tries to establish his social credentials by lacing his toast to Philip's success with a Latin quotation:

> He was agitated by the tender feelings of a paternal heart, he said, glancing benignly at Phil, who was cracking filberts. To see his son happy; to see him surrounded by such friends; to know him embarked this day in a profession which gave the greatest scope for talents, the noblest regard for industry, was a proud and happy moment to him, Dr Firmin. What had the poet observed? '*Ingenuas didicisse fideliter artes*' (hear, hear!) '*emollit mores*', – yes, '*emollit mores*'. (Thackeray 1904: 15.254)

According to Skilton and Osborne, Thackeray's allusion produces and reinforces 'a sense of upper middle-class Englishness' among the novel's readers (Osborne 2001: 129). The fact that the tag is here phrased in Latin is part of its discursive significance: 'Although Greek was a more reliable marker of social or intellectual superiority, phrases from Latin poetry were part of the currency of public life, recalled with comparative ease because authors such as Horace were drummed into schoolboys' (Hurst 2010: 488). Within the world of the novel, Dr Firmin shows himself to have been educated in the classics: this line from Ovid's *Epistulae ex Ponto* (2.9.47–8) is one of the first examples in the *Eton Latin Grammar* that students had to learn by heart (it serves as an instance of the rule that a sentence can function as a nominative or subject): 'To have learnt the liberal sciences thoroughly softens men's manners' (G. Taylor 1828: 48). The way in which Dr Firmin recalls his Latin theme is, furthermore, an extension of his untrustworthy character. He cannot recall the ending of Ovid's verse – '*nec sinit esse ferros*' or 'and does not suffer them to be rough' – a fact highlighted by his repetition, which signals that he knows something is missing.

Trollope's novels deploy Latin tags less regularly than Thackeray's, but still frequently. At the bottom of the same page in the *Eton Latin*

Grammar, we find a line from Terence's *Andria* (l. 552) – '*Amantium irae amoris integratio est*' or 'The quarrels of lovers are the renewal of love' (G. Taylor 1828: 48) – which Trollope uses as a title for chapter four in *Framley Parsonage* (which was published in the *Cornhill* a year before *Philip*) and chapter seventy-three in *Phineas Finn*. Trollope continues to play with tags in his late novels. In his last finished novel, *An Old Man's Love*, Mr Hall mocks his daughters because of their ignorance, assuming that they will not understand his reference to Virgil's *Eclogae* (1.15):

> 'And this is Mary. Mary considers herself to be quite the hope of the family; *spem gregis*. Ha, ha!'
>
> 'What does *spem gregis* mean? I'm sure I don't know', said Mary. (1998a: 89)

In a striking contrast, Mr Whittlestaff hopes that his ward, Mary Lawrie, will understand him when he makes an allusion to Horace (*Epistulae* 1.18.69) to illustrate his misgivings about going to a party at Mr Hall's: 'That young clergyman of [Mr Hall] will have told him everything. "Percontatorem fugito nam garrulus idem est". I've taught you Latin enough to understand that' (1998a: 99).[3] Whittlestaff's tag was a set phrase as well. In the 1828 edition of the *Eton Latin Grammar*, however, only the first two words are cited: 'Avoid an inquisitive person' (G. Taylor 1828: 60). Whittlestaff, a true enthusiast of the classics, can place the words in their proper context: 'for he is garrulous'. As these examples from *An Old Man's Love* indicate, Trollope tends to highlight the tag's exclusionary character.

Trollope does not just imitate Thackeray's play with tags, however. David Skilton observes that where 'Trollope frequently translates his tags in his text, . . . Thackeray can often be understood only by people with at least a rudimentary acquaintance with Latin vocabulary' (1988: 45). This distinction is a fundamental one. When Lord Hampstead declares 'I cannot conceive that I shall perish altogether' (Trollope 1985: 411), or Melmotte thinks, in free indirect speech, that 'he would not all die' (Trollope 1992: 685), these two very different characters are referring to a line of Horace: '*non omnis moriar*' (*Carmina* 3.30.6). Skilton identifies Harry Clavering's father's self-pity – 'I see a better path, and know how good it is, but I follow ever the worse' (Trollope 1994: 15) – as 'a schoolroom translation of Medea's famous soliloquy in Ovid's *Metamorphoses*' (Skilton 1988: 42): '*video meliora proboque deteriora sequor*' (7.20). Frank Houston translates this with his usual flippancy:

> *The better course I see and know –*
> *The worser* [*sic*] *one is where I go*. (Trollope 1989b: 305)

Hugh Osborne shows that Dr Wortle's contest with Mrs Stantiloup, to give a final example, is twice characterised by means of an allusion to '*flecti non potest, frangi potest*', a line from Seneca's *Thyestes* (l. 199): 'not being able to bend he would have to be broken', though he later resolves that 'she will not bend me' (Osborne 2001: 150; Trollope 1989c: 7, 98). Of course, Trollope may also be referring to Aesop's fable about the Oak and the Reed. He labours this allusion even more obviously in the name of *The Fixed Period*'s narrator, Mr Neverbend. Trollope's use of tags is, as such, circuitous and paradoxical: rather than appealing directly to the reader, he gives a short nod which the cognoscenti will understand and at which the uninitiated will not take offence.

Trollope's translated tags occupy a peculiar position within the Victorian debate on the extent to which a translation was supposed to be faithful, with Francis Newman's literal approach at one end of the spectrum and Matthew Arnold's more domesticating approach at the other. Osborne argues that Trollope's allusions are, in contrast to either model, part of a self-referential game. They are playful, seeking 'to act performatively as an index both of the translator's facility for translation and – by extension – of his rightful place within the community of gentlemen' (Osborne 2001: 159). In this view, both their form and function are essentially similar to that of quotations. There is, however, an element of undecidability in translations and allusions that is absent in quotations. Quotations can be seen, even if they are not understood, whereas allusions can pass by unnoticed. The skilled reader might find allusions where the author did not consciously intend to make them; it is difficult to tell where allusions end and originality begins – like Easter eggs, some will be found only when they have expired. As such, allusions will gradually erode the original. They are a sign that the distinction between the original and the present, the object and the subject, is being blurred. It might therefore be more productive to look at Trollope's allusions as forms of paraphrase or translation as conceived of by Benjamin. The Latin tags, in being paraphrased, are divested of their originality and made part of something new. Generating a surplus in meaning, Trollope's allusions thus evince a resistance to citationality. He rescues or redeems the Latin original – and does so without advertising his attempt, since this would imply that his own words would be at risk of becoming citational themselves.

Cousin Henry can be read as an amplified instance of this procedure. As we have seen, this short novel consists of a series of long, narrative improvisations upon one particular Ciceronian idea. The novel hints at this condition of its existence by means of a metafictional detail. It is telling that Indefer Jones's will 'lay still hidden within the folds' (1993b:

89) of a volume of Jeremy Taylor's sermons: the book of sermons encapsulates the principle of enfolding and unfolding that structures the novel. Goethe uses a similar motif in *Der Mann von fünfzig Jahre*, in which the beautiful widow, one of the novella's protagonists, is embroidering a briefcase, a *Brieftasche*, into which she weaves her memories and which she gives to the Major as a folder for his hunting poem. The will in *Cousin Henry* resembles the Major's poem insofar as both are literally enfolded. The Major's poem is not cited but summarised, just as the contents of Indefer Jones's testament are never stated explicitly.[4] *Der Mann von fünfzig Jahre* may seem a far-fetched point of comparison, but *An Old Man's Love* further reinforces the impression that in his late novellas Trollope is following Goethe's lead. There are many indications that *An Old Man's Love* is intended as a paraphrase of Goethe's *Der Mann von fünfzig Jahre*. Both Whittlestaff and the Major are explicitly fifty years of age. Both begin the story while looking into a mirror, trying to make sense of the discrepancy between their ageing appearance and their engagement to their ward or niece. They conceive of this engagement not as a matter of possessiveness: 'He wished more for her happiness than the pleasure of possessing her' (Goethe 2007: 57). In their attempts to convince their beloveds, Whittlestaff and the Major try out both citations and paraphrases of the classics. At one point the Major tries to find a suitable dedication in his book of Latin commonplaces. But when it dawns on him that using Ovid's description of Arachne implies that he would be addressing the widow as a spider, he thinks better of it and returns the poem in the *Brieftasche* without a dedication (Goethe 2007: 36). Horace is a particular point of reference for both, but other authors appear as well. The characterisation of Trollope's and Goethe's protagonists is thus strikingly similar, and so are their plotlines, insofar as their protagonists' plans are thwarted when a younger former lover suddenly bursts upon the scene. Finally, in more general terms, Trollope and Goethe share an interest in the limitations of a moral life in an immoral environment. But the way in which these characters develop and the plots are unravelled is different. Goethe's tale is brisk, enigmatic, and shorn of all psychological analysis, whereas Trollope's story hardly contains any action, revolving around a detailed description of the protagonist's mind. *An Old Man's Love*'s significance thus lies not only in its sophisticated, self-reflexive play with citations and paraphrases, but also in the operations of paraphrasis at a meta-level.

The detailed descriptions of Trollope's characters' minds are also paraphrastic, finally, in that these descriptions allude to the classical way of thinking in a portico culture. Just as the affluent Athenian citizen combined deep thought with walking, so Trollope's gentlemen tend to go for a walk when they are in the process of making a decision. It seems that gentlemen can only reach a conclusion if they, like their thoughts, are in motion; talking, in contrast, favours stasis.[5] In the first scene of *An Old Man's Love*, for instance, Whittlestaff agrees to become the *de facto* guardian of Mary Lawrie only after some mulling over during a stroll: 'In order that he might in truth make up his mind on the subject, he went out with his hat and stick into the long walk, and there thought out the matter to its conclusion' (1998a: 1). Similarly, Mr Peacocke in *Dr Wortle's School* feels that he needs a detour to decide whether he should reveal that Mrs Peacocke is in fact another man's wife. Peacocke makes this cluster explicit: 'I have walked all round by Bowick Lodge. I had something to think of before I could talk to you – something to decide upon, indeed' (1989c: 34). These characters have woven a classical practice into the fabric of their daily lives.[6]

Judicious Reading

In his works of literary criticism, *The Life of Cicero* in particular, Trollope's use of the paraphrase comes into its own as a genre. Trollope's biography of Cicero recounts Cicero's life as Cicero tells it in his own writings, since the 'man of letters is, in truth, ever writing his own biography' (1880: 1.32). This axiom provides the foundation for Trollope's paraphrastic methodology. His primary sources are Cicero's own writings, which he summarises, expands, evaluates, and translates. This approach is not as tedious and straightforward as it may seem, however. As with Trollope's allusions, it is not always clear when Cicero's voice dies down and Trollope's takes over. When Trollope translates Cicero's words, he usually cites his source and sometimes quotes the original in a footnote, but there are revealing exceptions to this rule. In the case of the following example, both are missing:

> 'Do not think', [Cicero] says, 'that I am complaining of all this because I myself am desirous of being engaged in public affairs. Even while it was mine to sit at the helm I was tired of the work; but now, when I am in truth driven out of the ship, when the rudder has not been thrown down but seized out of my hands, how should I take a pleasure in looking from the shore at the wrecks which these other pilots have made?' (1880: 1.345)

Although this passage fits neatly into Trollope's presentation of Cicero as an upright patriot, he is in fact trifling with the original. Cicero's original words – as they were available in Trollope's own day – reveal a more vindictive and partisan attitude:

> Atque haec sic velim existimes non me abs te κατὰ τὸ πρακτικὸν quaerere, quod gestiat animus aliquid agere in re p. Iam pridem gubernare me taedebat, etiam cum licebat; nunc vero cum cogar exire de navi non abiectis sed ereptis gubernaculis, cupio istorum naufragia ex terra intueri, cupio, ut ait tuus amicus Sophocles,
>
> κἂν ὑπὸ στέγῃ
> πυκνῆς ἀκούειν ψακάδος εὑδούσῃ φρενί
> (*Ad Att.* 2.7.4, Cicéron 1962: 1.228)

Having been stripped of his powers, Cicero says, in no uncertain terms, 'I desire to watch their shipwreck from the shore'. Trollope is fiddling with Cicero's words, turning a declaration into a rhetorical question. The Latin script had no punctuation, originally, so one might object that Trollope's interpretation is not impossible. Problematically, however, Cicero continues to emphasise his resentment in Greek: 'I desire, as your friend Sophocles says, "safe beneath the roof to hear with drowsy ear the splash of rain"' – a quotation from Sophocles' lost tragedy *Tympanistae*. This illustration makes a rhetorical question unlikely.

Trollope's *Life* is therefore not as objective as he makes it seem. This may not be too surprising, since he initially advertises the polemical intent of this work. In the biography's opening pages, Trollope takes aim at contemporary admirers of Caesar, James Anthony Froude in particular, who do not 'hesitate to load [Cicero] with infamy because of a playful word in a letter half jocose and half pathetic to his friend . . . and thus it comes to pass that their very meaning is misunderstood' (1880: 1.7–8).

After this initial skirmish, however, Trollope's attack on his contemporaries disappears almost completely. What follows is not a detailed study in which he proves Cicero's detractors wrong, but a redemptive reading, not just in the sense that Trollope seeks to salvage Cicero's reputation, but in that he seeks to imbue Cicero's words with their original intention. Not so much concerned with objective truth as with what Cicero himself held to be true, Trollope sets out to 'read between the lines, and interpret the words by creating for ourselves something of the spirit in which they were written and in which they were received' (1880: 1.390). Cicero's words cannot be elucidated without 'an insight into the humour of the man' (1880: 2.93). As such, Trollope's biography is an instance of phenomenology *avant la lettre* or, mutatis mutandis, proves that phenomenology very much harks back to certain forms of nineteenth-century literary criticism. Trollope calls this intra-subjective model of reading judicious:

> a judicious reader will discount a man's praise of himself. But the reader, to get at the truth, if he be indeed judicious, will discount them after a fashion

> conformable with the nature of the man whose character he is investigating . . . If a man praise himself for honour, probity, industry, and patriotism, he will at any rate show that these virtues are dear to him, unless the course of his life has proved him to be altogether a hypocrite in such utterances. (1880: 1.140)

The practical implementation of this theory of truth as essentially subjective runs up against some difficulties. First, Cicero's skill as a wordsmith presents a problem. On the one hand, it is only 'by the study of his own words' that one can feel the 'sanctity of his heart and morals' (1880: 1.143). Cicero's work must be studied 'in the original, for no translator can give its true purport' (1880: 1.386). At the same time, Cicero delights in creating illusions. The nature of Cicero's language does not follow the Keatsian assumption that truth and beauty ought to be identical:

> But with the Romans so great was the desire to shine that the reality was lost in its appearance. And so prone were the people to indulge in the delight of their senses that they would sacrifice a thing for a sound, and preferred lies in perfect language to truth in halting syllables. (1880: 2.333)

To translate Cicero's words is to miss their true purport, then, while to read them in the original makes one run the risk of being seduced. Paraphrasing Cicero's words gives Trollope a means of escape from this double bind: it peels off the veneer of Cicero's oratory in order to get at the sanctity of his heart and morals (see Sussman 2013: 888–91).

Second, entering the mind of an ancient Roman presents certain challenges. Trollope realises that 'now', nineteen centuries later, it has become impossible 'to decipher every intended detail' (1880: 2.167). He therefore decides to limit himself and 'simply to illustrate the life of Cicero by such facts as we know' (1880: 2.259). Again, there are two sides to this question. On the one hand, the 'facts we know' are furnished by contemporary writers such as Sallust and modern historians such as Mommsen who, so Trollope maintains, on the whole confirm Cicero's account of events. On the other hand, the 'facts we know' are facts Trollope's reader knows instinctively, because ancient Rome and Victorian Britain share many aspects. When elements in Cicero's prose are difficult to grasp because they refer to assumptions and facts that were part of the way in which the Romans saw their world, Trollope provides these with a commentary. Catiline, for instance, is glossed as Rush, the murderer (1880: 1.254); Cicero as a modern gentleman (1880: 2.300) and Robert Peel (1880: 1.367); troubles in Greece and Egypt as the protection of Turkey and the invasion of Zululand (1880: 1.175); democrats and oligarchs as Liberals and Conservatives (1880: 1.76); the

Acta Diurna as an official gazette (1880: 2.122); a house on the Palatine as a house in Park Lane (1880: 2.13); the great comic actor Roscius as Garrick, Siddons, and Talma (1880: 1.121). In this regard, Trollope's late writings about republican Rome are similar to Waterhouse's and Alma-Tadema's paintings with antique subjects, which 'stand for a self-aware statement about modernity' (Goldhill 2011: 16). Trollope is especially struck by the similarity between republican Rome and Victorian Britain in the problems that riddle their politics, such as the ballot (1880: 2.379), filibustering (1880: 2.14), hankering after the titles of office (1880: 1.345), and canvassing – the 'most degrading of all existing employments not held to be absolutely disgraceful' (1880: 1.130), words that recall the description in *An Autobiography* of his own failed attempt at Beverley (Trollope 1999a: 300–2).

Trollope's readers, then, are presented with a coherent image of Cicero's personality that strips his language of its beauty, and are encouraged to see Cicero's world through the lens of their own experience. This endeavour is made possible by paraphrases, which allow Trollope to kill two birds with one stone: through both actual passages of paraphrase and the exercise of paraphrasis he can, without arousing suspicion, phrase his material to make it fit his image of Cicero as an honest politician and riff on associations between past and present. Trollope thus weaves Cicero's words into a tapestry in which the threads out of which it is composed are not always clearly discernible. As a result, Cicero appears as a thoroughly modern subject:

> And with Cicero we are charmed by the modernness, by the tone of today, which his language takes. The rapid way in which he runs from scorn to pity, from pity to anger, from anger to public zeal, and then instantly to irony and ridicule, implies a lightness of touch which, not unreasonably, surprises us as having endured for so many hundred years. (1880: 1.160)

This description of Cicero's style is Trollope's interpretation – or invention – as much as it is a given. In fact, the 'tone of today' and the 'lightness of touch' that Trollope attributes to Cicero apply more to his own paraphrases than to Cicero's speeches, letters, and treatises. Yet this controversial statement is not directed against Cicero's detractors, as in the beginning of the *Life*. Trollope's aim is not polemical; rather, *The Life of Cicero* tries to save Cicero, to rescue his words from oblivion by presenting a Cicero as an old friend. The charming is Trollope's.

Public Schools

In a more immediate sense, this nostalgic use of paraphrasis served a pedagogical purpose. As George Meredith put it in a letter to John Morley in March 1877, Trollope's article on 'Cicero as a Politician' 'shows him to have a feeling for his hero. It reads curiously as though he were addressing a class of good young men. This is the effect of the style, or absence of style. One likes him for working in that mine: only – and yet I like a certain kind of open-mindedness' (Meredith 1912: 272–3).[7] The pedagogical slant of *The Life of Cicero* becomes clearer when we compare it to its predecessor, *The Commentaries of Caesar*, which appeared in Blackwood's *Ancient Classics for English Readers*. Like Collins's series in general, Trollope's volume is patently didactic. He aims 'to describe Caesar's Commentaries for the aid of those who do not read Latin' (1870b: 3, 18–19). The voice of the schoolmaster is manifest in Trollope's moral and religious comments, his imitation of Caesar's tenses and indirect speech (1870b: 37, 84), his concern with topography, and, in particular, his use of fables. Reducing complex historical processes to tales of the utmost simplicity – the wolf and the lamb (1870b: 30), the horse and the stag (1870b: 39), the monkey and the oyster (1870b: 75) – this technique adds a pedantic tinge to Trollope's book. Importantly, these elements are all paraphrastic. As Victoria Glendinning remarks, Trollope 'paraphrases, condenses, and adds his own commentaries to the *Commentaries*' (2010: 26). Small wonder that Charles Merivale called the book a 'comic Caesar' when Trollope sent it as a gift (Trollope 1983: 357; 1999a: 339). Yet Trollope takes this ungenerous remark as a compliment, confirming his belief that comedy was essential if his book were to be efficacious:

> With the leave of my sententious and sonorous friend, who had not endured that subjects which had been grave to him should be treated irreverently, I will say that such a work, unless it be light, cannot answer the purpose for which it is intended. It was not exactly a school book that was wanted, but something that would carry the purposes of the school room even into the leisure hours of adult pupils. (1999a: 340)

This passage indicates that the lightness of touch that Trollope finds (or pretends to find) in Cicero's work is, in fact, the kind of tone he himself was aiming for in his literary criticism. Significantly, Trollope also uses the term 'charming' to describe Collins's series as a whole, which he recommends 'as the most charming tales [young ladies] can read' (1999a: 338).[8] Trollope's 'comic Caesar' and, for that matter, 'comic Cicero' should ensure that the classics will be given a broader appeal.

The paraphrase is an especially helpful technique when addressing those 'who have never gone through – shall we say the farce or the fact? – of learning the two great dead languages' (Trollope 1870a: 665).

As such, Trollope's 'absence of style' in these books is a late solution to his long-standing concern with the public-school system, which had been under attack since the 1860s. On one front, Matthew Higgins had exposed abuses at Eton in a series of essays in the *Cornhill* in 1860, which almost singlehandedly led to the Clarendon investigation.[9] On another front, the place of the classics in the curriculum had been challenged by the ascent of science. Frederic William Farrar was not only an important clergyman and philologist, as we have seen in the previous chapter, but at one time also assistant master at Trollope's alma mater, Harrow. His experience as a teacher led him to question the merits of traditional Latin and Greek verse composition and to underscore the benefits of science education in a variety of publications such as his own contribution to *Essays on a Liberal Education* (1867: 207), a collection which he edited and which featured compositions by liberal lights such as John Seeley and Henry Sidgwick. In a later article, Farrar ups the ante, claiming

> that the educational value of [the classics] has been extravagantly overrated; that the evils of them (and their moral evils alone are very serious) are to this day resolutely ignored; that their yoke has been made needlessly heavy and needlessly humiliating; that taken alone it is doubtful whether they furnish the best mental discipline for any, but most absolutely certain that they do not furnish even a good discipline for all; and, finally that they remain to this day intrenched [*sic*] behind a mountain-heap of fallacies, of which no small number ought to have been banished ignominiously to the region of the most exploded errors. (Farrar 1868: 233–4)

In his essay on the 1864 report of the Clarendon Commission, Trollope agrees with Higgins and Farrar that the ignorance of pupils at the present time was lamentable. Yet his solution is different. Trollope concedes that reform is necessary, but advocates restraint. First of all, as Hugh Osborne has argued, Trollope's essay mimics Thomas Hughes's *Tom Brown's Schooldays* (1857) in that, by interrupting his essay with a nostalgic description of his days at Harrow and Winchester, he gives voice to a discourse of remembrance that 'inscribes memories of one's schooldays with a unilateral power to define and perpetuate a formative community of one's youth, an inclusive community which surrounds one even into adulthood' (Osborne 2001: 120). Trollope believes that the power to instil these memories is something worth preserving. Furthermore, he attributes the present state of affairs not to the subjects being taught but to the way in which this teaching takes place: 'boys have never been taught their lessons, but have simply been called upon to say them', a point that the Commissioners 'do not seem to insist on', though 'it cannot but be wished that they should have done' (Trollope 1865b: 482). Trollope thus wards off the measures proposed by the Commissioners – such as expanding the curriculum – by changing the conversation. Ignorance will remain, he argues, as long as teaching is left to older boys, or pupils themselves: 'what we require is not better masters at our schools – which we probably could not get – but more masters, which we certainly can get if we choose to pay for them' (1865b: 484). Trollope adduces St Andrew's College at Bradfield, where this practice has yielded results, though parents had to cough up £130 – £30 more than one paid at Harrow (Rae 1989: xii). Although Trollope's explanation of this increase is tortuous, at bottom it is clear that parents 'would either pay more, or go elsewhere for education' (Trollope 1865b: 485). Trollope denies that this would foster exclusivity by defending the present system of endowments, which will ensure that the

> son of the squire of the parish and the son of the parson are placed together at the same school, are educated in the same way, enjoy an equal footing, so that in after life they meet together with mutual sympathy, and on an absolute equality as gentlemen – though the school education of one has cost three times the sum expended on the other. This is what the old endowments do for us, and this inestimable benefit, let us hope, we may preserve. (1865b: 487)

Trollope continued to ponder how to change the actual conditions of public schools, as another late novella, *Dr Wortle's School*, attests. This novel presents an idyllic picture of school life: the food is good, the children are cared for, and there are four ushers for thirty boys. 'Bowick School is a curiosity', John Rae declares, noting that the school's lifestyle is inconsistent with Trollope's description of his days at Harrow and Winchester in his *Autobiography* (Rae 1989: xii). Perhaps, Rae notes, Dr Wortle's school reflects the happy interlude that Trollope spent at Sunbury. Reading the novel against 'Public Schools', however, reveals that Dr Wortle's school exemplifies the kind of reform that Trollope was hoping for: a reform that would not change the curriculum, but create a different kind of school. This message is emphasised by a satirical element in Trollope's representation. The novel plays with the image that *Tom Brown* installed in the public imagination of Dr Arnold as a short-tempered and righteous martinet, who, when vilified by the Tory press, did not hesitate to engage in controversy (Curthoys 2011). Like 'Black' Arnold, Dr Wortle is filled with moral certainty. He quarrels with the successive bishops of his diocese, the second of whom 'died, not, let us hope, by means of the Doctor' (1989c: 5). When a London weekly newspaper, *Everybody's Business*, suggests that Dr Wortle's defence of Mrs Peacocke is driven by a desire for the beautiful, creole American, Dr Wortle can scarcely restrain himself from shaming his bishop, who sent him the paper, by charging the newspaper with libel.[10] But unlike Arnold, though perhaps like Trollope, Dr Wortle is not feared but loved: 'If a tyrant, he was an affectionate tyrant' (1989c: 4).

Dr Wortle is not always taking the moral high ground, moreover. He has a guilty conscience: there are signs that his support for Mr Peacocke's wife is not fully disinterested. When she mentions that she ought to move out, for instance, Dr Wortle is quick to reassure her: '"You have been reading that dastardly article in the paper. It will have no effect upon me. Look here, Mrs. Peacocke" – then he got up and held her hand as though he were going, but he remained some moments while he was still speaking to her – still holding her hand' (1989c: 109). Furthermore, Dr Wortle has a blustering sense of decorum. 'He had been foolish enough to declare openly that he was in search of a curate who should have none of the "grace of godliness" about him' (1989c: 5) and 'was no doubt addicted to expletives in conversation' (1989c: 14). Elements such as these in combination with Dr Wortle's exaggerated sense of rectitude and his stiff-necked obstinacy make him at times look foolish. Or, as Trollope would say, human. Dr Wortle is not perfect, unlike Hughes's Dr Arnold. It is this that endears him to the reader. He is accorded praise in words that recall Trollope's Cicero:

> It may almost be said that he hated that state of perfection which would require no pardon. He was thoroughly human, quite content with his own present position, anticipating no millennium for the future of the world, and probably, in his heart, looking forward to heaven as simply the better alternative when the happiness of this world should be at an end. He himself was in no respect a wicked man, and yet a little wickedness was not distasteful to him. (1989c: 27)

There are contextual elements confirming the impression that Dr Wortle might be a parody of Thomas Arnold. The novel was written while Trollope was staying with Collins at the latter's rectory in Lowick, Northamptonshire (the same rectory where George Eliot wrote parts of *Middlemarch*, though this was before Collins received the living). Not only did this stay remind Trollope of Arnold because one had to leave the train at Rugby station in order to reach Lowick. More importantly, Collins had been one of the first pupils to be taught under Arnold's reformed system. When his days as a diocesan school inspector were over, he put himself forward as the unofficial chronicler of Britain's great schools. His essays were collected in *Etoniana* (1865) and *The*

Public Schools (1867). The latter is 'notable for its revisionist account of Arnold's influence at Rugby, Collins taking issue with Arnold's liberal eulogists, whom he thought had unfairly denigrated the latter's predecessors' (Reeve 2011: n. pag.).

The satirical note in Trollope's portrait of a headmaster can be understood as an echo of Collins's views, but it also brings to mind another school inspector, Thomas Arnold's son Matthew. Matthew Arnold's 'The Twice-Revised Code' (1862) responds to a very different context and is much more closely argued than Trollope's essay, but he, too, emphasises the need for good and qualitative teaching that Trollope advocates in 'Public Schools' and *Dr Wortle's School*. Arnold argues that it is the taxpayer who should pitch in, whereas Trollope targets the nobility, but this is due to the schools they are talking about – Arnold considers elementary schools in general, Trollope public schools (though Bowick school is, significantly, a preparatory school). Furthermore, Arnold shares Trollope's belief in the importance of the ability to produce a good paraphrase, an ability which he singles out in his defence of the humanities in his famous Rede lecture 'Literature and Science' (Arnold 1882: 228). This returns us to the first point in Trollope's essay. Trollope's paraphrases of Cicero's and Caesar's works can be understood as attempts to remedy this deficit in classical knowledge for adults who had the misfortune of being taught by their fellow pupils rather than their masters; even more, they teach that knowing how to put this knowledge into simpler words is the stuff that a community is made of.

Notes

1. Henry Jones is not the only character in this novel to grapple with Ciceronian ethics. Isabel Brodrick's stubborn refusal to marry William Owen recapitulates Cicero's warning that 'it is a hateful fact that loftiness and greatness of spirit all too easily give birth to wilfulness and an excessive desire for pre-eminence' (Nardin 1996: 95; *De Officiis* 1.64).
2. The interplay between polemic and salvation, or rescue, is typical of late style, as Adorno suggests and 'performs' in 'Parataxis: On Hölderlin's Late Poetry' (see Savage 2010).
3. Trollope fictionalises his attempt to make the classics accessible to women and girls in *An Old Man's Love*. The novel's protagonist, Mr Whittlestaff, seems stern and severe, but is in fact effeminate. He is introduced to the reader as he looks into a glass, which characterises him as unmanly (Heath 2006: 30). His intention not to burden his wife with children further emphasises his femininity. Portraying education in the classics as the domain of the weak and the excluded, *An Old Man's Love* heralds the emerging affinity between the classics and marginalised sexualities.

Towards the fin de siècle, Aesthetic Hellenism was increasingly associated with homosexuality – one thinks of John Addington Symonds, one of Walter Pater's fellow students, and Oscar Wilde and Gerard Manley Hopkins, who were taught by Pater. But educated women, too, found in the study of Greece a tool with which they could undermine the classics as an exclusively male field of knowledge. Vernon Lee's art criticism, modelled as it is on Pater's work, insists on physical experience more than bookish precision, sensual impressionism more than academic accuracy. Her emphasis on the aesthetic and imaginative dimensions of the archaeological object can 'be seen to have aided a popularising turn in classical studies, opening Victorian classicism to the intervention of women and social groups that had traditionally been excluded from institutionalised education' (Evangelista 2009a: 32). The young Virginia Woolf, who was taught Greek by Pater's sister Clara, was imbued with a deep admiration for Greek culture: 'They could march straight up, with their eyes open; and thus fearlessly approached, emotions stand still and suffer themselves to be looked at' (Woolf 1966a: 10). These two marginalised groups were occasional allies: under the editorship of Oscar Wilde, the *Woman's World* made the reception of ancient Greece accessible and amenable to the New Woman. Through a discussion of vase-paintings representing Sappho, for instance, Jane Ellen Harrison illustrates the 'unreliability of legends about Sappho' and simultaneously 'discusses the role of collegiate life in reviving the social instincts that had allowed Sappho to flourish' (Hurst 2009: 49). On the interaction between Aestheticism and Hellenism, see Evangelista (2009b) and Østermark-Johansen (2009). On Hellenism and gender, see Dowling (1994), Hurst (2006), and Prins (1999).

4. This is a motif in Trollope's fiction. In *John Caldigate*, for instance, the fact that the title character addresses Euphemia Smith as 'Mrs Caldigate' on an envelope is sufficient evidence for his bigamy; the letter that this envelope supposedly contained, however, is never produced or described. *The Fixed Period* elaborates this principle in a different way: 'the only one of [Trollope's] novels which contains within itself a fictional account of its own creation' (Skilton 1973: 41), the novel envelops itself: it is a paraphrase of its own origins.
5. Female characters, interestingly, tend to reflect while they are sitting. For some exemplary passages of women composing themselves, see *The Way We Live Now* (1992: 229, 262) or *Ayala's Angel* (1989b: 398, 448). Other Victorian novelists made this distinction as well. In Dickens's *The Mystery of Edwin Drood* (1870), Mr Crisparkle corrects Neville Landless's choice of a walking stick. 'You don't rest upon it; you merely balance with it' (2005: 133). Landless explains that, recently arrived from Ceylon, he has 'not lived in a walking country' (2005: 134). The 2012 BBC adaptation ignores the gender ideology that accompanies this practice, giving the line to Landless's sister, Helena.
6. When the idea of a portico culture was introduced in the domestic architecture of Rome, it underwent some changes: 'the Romans gave rather more weight, and concentration, than the Greeks to the walking itself. You wouldn't have caught the stereotypical Roman absent-mindedly falling into a well, like the Greek sage Thales, while wandering about, lost in his

own thoughts' (Beard 2012: 3). Timothy O'Sullivan argues that different forms of walking gradually crystallised into an 'art of physiognomy' (2011: 20–1). For the Romans, the way one walked was an indicator of one's character: 'how you walk defines who you are' (O'Sullivan 2011: 13). Slaves move quickly, women slowly, gentlemen statelily, revolutionaries capriciously. The Latin language reflects this practice. The word *incessus* literally means 'gait' but is usually translated as 'bearing' or 'demeanour'. Wrecked on the shores of Africa, for instance, Virgil's Aeneas embarks on a reconnaissance mission and meets a huntress, whom he immediately recognises as a goddess in disguise. She is, in fact, his mother, Venus. To Aeneas's perpetual frustration, she refuses to make herself known, though the signs are clear:

> Dixit et avertens rosea cervice refulsit,
> Ambrosiaeque comae divinum vertice odorem
> Spiravere; pedes vestis defluxit ad imos;
> Et vera incessu patuit dea. (1.402–5)
>
> Thus she spoke. Turning away, she gleamed from her rosy neck, and the heavenly tresses wafted a divine fragrance from her head; her clothes flowed all the way down to her feet, and by the way she walked she was clearly a true goddess. (O'Sullivan 2011: 11)

Trollope cites Virgil's passage in three novels, thus alluding explicitly to the Roman understanding of walking as an index of one's character. These citations are all ironic, however. This qualification is significant, as the following chapter will show: the eye cannot reveal what goes on in the mind, which is, for Trollope, what really matters. In *The Bertrams*, Trollope uses Virgil's words to emphasise that Caroline Waddington, his '*donna primissima*', walks like a Roman woman. But as the passage continues, he specifies that the Roman way of walking has been preserved only in Spain – the area that, according to Strabo's account, lacked this very skill (see O'Sullivan 2011: 1): 'But perhaps the most wonderful grace about her was her walk. "Vera incessu patuit Dea". Alas! how few women can walk! How many are wilfully averse to attempting any such motion! They scuffle, they trip, they trot, they amble, they waddle, they crawl, they drag themselves on painfully, as though the flounces and furbelows around them were a burden too heavy for easy, graceful motion; but, except in Spain, they rarely walk. In this respect our heroine was equal to an Andalusian' (1993a: 88–9). In *Framley Parsonage*, the phrase serves to mark the difference in appearance between 'brown' Lucy Robarts and her 'Greek' sister Blanche. In conclusion, Trollope suggests that this difference does not go for much: 'She was not like Blanche; for Blanche had a bright complexion, and a fine neck, and a noble bust, "et vera incessu patuit Dea" – a true goddess, that is, *as far as the eye went*' (2004: 139, my emphasis). Trollope's last explicit reference, in *Marion Fay*, to this line from the *Aeneid* adds a second layer to his playful engagement with the concept of walking. The Marchioness of Kingsbury 'could be very eloquent with silence, and strike an adversary dumb by the way in which she would leave a room. She was a tall, handsome woman, with a sublime gait. "Vera incessu patuit Dea"' (1985: 18). Lady Kingsbury is, first of all, as fickle as Venus, though certainly not as benevolent. In addition, though she may have a stately walk, she does not possess the gift of self-reflection that this walk should encourage.

7. Morley himself favoured a polemical use of paraphrasis. When he criticises what, 'in [his] opinion [and that of] his liberal friends, official Christianity stood for even in his own time', he does so 'obliquely through a summary of Voltaire's objections' using 'the ventriloquial method so beloved of himself and of Leslie Stephen' (Willey 1969: 263).
8. In his writings on the classics, Trollope often expresses support for the rights of women – rights such as property (1856: 43), freedom (1870b: 94), and divorce (1880: 2.170). Yet his thinking on the education of women is marked by contradictions. Trollope's avowal that *The Commentaries of Caesar* was aimed at girls and ladies is at odds with the fact that the audience which he addresses in his text is predominantly male: he will, for instance, not 'upset the teachings of our youth' (1870b: 4). In other descriptions of his intended female audience, Trollope is more disparaging: a 'well educated girl who had read [*The Commentaries of Caesar*] and remembered it would, perhaps, know as much about Caesar and his writings as she need know' (1999a: 339). His language here echoes *Sesame and Lilies*, in which Ruskin candidly maintains that girls 'should be served lighter intellectual food' (de Graef and Gilleir 2010: 18). As Trollope's biting review of *Sesame and Lilies* attests, however, he intensely disliked Ruskin's social ideas (1865a). Trollope plays a similar trick in his 1868 lecture on the 'Higher Education of Women', in which he skirts the more pressing issue of institutional reform by agreeing that upper-class women 'whose circumstances do not require them to earn their daily bread' and who are otherwise occupied with needlework are right to desire 'mental employment and material employment' (1938: 73). Finally, in *An Autobiography* Trollope uses a Horatian ode in which he has altered a line to illustrate how a boy 'who learns with accuracy the prosody of a Sapphic stanza' will spot this change in metre, while a girl 'endowed with gifts of music, well instructed in her art, with perfect ear' will 'find no halt in the rhythm' (1999a: 236). It is curious, however, that as an example Trollope should choose a stanza that was purportedly invented by a woman. All these paradoxes give the impression of Trollope sitting on the fence, which explains, perhaps, the exhaustive literature on his concern with issues of gender; see, for instance, Markwick (1997, 2007), Denenholz Morse (1987), Nardin (1989), and Skilton (2010).
9. Trollope congratulated George Smith when these essays first appeared; Higgins eventually became a good friend and was a fellow-member of the Cosmopolitan (Trollope 1983: 130). Dedicated to Higgins, Thackeray's *The Adventures of Philip* (1862) participates in this conversation as well.
10. On Mrs Peacocke's creole background, see Denenholz Morse (2013: 133–65).

Chapter 7

'An Admirable Shrewdness': Character and the Law

> For when the Gentiles, which have not the law, do by nature the things contained in the law, these, having not the law, are a law unto themselves. (Romans 2.14)

> I was considerably impressed with [Trollope's novels] in the early eighties when I chanced upon a novel entitled *Phineas Finn*. I haven't seen them since, to tell you the truth, but I have preserved a strong impression of a notable gallery of portraits rendered with that same intimacy of technique (if technique is the word) in which I believe the secret of his fascination lies. (Conrad 2007: 304)

The 'greatest of superficial novelists' (James 1971: 481), Charles Dickens tends to see his characters' appearance as a substitute for their character: 'it is true that Dickens can appear to skimp on his characters' personalities, and even what they look like from the neck up, when compared to the loving attention he lavishes on their outfits' (Douglas-Fairhurst 2011: 59). Trollope, in contrast, is interested in what lies beneath the surface.[1] His skill as a storyteller resides in his ability to probe the depths of his characters' minds, often catching them as they are in the process of doubting.[2] Trollope uses various stylistic means to this end, such as the description of his characters' movements or the strategic placement of certain conjunctions:

> [The] process of approximation and qualification which is inseparable from any attempt to balance up the conflicts and complexities of human character and motives . . . is closely linked with a recurring cadence which seems to be specially characteristic of Trollope. It is unobtrusive, indeed, yet in its own way powerful, and its power depends on nothing more than a very skilful use of the small word *but*, together with those meanings of *and* which the dictionaries call 'adversative', and occasionally such other conjunctions as *though* and *unless*. (Davies 1960: 76)

More important than setting or conjunctions, however, is the free indirect discourse in which these are enmeshed. Free indirect discourse presents the thinking process as a character experiences it while dressing it for communication to the reader. Although this 'intimacy of technique', as Joseph Conrad calls it, is also a characteristic feature of Trollope's earlier work, it is telling that it becomes more prominent in the late novels, especially in his novellas, at the expense of action, dialogue, and the narrator's commentary. 'Even in a work of characteristically Trollopian realism such as *The Prime Minister*', David Skilton notes, 'the narrator helps readers make up their minds about the significance of the action far less than in his earlier novels, and leaves more play for an unmediated reading of the characters' states of mind' (1998: ix).[3]

Trollope's increasing interest in the exploration of individual states of mind is part of his late style: creating a delicate counterpoint between the voice of the narrator and the voice of a character, this mode sketches a process of deliberation that lies partially outside subjectivity. Free indirect discourse thus heightens the turn inward that typifies lateness. To be more precise, as Martin Jay points out in his reading of Valentin Nikolaevich Voloshinov, free indirect discourse harbours a 'conflict between the evaluative orientation of the character whose speech is reported, and the narrator whose smooth narration is disrupted by its representation' (Jay 1998: 56). As a result, 'experience without the subject turns out to be experience with more than one subject inhabiting the same space' (Jay 1998: 56). The following passage from *Is He Popenjoy?* can illustrate these theoretical reflections:

> But [Lord George] was very angry with his brother, and did not in the least wish to see him. Nor did he think that by seeing him he could in any degree render easier that horrible task which would, sooner or later, be imposed upon him, of testing the legitimacy of his brother's child. And there were other reasons which made him unwilling to leave London. He did not like to be away from his young wife. She was, of course, a matron now, and entitled to be left alone, according to the laws of the world; but then she was so childish, and so fond of playing bagatelle with Jack De Baron! He had never had occasion to find fault with her; not to say words to her which he himself would regard as fault-finding words though she had complained more than once of his scolding her. (1998b: 178)

Subtly alternating his conjunctions, Trollope creates a form of language in which the voices of his narrator and Lord George are simultaneously present, though the balance is continually shifting. The exclamation of the fifth sentence accentuates George's mind; in the declarative sentences which surround this interjection, the narrator's reflections – partly mediated in indirect discourse – shine through more clearly. Trollope thus represents a form of subjectivity in which it becomes difficult to distinguish whose voice we are hearing and in which the individual element is no longer clearly distinct.

Lord George's worry about the power of the law – as regards both his brother's son and his control of his wife – hints at a particular feature of Trollope's representation of consciousness; his focus on the delineation of character, that is, stands in a productive tension with his representation of 'the laws of the world'.[4] Trollope, as critics have noted, tends to be on his characters' defence team. As Virginia Woolf remarks, 'there is an admirable shrewdness, like that of a family doctor or solicitor, too well acquainted with human foibles to judge them other than tolerantly' (1966b: 63); Ruth apRoberts similarly notes that Trollope is famously an 'advocate for each one of his characters' (1971: 53). Trollope's advocatory, non-judgemental stance is partly the result of his emphasis on free indirect discourse and character. Since 'Trollope's gift of speaking for the characters . . . erases the distinctions between good and bad' (J. H. Miller 2001: 90), it challenges the fundamental distinction on which the law relies. The law adheres to 'the dogma of the natural guilt of human life', to which character opposes 'a vision of the natural innocence of man' (Benjamin 2004d: 206). In the passage of free indirect discourse we have already examined, for instance, Trollope allows Lord George, who to all intents and purposes seems determined to destroy his own marriage, to exonerate himself and justify his own intentions.[5] The purpose of this passage is thus not to make the reader condemn Lord George or sympathise with his plight; instead, the reader gets an impersonal picture of the back-and-forth movement taking place within his mind. Because this picture has no other purpose than to amuse the reader and thus takes on 'only the interest shed by the light of character' (Benjamin 2004d: 205), Trollope's representation of consciousness produces a non-legal conception of human subjectivity.

A closer look at the representation of the law in Trollope's late novels confirms the tension between his view of subjectivity and the law's. Trollope's representation of the law took on a new life after the public debates which followed the Judicature Acts of 1873 and 1875.[6] Although these Acts' objective to fuse equity with the common law was largely an institutional matter, the popular mind perceived the disappearance of equity as an attack on the assumption that the law was supposed to serve natural justice.[7] Public opinion thus believed that the proposed reform challenged the theory of natural law. This belief was misguided as well as belated: by the mid-nineteenth century, the British legal system had already shifted its allegiance to very different, positivist principles.

Natural law theory can be dated back to antique and Catholic philosophies and was developed most fully, as Frederic Harrison indicates in his 1878 overview of the *status quaestionis*, by Enlightenment thinkers such as John Locke and William Blackstone, who tried 'to clothe law and judicial authority with a moral or metaphysical dignity' (1878a: 480). In the course of the late eighteenth and early nineteenth century, this theory was challenged and eventually replaced by the positivist conception of the law. According to Jeremy Bentham and John Austin, the law rests not on an idea of justice but on the command of the sovereign, 'an unlimited power, itself free from law and the source of law' (Harrison 1878a: 477). This conception of the law, which was foreshadowed by earlier opponents of natural law theory such as Jean Bodin and Thomas Hobbes, rests on the idea that 'the bases and sanctions of law and morals are, for logical proposes, totally distinct' (1878a: 481). If Harrison is right in asserting that by the end of the 1870s Austin's propositions had become 'ordinary truisms' (1878a: 481), then the outrage at the Judicature Acts was directed at a *fait accompli*. Trollope, however, refuses to subscribe to either doctrine and challenges, as such, 'the normative ideal of a liberal politics', the rule of law, which 'guarantees individual rights against the state, organises and limits the exercise of state power, and provides the conditions for market transactions' (Kahn 2005: 11).

In *Mr Scarborough's Family*, for instance, the honest lawyer Grey, for whom the laws are 'as Holy Writ' (1998c: 426), is deceived by his client, Mr Scarborough. His conception of the law hangs on the conviction that 'the Law and Justice may be made to run on all fours' (1998c: 430), but his need to confess his doubts and misgivings to his daughter Dolly, who 'felt herself to be the Conscience of the firm' (1998c: 123), indicates that this conception does not pass muster in the modern age. If *Mr Scarborough's Family* thus nevertheless conveys a certain nostalgia, *John Caldigate* provides a more cutting critique. After his return from Australia and his marriage to Hester Bolton, John Caldigate is accused of bigamy by his Australian partners, Euphemia Smith and Timothy Crinkett. Their motive is not justice, however, but redress for the fact that Caldigate had unwittingly sold them his gold-mine just before it was depleted. Nevertheless, all the Boltons except Hester are eager to take a stand against him. Mrs Bolton, in particular, does not buy the story of Caldigate's moral reform; from the moment of Caldigate's return, she believes that he intends to deceive her family, even though there are no facts to support her feelings. Instead, Mrs Bolton incessantly quotes and twists the Gospel in order to justify her sense of superiority, not hesitating to introduce a biblical 'commonplace as to the world's condition into a particular argument as to [her] daughter's future life' (1995b: 142). As a result, the Enlightenment idea that the law should rest on a higher, metaphysical order – an idea which Grey embodies in a more positive albeit naive way – is distorted: 'At Puritan Grange the matter was argued rather by rules of religion than of law; but as the rules of law were made by those interested to fit themselves to expediency, so were the rules of religion fitted to prejudice' (1995b: 434). *John Caldigate* thus attacks the assumption, inherent in natural law, that ends justify the means. As Walter Benjamin mentions in his 'Critique of Violence', natural law sanctions one to 'judge all existing law only in criticising its ends' (2004b: 237). Indeed, when the law fails Mrs Bolton, she has no qualms about resorting to force in the private sphere. Since Hester Bolton refuses to abandon her husband, her family effectively kidnaps her, taking away her bonnet and boots and locking all the doors after having invited her to the Grange. In short, *John Caldigate* censures the doctrine of natural law for its inclination to violence.

Furthermore, *John Caldigate* suggests that an adherence to natural law is profoundly illiberal because it tends to produce a form of half-belief. When she is told that Caldigate's verdict will be reversed by means of a royal pardon, for example, Mrs Bolton's reply illustrates her mistaken belief, or half-belief, that this pardon depends on her Majesty's sentiments: 'If the Queen were told the truth she would never do it . . . The Queen is a mother and a woman who kneels in prayer before her Maker. Something should be done, so that the truth may be made known to her' (1995b: 435). These sentiments are naive and express wishful thinking rather than a real understanding of the law. Trollope further reinforces this impression by modelling Caldigate's trial on the most famous trial of the decade, the Tichborne case.[8] The Tichborne case revolved around Arthur Orton, a butcher's son from Wapping, who had emigrated to Australia and who, upon his return to Britain, claimed to be Sir Roger Tichborne, a wealthy heir long thought to have drowned at sea.[9] Trollope alludes to this trial when his Australian troublemaker, Euphemia Smith, declares that she would 'sooner have fourteen years for perjury, like the Claimant' (1995b: 429). The Claimant's case was taken up vigorously by the lower classes, who sympathised with Orton, not because they believed that he really was Sir Roger, but because they felt that the aristocracy should be made to bite the dust. As one reporter for the *Saturday Review* noted, 'They would probably not have insisted so strongly on his being Roger if they had not half believed him to be Orton' (quoted in Thomas 2004: 108). It is not that Orton's supporters thought in values rather than facts; more precisely, they 'refuse the fact-value distinction that underlies . . . the liberal tradition at its largest levels' (Thomas 2004: 108).[10] Paradoxically, Trollope sketches this state in great detail; through free indirect discourse, the reader is made to experience and share Mrs Bolton's half-belief. Trollope thus pardons her even though she herself lacks the very faculty of forgiveness. As such, his representation of Mrs Bolton's perversion of natural law can be read as a swipe at the public opposition to positive law.

Trollope's portrayal of positive law contains negative elements as well, however. The judge in Caldigate's trial and the lawyers representing him are only concerned with the means and procedure of the trial, not with its societal function. This separation of legality and justice, a key tenet of legal positivism, in the end serves to condemn a man who, in fact, does not live up to the requirements of *mens rea* and *actus reus*: although both Caldigate and the narrator remain suspiciously vague about the actual affair, all the evidence adduced turns out to be manufactured. When this emerges, however, it makes no difference: Caldigate is 'guilty of bigamy in consequence of the verdict, even though he should never have committed the offence' (1995b: 433). The legal fiction of the Queen's pardon allows justice to be done, but it remains an 'awkward remedy' (1995b: 417) for a problem that is inherently structural.[11] This may clarify why Trollope's novels tend to convey a feeling that the law is always in a state of corruption and 'dinginess'. *John Caldigate* suggests that this sense of decay does not originate in the law's delay, but in the law's tendency to assume that all its subjects are guilty: 'The Judge begins with the idea that the man before him would hardly have been brought there had he not been guilty' (1995b: 288). To use Benjamin's terminology, 'the judge can perceive fate wherever he pleases' (2004d: 204). This means that guilt follows condemnation rather than condemnation guilt. The tense of the law, as such, is the future perfect: its violence, such as that exercised by the policeman, is violence that will have been legitimate, as when Mr Justice Bramber reflects, in spite of new evidence, that 'the law had got hold of [Caldigate], and had made him guilty, and the law need not now subject itself to the normal human weakness of a jury' (Trollope 1995b: 423).

Mr Scarborough's Family is even more scathing in its critique of positive law. When the dying Mr Scarborough disinherits his older son, Mountjoy, by producing a certificate which proves that he and Mountjoy's mother were married after Mountjoy's birth,[12] his younger son, Augustus, does not respond with outrage at the fact that his own mother should have been made to bear a bastard, but that he should have nearly been robbed of what was rightfully his:

> The making of all right and wrong in this world depends on the law. The half-crown in my pocket is merely mine because of the law. He did choose to marry my mother before I was born, but did not choose to go through that ceremony before my brother's time. That may be a trifle to you, or to

> my moral feeling may be a trifle; but because of that trifle all Tretton will be my property, and his attempt to rob me of it was just the same as though he should break into a bank and steal what he found there. He knows that just as well as I do, but to suit his own purposes he did it. (1998c: 35)

Augustus Scarborough's complaint has all the characteristics of positive law. He oversteps the mark, however, by feeling – and voicing out loud – 'that the squire ought to complete his work by dying' (1998c: 139), not knowing that his father has a second card up his sleeve. Once Scarborough has tricked Augustus into paying off his brother's debts for a fraction of their total value, he produces an older certificate, thus reinstating Mountjoy as heir. The reader rejoices when Scarborough fulfils his desire to 'set all laws at defiance' (1998c: 298).

If in Trollope's late novels both positive law and natural law are shown to be imbricated with violence, Mr Scarborough represents an alternative: 'Mr Scarborough hated the law – because it was the law and endeavoured to put a restraint upon him and others. Augustus liked the law – unless when in particular points it interfered with his own actions. Mr Scarborough thought that he could do better than the law. Augustus wished to do worse' (1998c: 152).[13] In other words, Scarborough believes in freedom, our ability to shape our own future. He turns himself into the protagonist of a world governed by the principles of character, 'an individual whom, if we were confronted by his actions in life instead of by his person on the stage, we would call a scoundrel' and whose actions affect his public 'never in themselves, never morally', but only 'insofar as they reflect the light of character' (Benjamin 2004d: 205). As such, Scarborough perplexes other characters, whose attempts to grasp his character in moral terms are bound to fail.[14] The aggrieved Grey complains that Scarborough 'is the greatest rascal that [he] ever knew' but 'yet he did not regard him as an honest man regards a rascal, and was angry with himself in consequence' (1998c: 304). Or as his physician Merton says, 'he has within him a capacity for love, and an unselfishness, which almost atones for his dishonesty; and there is about him a strange dislike to conventionality and to law which is so interesting as to make up the balance' (1998c: 416). The reader, too, is left in the dark; Scarborough is one of the few characters whose thoughts are not represented through free indirect discourse. Like the narrator, he stands above the distinction between guilt and innocence.

His dislike of the law notwithstanding, Scarborough is better at manipulating its rules than all other characters; he is implicated within the world of the law even though he tries to transcend it. One could fruitfully describe his actions as a manifestation of divine violence, 'a different kind of violence . . . that certainly could be either the justified or the unjustified means to [just] ends but was not related to them as means at all but in some different way' (Benjamin 2004b: 247). If positive law and natural law are the obverse and reverse of a single coin that denotes legal violence, divine violence must be thought of as the edge, revealing itself only sporadically, and always in danger of tipping over. Turning the tables on the law without initiating a new game, Scarborough's actions can be categorised under this heading. Divine or pure violence has become a notoriously difficult notion, partly because Benjamin does not discuss it 'in its own right but only via examples of *manifestation*' (Blumenthal-Barby 2009: 733). Though potentially pure, it is indirectly 'implicated in the problematic nature of law itself' (Benjamin 2004b: 243): the law will always tolerate a degree of violence outside itself as a safety-valve, thus suspending the challenge manifested by this violence's law-making potential. Trollope provides a sophisticated instance of this bastardisation in *John Caldigate*, when Hester, being held captive, resists her family by means of a peaceful rebellion. Refusing to eat except what is necessary to sustain her baby, she sits in front of the main door for two days, after which the Boltons have no choice but to release her. Like divine violence, Hester's strike 'only expiates' and is 'lethal without spilling blood' (Benjamin 2004b: 249–50). But because her act of divine violence is also a material manifestation, her revolt initially bolsters her mother's claims and the legal violence that these cause: to abstain from force to achieve a certain end is, after all, to exert violence in the form of extortion (Benjamin 2004b: 239). Nevertheless, it is because Hester continues to believe that her husband's sins can be atoned for that his innocence is eventually proven. In the face of public opinion, she continues to assert that Caldigate never meant to deceive her, although she is sceptical enough to realise that he may have erred in his ways: 'he had been on the brink, but had been wise in time. That was her creed' (Trollope 1995b: 394). In contrast to her mother's inflexible individualism, then, Hester holds fast to a 'promise of a divine affirmation of the human, more total than humans can ever attain unaided' (Thomas 2004: 111).

So does Dr Wortle, to give a final example. Dr Wortle first congratulates himself on having found an excellent new classics teacher, until he discovers that the previous husband of Mr Peacocke's American wife, Colonel Ferdinand Lefroy, may be still alive. Partly to spite Dr Wortle, his fellow citizens roundly condemn the Peacockes. The combative Dr Wortle, however, takes up the cudgels, even though he knows that his position is a weak one according to the 'law of God and man' (1989c: 70) and 'the strict law of right and wrong' (1989c: 77, 99). Yet, like Hester and Scarborough, he believes that men are naturally innocent, which allows him to transcend this legal perspective:

> He could not bring his conscience and his inclination to come square together. And even when he counselled himself to yield to his conscience, his very conscience – a second conscience, as it were – revolted against the first. His first conscience told him that he owed a primary duty to his parish, a second duty to his school, and a third to his wife and daughter. In the performance of all these duties he would be bound to rid himself of Mr Peacocke. But then there came that other conscience, telling him that the man had been more 'sinned against than sinning', – that common humanity required him to stand by a man who had suffered so much, and had suffered so unworthily. (1989c: 69)

Dr Wortle's defence of Mr and Mrs Peacocke, Hester Caldigate's belief in her husband's conversion, and Mr Scarborough's manipulation of the laws of entail are all manifestations of divine violence. Instead of judging, these characters intervene. As such, their actions resemble Trollope's 'perfect delineation of character' (Trollope 1999a: 166). Because it interweaves the voices of narrator and character, Trollope's use of free indirect discourse does not posit a foundation, but transcends the binary distinction between right and wrong. If the Enlightenment perfected natural law theory and the Victorian age witnessed its replacement by positive law, then Trollope falls back on a form of language which challenges the conditions of possibility of both by sketching subjectivities rather than subjects, thus stressing his characters' essential innocence.

Notes

1. Trollope had mixed feelings about Dickens's melodramatic realism (Trollope 1999a: 247–9), memorably satirising him as Mr Popular Sentiment in *The Warden*. Trollope's stance vis-à-vis physiognomy is different as well. Although his characters are often introduced with a description of their face and demeanour, these descriptions are conventional and repetitive. The very fact that there is a clear method in Trollope's use of physiognomy, with 'good' girls being brown and imperfect, and 'bad' girls white and beautiful (Ammar 2010), makes the interpretive value of his comments limited. In his earlier work, there are 'Dickensian' exceptions, such as George Vavasor who, 'when he was angry or disappointed . . . would so contort his face that the scar would, as it were, stretch itself out, revealing all its horrors' (Trollope 1989a: 35). Such legible faces are rare in Trollope's late fiction.
2. This is a central motif in Trollope's work, which is 'structured by vacillation or unresolvable opposition' (Shuman 2000: 84). This principle also determines the way in which Trollope approaches various areas of life: 'The principles of legislation do not concern Trollope nearly so much as the *process*.

Walpole's image of "the doors of the House of Commons ever swinging backwards and forwards" is appropriate enough here. It must be the process of arriving at the decision, the ways to and from it, rather than the decision itself, that will occupy the novelist. If it were not so, we would be quick enough to accuse him of propagandising' (J. McMaster 1978: 39).

3. The first critic to comment extensively on free indirect discourse in Trollope's novels was Bill Overton (1982: 105–20); more recently, J. Hillis Miller has suggested that Trollope's use of free indirect discourse creates a kind of transparency between novelist and reader that is also present between the novel's different characters (J. H. Miller 2015: 52–8). Interestingly, both Overton and Miller take *The Last Chronicle of Barset* as their example. In the late novels, however, such intersubjective transparency is often absent.
4. This proposition tallies with recent investigations into the relation between Victorian literature and the Inns of Court, which literary critics versed in the legal arts have described as a professional rivalry or a functional supplement (Dolin 1999; Peters 2005; Rodensky 2003; Schramm 2000). Scholars more attuned to the rhythm of cultural history have similarly claimed that literary texts intervened in legal debates without being entirely determined by these (Finn 2002; A. H. Miller 1995; Pettitt 2005; Poovey 1995). For an older overview of the overlap between Victorian jurisprudence and public discourse, see Collini (1993a: 251–307). These critics posit a dynamic relation between Victorian law and literature, which earlier critics' Foucauldian approach could not accommodate; for an overview, see Petch (2007) and Pettitt (2005).
5. Benjamin indicates that the novel can articulate moments of decision by means of a verbal form, *eine sprachliche Gestalt*, that closely resembles free indirect discourse (Leacock 2002: 282). Martin Jay has confirmed this impression, arguing that free indirect discourse provides an unexpected means for expressing the *Erfahrung* that Benjamin's 'Program of the Coming Philosophy' admonishes us to recover (2004a). Free indirect discourse, that is, can simulate *Erfahrung* (a form of collective, unconscious experience) by embedding character in a form of language that does not serve the purpose of either communication or information.
6. Seminal studies of Trollope's legal language have largely and understandably ignored his interest in legal theories, instead focusing on his historical and practical understanding of the law as an institution (see Lansbury 1981 and R. D. McMaster 1986).
7. Equity 'had entered the English legal system in the Middle Ages as the Chancery, a department of state administered by the Chancellor to whom the sovereign delegated the exercise of the royal prerogative of Grace' (Petch 1997: 123). The Chancellor's task was to represent the conscience of the king. In the course of their history, the Equity Courts developed an adversarial relationship to the common law, which led to the misunderstanding that their function was to serve 'the conception of some broader and more reasonable system of justice than that which is embodied in any actually existing laws' (Stephen 1861: 475). Josiah Smith, among many others, tried to correct this view: 'In the most general sense, Equity is synonymous with natural justice. But Equity as contradistinguished from Law,

and as administered in our Courts of Equity, has a much narrower and an otherwise different signification' (Smith 1845: 3). Its province was that of the trust or property law.

8. There is another possible model: the Yelverton affair, one of the most famous cases in nineteenth-century Irish law, which led to the enactment of the Matrimonial Causes and Marriage Law Amendment Act of 1870. The case was instituted by Theresa Longworth, an English Catholic, who met Major Yelverton, heir to an Irish peerage, in the Crimea. He pursued her and eventually went through a form of marriage with her before a Catholic priest in Ireland. They lived in Scotland as man and wife, but he deserted her when he met Emily Forbes, whom he married. Theresa then sued to be recognised as his wife. Irish and Scottish courts found in her favour, but the House of Lords ruled against her. Major Yelverton cut a very poor show in the witness box, adopting the strategy of declaring that his intentions to her had always been dishonourable. The Yelverton affair influenced, among others, Mary Elizabeth Braddon's *Lady Audley's Secret* (1862) and Wilkie Collins's *Man and Wife* (1870). For more details, see Schama (2010). My thanks to Patrick Maume for this suggestion.
9. Sir Roger Tichborne was last sighted in Rio de Janeiro in 1854, but had not been heard of for more than a decade, until Orton appeared on the scene in the late 1860s. Under the name of Thomas Castro, Orton had been plying his father's trade in Wagga Wagga, Australia, where he began to pose as Sir Roger. Lady Tichborne, Sir Roger's mother, immediately recognised him as her son on meeting him in Paris in 1867. A year later, with Lady Tichborne dead, the Tichborne family refused to honour his alleged rights, and Orton took them to court. Although Orton's bearing and manners made his suit ridiculous, he had in some way become privy to many of the family's secrets. For more detailed accounts of this event, see McWilliam (2007) and the bibliography in Thomas (2004: 198, n. 2).
10. For a different exploration of half-belief in terms of lingering, see Plotz (2011).
11. As the common law's extensive body of rules recognised only certain forms of action, lawyers had to circumvent these by developing 'legal fictions'. Such fictions, as Henry Sumner Maine understood them, 'signify any assumption which conceals, or affects to conceal, the fact that a rule of law has undergone alteration, its letter remaining unchanged, its operation being modified' (Maine 1861: 26). Maine is the representative of a third theory in legal thinking, the historical school. Because sovereignty is always subject to 'the mass of historical traditions' (Harrison 1878a: 489), the historical method sets out to examine the function of the law at a particular time and place. Whereas positive law can predict, the historical method can explain. Victorian lawyers had little patience for such explanations, however. Although Harrison admits that 'it is of immense importance to respect those practical methods . . . which have been sanctioned by so many centuries of actual experience' (1878b: 703), the historical method nevertheless is 'merely an instrument' (1879: 124). James Fitzjames Stephen similarly jokes that Maine 'would hardly defend a client on the ground that he could show, by the application of the historical method, how the case against him had grown up' (Stephen 1861: 482).

12. On the topic of legitimacy in Trollope's oeuvre, see Taylor (2009).
13. Ayelet Ben-Yishai proposes that Trollope found an alternative to the inefficacy of both positive and natural law in the mediating role of the common law, which could 'renegotiate a new commonality' (2010: 166): laws based on the decisions of judges incorporate change and can therefore adequately take care of the community's needs. Ben-Yishai's distinction between legal codification and a common law deals with the law's institutional embodiment, however, not the law's conditions of possibility.
14. Like most Victorianist writing in this field, the present chapter turns a cold shoulder to the ahistorical claims put forward by the Law and Literature movement, such as Martha Nussbaum's, whose 'analysis of the form of Victorian fiction as a training process in ethically valuable cognitive habits' separates 'novel-reading from other experiences of consumption and other practices of everyday life' in a way that the eighteenth-century language of moral sentiments did but Victorian theories of the novel certainly did not (Dames 2007: 18).

Chapter 8

'A Poise So Perfect': Tact as Love

> The new stage of courtesy and its representation, summed up in the concept of *civilité*, was very closely bound up with this [psychological] manner of seeing, and gradually became more so. In order to be really 'courteous' by the standards of *civilité*, one was to some extent obliged to observe, to look about oneself and pay attention to people and their motives. In this, too, a new relationship of person to person, a new form of integration is announced. (Elias 2000: 67)

The beginning of modernity was accompanied by the predominance of vision over the other senses. As Norbert Elias has shown, clothing and manners were cultivated and codified in an attempt to externalise subjectivity. For Victorian liberals, this situation presented both opportunities and a source of anxiety. Since the Victorian citizen was aware that he or she was observed by others who were aware that he or she was also observing them, this interplay removed externally imposed barriers to individual freedom and replaced these with an autonomously regulated mechanism that encouraged the citizen to behave well, thus providing a form of positive liberty (Otter 2008). At the same time, advances in Victorian physiology indicated that the potential of this perspective was limited because it hypothesised that attention was regulated by the nervous system, which meant that observation was guided by reflexes rather than the will, instinct rather than intention (Dames 2007): the Victorians 'feared that these signs [encoded in their clothes and their speech] were equally beyond their power to mould, but would instead be manifest to others in involuntary tricks of speech, body gesture, or even how they adorned themselves' (Sennett 1976: 25). This anxiety gave a renewed impetus to the rules of politeness and the study of physiognomy: a thorough knowledge of these codes provided guidelines with which to interpret 'unconscious' signs. Unlocking a knowledge that was 'potentially open to all' (Otter 2008: 51), politeness and physiognomy created the possibility of a 'democratisation of observation' (Hartley 2001: 41).

This possibility could only be realised in a public sphere where the conditions for sight and observation were excellent. Poorly lit and mired in fog, however, early nineteenth-century London presented all sorts of problems for those who wanted to foster liberal subjectivity through vision. In an attempt to rectify this situation, liberals fully supported innovations in medicine and technology.[1] The city was remodelled to redirect citizens' attention from their environment to one another: 'Maps, along with street signs, house numbers, and streetlamps, allowed the individual, when alone in the city, to be secure, mobile, and autonomous' (Otter 2008: 54). The suburb, a new kind of environment, was designed in the manner of an oligoptic space such as the museum, the library, the zoo, the hospital, the park, or the boulevard: in contrast to a panoptic institution such as the prison, these spaces lack 'a central, dominant vantage point. This makes an oligoptic space an arena within which a small group of people observe each other: it is a place in which mutual oversight takes place' (Otter 2008: 74). The Victorian novel, too, was a cog within this apparatus, for it taught its readers the codes of politeness:

> Much of the elaborate etiquette that we think of as distinctly Victorian – rituals of introduction, calling cards, the chaperoning of unmarried women, intricate decorums of dress – is at root a strategy for coping with social mobility, by affirming one's own claims to recognition while at the same time maintaining a distance that allows one to 'place' new acquaintances (Davidoff 1973). The Victorian novel developed into a form uniquely suited to represent these dynamics, capturing the textures of social interaction, aspiration, and anxiety, within which social hierarchy could seem both a stimulus and a barrier to personal achievement. (Adams 2012: 7)

Trollope's late novels, however, evince a certain scepticism about this endeavour. Characters who try to relate to others through the use of visual signs and codes of politeness are portrayed as fundamentally misguided. In the words of a contemporary reviewer, 'Mr Trollope shows in his own inimitable way that this very conventionality is the price we pay for our high civilisation, this instinctive repressiveness is the silent police which keeps the discordant social elements in order' (Smalley 1969: 407). This is apparent even in small details, such as Trollope's representation of characters' eyesight. When characters wear spectacles, these are often meant as an emblem of their short-sightedness in ideas.[2] Consider Olivia Q. Fleabody, the American feminist in *Is He Popenjoy?*, whose spectacles 'make the beholder feel that there is before him a pair of spectacles carrying a face, rather than a face carrying a pair of spectacles' (1998b: 130). In contrast, Lady Sarah Germain, who does not wear spectacles even though she is shortsighted (1998b: 33), 'was very just' even though 'she was hard' (1998b: 365). The representation of spectacles as unnecessary encapsulates Trollope's distrust of the idea that visual signs can give others clues about one's moral qualities. By contrast, Trollope suggests that one should cultivate a disposition that would recognise and accept the ultimate unknowability of others.

One name for this different, disenchanted disposition is tact. As David Russell has argued, tact enjoins the subject to pre-empt disagreement by 'widen[ing] the promise of relations now, rather than envisioning total ends for the progress of the present' (2012: 206). The subject must attend to 'the conditions of the medium, the middle spaces that affect how life "comes to" one, and the way it can be diminished by dogma' (Russell 2012: 205). This sociability requires one to nurture reserve, which is the opposite of the detachment from one's surroundings that the codes of politeness require. Instead, the reserve of tact allows one to appreciate the singularity of each individual encounter:

> The word attained wider currency in shifting register from politesse to politics, and from a model of social interaction that achieved its metaphorical expression in terms of a visual reading of social signals to a more cautious and tactile feeling one's way in less certain social conditions, no longer governed by absolutist hierarchies of status. (Russell 2012: 180–1)

This form of sociability had no place in Victorian liberalism, which situated it in places where liberal citizens allegedly feared to tread: 'while the suburb, the library, and the boulevard were sites where visual command could be exercised, the slum, the court, and the alley were spaces where this command crumbled and gave way to something more tactile and intimate' (Otter 2008: 19).

David Russell also posits that the promotion of a tactful disposition is the prerogative of the essayist, not the novelist. Whereas the essay is deliberately muddled, the Victorian novel is all too knowing: focusing on hierarchy rather than equality, etiquette rather than manners, the novel teaches caution, not reserve. Only with the development of forms of focalisation in the work of Henry James, so the story goes, does the novel acquire a degree of tact.[3] In the case of Trollope as well, however, the novel and the essay may be not incommensurable. This chapter examines a formal innovation that is particular to the late novels, the depiction of 'perfect' love, with which Trollope represents a tactful form of sociability.

The Psychology of Seeing

Trollope's characters are usually very sensitive as to how, where, and with whom they are seen. In *Is He Popenjoy?*, for instance, Lady George Germain's rides with Captain Jack de Baron in Hyde Park are supervised. She knows that his name has been mixed up with too many women, including Miss Augusta Mildmay, but tells herself that, being a married woman, she can enjoy his flirtations without compunction. Nevertheless, she does realise that others may think differently:

> 'Now, Captain de Baron, would you like to be a dog?' This she said turning round and looking him full in the face.
>
> 'Your dog I would'. At that moment, just over his horse's withers, she saw the face of Guss Mildmay who was leaning on her father's arm. Guss bowed to her, and she was obliged to return the salute. Jack de Baron turned his face to the path and seeing the lady raised his hat. 'Are you two friends?' he asked.
>
> 'Not particularly'.
>
> 'I wish you were. But, of course, I have no right to wish in such a matter as that'. Lady George felt that she wished that Guss Mildmay had not seen her riding in the park on that day with Jack de Baron. (1998b: 127)

Lady George feels uncomfortable chiefly because she knows that Augusta Mildmay has set her heart on marrying the Captain, but also because she knows that her husband, Lord George Germain, thinks that by flirting with Captain de Baron – and the sexual undertone of their dialogue hardly needs comment – she subjects herself (and him) to calumny.[4] Lord George therefore proposes to retreat into the country, a command that Lady George does not obey, since such a retreat would be perceived as a tacit confession of impropriety. Matters take a turn for the worse at Mrs Montacute Jones's ball when, dancing the Kappa-Kappa, Lady George trips and 'could hardly have been saved without something approaching to the violence of an embrace' (1998b: 303). Jack de Baron has the decency to catch her and Lord George, in his jealousy, reprimands her conduct in front of all assembled. Lord George realises only belatedly that it is his intervention that has really disgraced her, however. Having buried himself in the country for thirty years, he does not know how to behave in an oligoptic space. Lady George, in contrast, can compose herself when necessary; her reaction saves herself and her husband from shame.

Marion Fay, too, dwells on the nature of oligoptic spaces.[5] Trollope began *Marion Fay* in the winter of 1878 against the background of a first attempt to illuminate the City of London with electrically powered lanterns:

> The City operated as something of a laboratory for electric lighting. It was first illuminated electrically in late 1878, when Jablochkoff candles were displayed at Billingsgate Market, Holborn viaduct, the Embankment, and the office of the *Times*, while a larger-scale experiment took place with arc light in 1880. (Otter 2008: 244)

This fact makes its way into the novel when Lord Llwddythlw ascribes his negligence in visiting his fiancée, Lady Amaldina, to the fact that he had 'to meet five or six conservative members later on in the afternoon as to the best thing to be done as to Mr Green's Bill for lighting London by electricity' (1985: 327). Llwddythlw's concern is not a standalone issue: electric lighting was part of a larger push in urban developments such as the expansion of suburbs in North London, where most of the novel is set. The novel's heroine, Marion Fay, lives at 17 Paradise Row, Holloway; her father, Zachary Fay, commutes to the newly illuminated City, where he works as a senior clerk. The novel weaves this area into the names of its characters. One of the Fays' neighbours is a Post Office clerk, George Roden, which 'is also the name of a real street in Holloway' (J. H. Miller 2001: 88). Having first met one another at a political debating society, Roden strikes up a friendship with Lord Hampstead, whose visits to Holloway are facilitated by the closeness of Hendon Hall, his father's 'lovely suburban seat', 'half town half country' (1985: 4, 6). Holloway, Hampstead, and Hendon were rural up to the middle of the century, when the area began to be built up in tandem with the opening of new railway stations. Given this oligoptic setting, it is not a coincidence that *Marion Fay* was the only novel for which Trollope drew up a geographical sketch in his drafts: we might read this as a sign of his intention to envisage a space in which self-control had been optimised.[6] In fact, however, Trollope's decision to set his story in this suburban locale serves to offset his criticism of the politics of vision.

On the one hand, the inhabitants of this suburb exploit the codes of physiognomy. The visits of an heir to a Marquisate to this modest street create a sensation, an effect of which Hampstead is initially oblivious. At first he is mistaken for a Post Office clerk, but when he arrives with a horse and groom, Paradise Row is 'awe-stricken' (1985: 40). The women observing Hampstead are skilled readers of the street. Nothing is known about George Roden's mother, for example, but they successfully guess the identity and background of one of her friends, Mrs Vincent (1985: 33). On the other, they themselves are unwilling to be observed and identified. Sneaking behind their curtains, Mrs Demijohn, her niece Clara, and Mrs Duffer operate under the cover of anonymity, thus turning supervision into surveillance:

> [Hampstead] had become somewhat abashed and perplexed as to his visits to Paradise Row, having learned to entertain a notion that some of the people there looked at him. It was hard, he thought, that if he had a friend in that or any other street he should not be allowed to visit his friend without creating attention. He was not aware of the special existence of Mrs Demijohn, or of Clara, or of Mrs Duffer, nor did he know from what window exactly the eyes of curious inhabitants were fixed upon him. But he was conscious that an interest was taken in his comings and goings. (1985: 121)

At one point Miss Demijohn even sends an anonymous letter to Hampstead's parents to inform them of their son's entanglement 'in what [she] think[s] to be a dangerous way with a young woman living in a neighbouring street to this' (1985: 222). This parochialism is at odds with the liberal quality of self-criticism that the structure of the suburb ought to stimulate.[7] Hampstead, in contrast, does not seem to have taken the lessons of physiognomy to heart: 'He did not see why a man on horseback should attract more attention at Holloway than at Hyde Park Corner' (1985: 40).

A similar element of perversion is apparent in these characters' disregard for politeness. Clara Demijohn, for instance, vehemently appeals to the standards of bourgeois respectability. To her thinking, it is unseemly that Hampstead walks Marion Fay home:

> I saw it! They came out together from No. 11 as loving as could be, and he walked up with her to their own house. Then he seized her hand and held it – oh, for minutes! – in the street. There is nothing those Quaker girls won't allow themselves. They are so free with their Christian names, that, of course, they get into intimacies instantly. I never allow a young man to call me Clara without leave asked and given. (1985: 125)

In reality, however, it is Clara Demijohn who gets into intimacies. In the course of the novel, she gives leave to at least three men (Samuel Crocker, Daniel Tribbledale, and a certain 'Pollocky of the Highbury Gas works'), with the suggestion of more in the past. In the street, too, she cannot keep her distance. She has no qualms about throwing herself in Crocker's way 'in the gloam of the evening' (1985: 207). This transgressive behaviour ties in with her talent for observation without self-reflection: she is 'attracted by the easy air with which [Crocker] cocked his hat and swung his gloves' (1985: 207). In such circumstances, courtesy takes a back seat: 'No doubt, as in all such cases, it was the gentleman who spoke first', the narrator comments. 'Let us, at any rate, hope so for the sake of Paradise Row generally' (1985: 208). As a result of this nocturnal encounter, Miss Demijohn trades Daniel Tribbledale's affections and limited means for the prospects offered by Crocker.

Crocker certainly matches her in his lamentable attempts at gentility; he is a master of the faux pas. Invited by Lord Persiflage to Castle Hautboy for a party because he is the steward's son, for example, he tries to ingratiate himself with Lord Hampstead by alluding to the as yet unsanctioned 'matrimonial alliance' (1985: 100) between Hampstead's sister, Lady Frances, and George Roden. Crocker's allusion offends Hampstead's feelings: 'how grievous a thing it was that a girl's name should be made so common in the mouths of men!' (1985: 89). Wonderfully oblivious to his own blunder, Crocker is unable to perceive Hampstead's disgust. This is a theme for fun that recurs in Trollope's late novels; the Honourable Mr Traffick in *Ayala's Angel* is an even better example of such pachydermatous behaviour. When Sir Thomas Tringle tells Traffick to his face once and for all to leave his house, the latter retorts, 'Am I to understand that you wish your child to leave your roof during this inclement weather in her present delicate condition?' (1989b: 481).

Nor do Crocker's faux pas limit themselves to a failure in self-criticism. His appearance and clothing, for one, draw too much attention to themselves: the narrative repeatedly stresses his yellow gloves.[8] Most telling, perhaps, is his mode of address. Like Clara Demijohn, he professes to know the finer points of etiquette:

> 'And how does he address you?' asked Clara – also with something of awe.
> '"Dear Crocker" – just that. I always say "My dear Lord Hampstead", in return. I look upon "Dear Hampstead", as a little vulgar, you know, and I always think that one ought to be particular in these matters'. (1985: 213)

But when faced with bringing these rather dubious notions into practice, Crocker is, unsurprisingly, all too particular. His masterpiece is a letter addressed to 'Right Honourable, The Lord Hampstead', which he ends as only a diplomat would: 'I have the honour to be, My dear Lord Hampstead, Your lordship's most obedient, Very humble servant, Samuel Crocker' (1985: 192). Crocker's efforts to make his language attentive fail by dint of trying. Hampstead rightly treats this as a joke: he realises that there is no malice in Crocker's behaviour. But it is no laughing matter for those whose position is more vulnerable, such as Marion Fay, who is lost for words when Clara Demijohn has the audacity to run across with a newspaper and tell her (incorrectly, as it turns out) that Hampstead got himself killed out hunting: 'Why would not the cruel young woman go and leave her to her sorrow? Why did she stand there looking at her, as though desirous to probe to the bottom the sad secret of her bosom?' (1985: 294). Characters such as Clara Demijohn and Samuel Crocker thus show that there are limits to the kind of attention that the distance created by the suburb was meant to foster: 'perceptual control was vastly simpler when undertaken within the walls of institutions than outside in the more unruly streets' (Otter 2008: 98).

The Art of Surprise

Marion Fay and Lord Hampstead present an alternative to the sociability of etiquette. They observe not with the public gaze but through the private eye. Hampstead does not lurk about in Paradise Row to get a second glimpse of Marion, but instead invites her to his house. As a result, he is not anonymous: 'I hardly knew whether I was glad that he should observe me so much – or offended at his persistence. I think that I was glad, though I told myself that he should not have glanced at me so often' (1985: 184). Such intimate encounters also allow him to appreciate what cannot be seen from behind a curtain. Hampstead finds out that Marion's face rivets his attention because it resists interpretation:

> And there was a fleeting brightness of colour which went about her cheeks and forehead, and ran around her mouth, which gave to her when she was speaking a brilliance which was hardly to be expected from the ordinary lines of her countenance. Had you been asked, you would have said that she was a brunette – till she had been worked to some excitement in talking. Then, I think, you would have hardly ventured to describe her complexion by any single word. (1985: 111)

Marion's complexion is not fixed, but shifts, flits, flutters; it is full of subtle and fleeting expressions. Physiognomy has no rules for this situation; each street lantern would show the observer a new face, as it were. This is in keeping with a fixture of Trollope's fiction: female beauty requires repeated viewing because it only dawns on the perceiver in retrospect (Jöttkandt 2006). To see Marion Fay's face for what it really is, she must be excited. Indeed, Hampstead chances upon Marion when he visits Roden and she is about to leave. Her complexion catches Hampstead's attention inadvertently. It is a *vision fugitive*: Hampstead 'would have declared that some divinity of grace had been the peculiar gift which had attracted him. And yet that rapid change of colour had not passed unobserved, as she told him that she was sorry that he did not go to church' (1985: 111). Her clothes, the traditional Quaker dress, send paradoxical signals as well:

> The close brown bonnet and the little cap, and the well-made brown silk dress, and the brown gloves on her little hands, together made, to [Hampstead's] eyes, as pleasing a female attire as a girl could well wear. Could it have been

> by accident that the graces of her form were so excellently shown? (1985: 108)

On the one hand, Marion's dress does not draw attention to itself, but creates interest by being inconspicuous, invisible, merely accentuating the body that it covers. The plain and simple costume of a Quaker, indeed, 'emphasises stillness, silence, and the wearer's interiority' (Keen 2002: 215). At the same time, by the mid-century the Quaker dress had acquired erotic overtones because of an effort to funnel the unruly energy that Quakers represented 'back into the domestic sphere' (Keen 2002: 212).[9] Hampstead succumbs to this idea. Marion is attractive, then, despite her best intentions.

Hampstead, too, disregards the rules of physiognomy. He does not 'walk about the streets with a chimney-pot hat' (Trollope 1985: 10), the sign of a gentleman. At the same time, his attachment to his horse and groom marks him out as a man of means. Paradise Row cannot make sense of this contradiction. It is in his disregard for the codes of politeness, however, that Hampstead sabotages the sensibilities of seeing most ingeniously. If Marion Fay's mode of dress creates a desire for intimacy, so does Hampstead's mode of address: he encourages those he knows familiarly to use his Christian name. Characters who have the courage to stray that far from convention are few and far between. Only George Roden calls him John; his little step-brothers, toddlers as they are, call him Jack. This is a reflection of Hampstead's political principles. Hampstead has grasped the axiom that forms of address are essential cogs in the mechanism of social interaction. He knows that they are meant to produce difference. So does his prudish mother-in-law, Lady Kingsbury, whose efforts to teach her darlings to use the more respectable 'Hampstead' are in vain (1985: 24). Similarly, she says 'a word in haughty anger' when Roden is talking to Lady Frances (her step-daughter) and 'she hear[s] the name "Frances" without the prefix "Lady"' (1985: 8). What offends her is the breach in decorum itself as much as its implication that it can only mean that the two have fallen in love. These examples illustrate how forms of address are performative rather than constative. They effectively bring a relationship into being.

This axiom is an essential ingredient in Trollope's story-worlds, where relationships are never static, but change with each and every encounter:

> Trollope's supreme mastery lies in the shifting situation . . . This is where his originality lies: no English novelist before him had so fully exploited the drama of scenes where relationships alter by conscious design . . . or slip by subtle inadvertence, or slide headlong towards intimacy in a manner neither willed nor desired. The most compelling of his scenes are often those in which

> a character enters a room or a garden intending to effect one kind of dramatic encounter, only to find that the scene evolves beyond his control and, what is more, beyond anything that his most careful meditation could have predicted. The analogy with chess is here at its strongest. (Watson 1973: 228)

Characters with fixed intentions rarely succeed in forcing checkmate. Indeed, attempts to change another's opinion are likely to backfire: 'Trollope, doubtful of such ideas about stable laws of human nature and inclined, rather, to suspect that people leap in unpredictable ways under pressure, thinks the discerning teller of tales ought to help us discern that tales offer suspect revelations' (Swingle 1991: 249). Some characters, however, break out of this web of arbitrariness. They know that one must trust to chance in order to override the rules of the game. Hampstead knows this, which may clarify why, having seen Marion Fay, he sets out to win her heart rather haphazardly:

> He would go over to Paradise Row, and call on Mrs Roden. He would then explain to her what had taken place between him and George, and leave some sort of apology for the offended Post Office clerk. Then he would ask them both to come over and dine with him on some day before his sister's return. In what way Marion Fay's name might be introduced, or how she might be brought into the arrangement, he must leave to the chapter of accidents. (1985: 121)

Hampstead adapts himself to the situation; he does not try to control it. As such, his invitation itself surprises and puzzles Marion and her father. Hampstead's manipulation of forms of address and his faith in chance, in short, show that he is tactful. Instead of following the rules of etiquette, he cultivates the art of surprise.[10]

We witness an example of tact in action when the Fays and the Rodens visit Hendon Hall. In a scene that Trollope reprised from *The Duke's Children* (2011: 329), Zachary Fay censures the young lord's use of slang during dinner. This occasion could give rise to conflict, but Hampstead turns it into an occasion for comedy:

> 'I suppose you found it awfully cold', [Hampstead] said.
>
> 'I do not know that we were awed, my lord', said the Quaker. 'But the winter has certainly set in with some severity'.
>
> 'Oh, father!' said Marion, rebuking him.
>
> 'Everything is awful now', said Hampstead, laughing. 'Of course the word is absurd, but one gets in the way of using it because other people do'. (1985: 145)

Hampstead does not take issue with Mr Fay's censure, but counters with laughter and evasion. His manners rely not on etiquette or politeness but on surprise and compromise. Accordingly, Hampstead has removed all visual signs of status and hierarchy: 'If the Quaker himself expected much of that gilding of which he had spoken he was certainly disappointed. The garniture of Hendon Hall had always been simple, and now had assumed less even of aristocratic finery than it used to show when prepared for the use of the Marchioness' (1985: 145).

The association of tact with equality Trollope may have borrowed from the criticism of Matthew Arnold. There are, indeed, some contextual indications that Trollope came under Arnold's spell while conceiving *Marion Fay*.[11] In any case, Arnold would have applauded Hampstead's efforts. Hampstead's opinions clearly hark back to Arnold's idea that it 'is by the humanity of their manners that men are made equal' (Arnold 1993a: 223). This becomes even clearer when we turn to Trollope's depiction of love.

Trollope's depiction of love involves a number of concepts and phrases that are recognisably Arnoldian. Arnold maintains that to 'handle [poetry] properly there is needed a poise so perfect that the least overweight in any direction tends to destroy the balance. Temper destroys it, a crotchet destroys it, even erudition may destroy it . . . The critic of poetry should have the finest tact' (Arnold 1960: 174). What Arnold here calls tact, Trollope calls love.[12] Trollope's *Autobiography* points us in this direction: 'If the novelist therefore can so *handle* [love] as to do good by his *handling*, as to teach wholesome lessons in regard to love, the good which he does will be very wide' (1999a: 224–5, my emphasis). Trollope's repetition of this eminently tactile word 'handling' in a pedagogical context suggests a proximity between the theory of his writing and the ethos of Arnold's criticism. Trollope's novelistic portrayal of love mirrors Arnold's essayistic handling of poetry: as Arnold is clever in his definition of tact, so Trollope is tender in his descriptions of love.

The Unconscious

In 'On Translating Homer', Arnold argues that the critic must take care not to be overwhelmed when interpreting a subject that inspires an array of emotions:

> To press to the sense of the thing itself with which one is dealing, not to go off on some collateral issue about the thing, is the hardest matter in the world. The 'thing itself' with which one is here dealing – the critical perception of poetic truth – is of all things the most volatile, elusive, and evanescent; by even pressing too impetuously after it, one runs the risk of losing it. (1960: 174)

To be tactful is to hold back yet to press on. The critic should therefore cultivate reserve. Poetic truth, 'the thing itself', cannot be grasped by actively looking for it but must be felt intuitively, reflexively, unconsciously. As such, critical tact gives us an example of what Christopher Bollas has called an aesthetic of handling (Russell 2013: 27). In this theory, we relate to objects without the language or consciousness to know them: 'While we do know something of the character of the object which affects us, we may not have thought it yet' (Bollas 1989: 3). These impressions leave their mark upon the ego. To 'see the object as in itself it really is' (Arnold 1960: 140), in this view, means to look at the level of the relational, the pre-reflective level of knowledge at which relations are still being made up and objects still have a role to play. Such a form of tact demands that we look at a poem, an object, a word, a person, as if for the first time, like a child.

Arnold's wish to 'press to the sense of the thing itself' corresponds with Trollope's delineation of the recognition of love, as can be witnessed in the following scene, in which Hampstead asks Marion to poke his fire:

> 'Coals were made to be poked. I feel sure of that. Do take the poker and give them one blow. That will make you at home in the house for ever, you know'. Then [Hampstead] handed the implement to Marion. She could hardly do other than take it in her hand. She took it, blushed up to the roots of her hair, paused a moment, and then gave the one blow to the coals that had been required of her. 'Thanks', said he, nodding at her as he still knelt at her feet and took the poker from her; 'thanks. Now you are free of Hendon Hall for ever. I wouldn't have any one but a friend poke my fire'. (1985: 147)

This scene is a variation on a theme. The poker fulfils a function that is normally occupied by books which, as physical objects, can forge a connection: what 'interests Trollope . . . isn't the relation between a person and a text so much as the relation, or lack thereof, that two persons can establish only in the presence of a printed party' (Price 2012: 60). Trollope's substitution of the poker for a book draws the reader's attention to the tactile nature of this encounter, mediated as it is through an object. Hampstead's request points towards the handling that tact is supposed to encourage. Marion's response, indeed, is unconscious and instinctive. By granting Hampstead's wish, she knows that a form of knowledge is about to unveil itself, but as yet she can only see its contours and not its substance. The event leaves a trace in her unconscious: 'Not for a moment did her mind run away, as they were taken homewards, from the object of her unconscious idolatry' (1985: 155). The poker, in short, is an 'unthought known', an object that creates a space for the play of thought in the realm of the unconscious. This unconscious dimension is re-emphasised at the end of the novel, when Hampstead has been told of Marion's death and he returns to the poker as a souvenir of their love. R. C. Terry makes light of this moment: '*Marion Fay* ends with the most ridiculous scene of Trollope's entire work as Lord Hampstead tiptoes from the chamber of his dead love carrying his only keepsake of her: a poker she had once touched. Freudians have not, so far as I am aware, dealt with this intriguing detail' (Terry 1977: 86). Even though Terry's description is not quite accurate in its detail (Hampstead tiptoes in his own house), it is an important point. A Freudian, Terry suggests, would have a few interesting things to say about an object that is unambiguously phallic. More generously, however, a Freudian might also conceive of the poker as a joke – a fact that Marion hints at: 'Of course it was a joke! but I wish I hadn't done it' (1985: 147). Jokes, as Freud argued, originate in the play of words and ideas. Hampstead's words, indeed, are charged with *double entendre*. It is not difficult to see why Marion should blush. Hampstead's joke allows him to imagine himself as the spectator of an act of sexual aggression; his joke is one that Freud would categorise as obscene (Freud 2002: 94–9).

Not all the characters appreciate Hampstead's jokes, however, because they are taboo-breaking. Their attitudes to Hampstead thus give the concept of tact that Trollope develops a negative correlative. Like tact, the taboo draws its power from the traces that mark our unconscious. Etymologically, too, the taboo shares an important element with tact: touching. Nevertheless, the two are radically opposed. Whereas tact fosters play and association through intimacy, the taboo nurtures neurosis and prohibition: 'the principal prohibition, the nucleus of the neurosis, is against touching; and thence it is sometimes known as "touching phobia" or "*délire du touche*"' (Freud 1961: 27). In *Marion Fay*, Freud's theory that in modern society the fascination with the gruesome and the taboo has been channelled into admissible forms is exemplified by Lady Kingsbury. She is horrified when she sees Hampstead play with her children: 'When I think of what he is, and to what he will reduce the whole family should he live, I cannot bear to see him touch them' (1985: 140). Taken at face value, Lady Kingsbury's neurosis is a case of the 'taboo against marriage between members of different classes' (J. H. Miller 2001: 88), but it can actually be traced back to two deeper obsessions. On the one hand, she believes that Hampstead is a degenerate, a half-caste. The son of an aristocrat and a commoner, his blood is impure (Trollope 1985: 140). On the other hand, her response may have psycho-sexual roots. Being more than thirty years of age, she has had to settle for a position in which she is not 'the mother of her husband's heir' (Trollope 1985: 78). Her stepson, in contrast, embodies all that she would have wished for, but such a union would be tinged with incest.

Trollope's portrayal of religion further emphasises the repressive powers of the taboo. Freud postulates that taboos forbid certain forms of physical contact in order to suppress primordial desires. Religions institutionalise these prohibitions by expressing a certain ambivalence about them: religious rites such as the sacrificial meal provide re-enactments of the forbidden something that the individual longs for. Trollope's novel makes this ambivalence explicit. If the two core examples of primordial desires are incest and patricide, and Judaism and Christianity suppress the latter through the command that 'thou shalt not kill', then, daringly, Lady Kingsbury's chaplain turns this tenet inside out. Influenced by the Marchioness, Mr Greenwood warms to the idea of getting Hampstead out of the picture. Wishing for something that he professionally ought to forbid, Greenwood is caught on the wrong side: he lets one taboo (the sin of murder) be overruled by another (the sin of miscegenation). This goes against all that Christianity should stand for. As Jill Durey notes, 'to have a clergyman contemplate murder, as *Marion Fay* has, is to commit the ultimate taboo' (2002: 105). When an opportunity for using his pistol presents itself, however, Greenwood is held back by a mixture of suspicion and self-interest. Greenwood, then, does not repress taboos in the way that the Marchioness does, but uses them to his own advantage. Trollope's cynical portrayal of the chaplain is a long way from the gentle satire of the Barchester series: it shows that when taboos do not lead to neurosis, they can always lead to hypocrisy – but certainly not to tact.

Yet another sign of Trollope's criticism of the taboo is his negative portrayal of self-sacrifice. Following in the footsteps of William Roberson Smith, Freud claims that clansmen of totemic religions 'renewed and assured their likeness to the god' by means of 'the sacramental killing and communal eating of the totem animal' (Freud 1961: 138, 39). The totem animal could not be touched on any other occasion. Neurotics have a similar ambivalent relation to their desires, which is why Lady Kingsbury wants to see Hampstead dead. Marion, in contrast, wants to solve her ambivalent relation to Hampstead by killing herself. This, too, is a familiar theme. In Trollope's novels, women in love often refuse to acknowledge their love for the benefit of the other and imagine (not without satisfaction) that they are sacrificing themselves. Consider, for instance, Eleanor Harding in *The Warden*, believing that her father will be pleased should she convince John Bold of his error without confessing her love; Lucy Morris in *The Eustace Diamonds*, telling Frank Greystock that he would do better with himself by marrying Lizzie

Eustace; or Isabel Brodrick in *Cousin Henry*, rejecting William Owen's suit because of her new-found poverty. Dominated by the 'spirit of self-sacrifice' (Trollope 1985: 204), Marion Fay insists on the language of martyrdom as well. Her name being an archaic version of 'faith', J. Hillis Miller suggests that Marion harks back to a strand in Christianity and Judaism that has its roots in the story of Abraham and Isaac. Marion listens to her conscience just as Abraham obeys God: 'She was not bound to listen to any other voice but that of her own conscience. She was bound not to subject him to the sorrows which would attend him were he to become her husband' (J. H. Miller 2001: 96; Trollope 1985: 390).[13] Marion's story illustrates that Hebraic principles are tainted: like most of Trollope's heroines, she experiences true love only when the artificial obstacles erected by a misguided idea of self-sacrifice have been taken down. Her sacrifice is 'imperfect': 'she had only half carried out her duty' (Trollope 1985: 332, 331). Trollope thus satirises the language of Hebraism and the power of conduct, as Arnold would put it.[14]

The Sublime

If the presence of taboo enhances the general contours of the concept of tact through contrast, Trollope introduces an even more important foil for the more specific theory of tact as love. This foil is the theory of love as a response to the sublime. Enlarging on J. Hillis Miller's observations, Sigi Jöttkandt has argued that women in Trollope's fiction react to the sight of male beauty in a way that structurally resembles the recognition of the sublime.[15] In particular, Trollope's portrayal of female love is marked by a number of characteristics of the sublime as Edmund Burke defines it in his *Philosophical Enquiry into the Origin of Our Ideas of the Sublime and Beautiful* (1757). Burke's empirical sublime is characterised by sensorial overkill: it is obscure, vast, incomprehensible. Intense darkness can produce this experience, but so can intense exposure to light, 'such a light as that of the sun, immediately exerted on the eye, as it overpowers the sense' (Burke 1834: 1.45). For the viewer, the intense light of the sublime excites a sense of self-annihilation and self-forgetting: 'we submit to what we admire' (1834: 1.55). It cannot be experienced consciously or felt in the moment, but only reflected upon afterwards. As a result, the sight of the sublime often causes writers to confront the nature of language itself. Only through language can they come to grips with their experience: 'the writing of the sublime encounters its topic as something other and more than a mere topic, namely, as a kind of event in the very process of thinking and writing it' (Balfour

2006: 332). Writing about the sublime, in this view, is performative: it seeks to bring the sublime back to life.

In Trollope's fiction, Jöttkandt argues, the male object is in many ways similar to a manifestation of the sublime. This theory sheds a different kind of light on the poker scene. Marion Fay does not realise what she has just experienced, trying to dismiss it as a joke: it is only on her way home that she can make sense of what she has felt. The scene thus exemplifies J. Hillis Miller's claim that in Trollope's novels, love 'seems always to have happened already, at some time anterior to whatever time anyone is aware of it' (J. H. Miller and Asensi 1999: 301). Furthermore, Hampstead seems to be surrounded by a halo. When Marion is adamant that marriage is out of the question, Hampstead reflects that all 'lightness and brightness had gone from him' (Trollope 1985: 400): she 'had bade him retrick his beams and take the light and the splendour of his sun elsewhere' (1985: 438). One might object that this is rhetorical veneer – Trollope alludes to Milton's *Lycidas* (ll. 168–70) – but more is at stake. Marion initially refuses to acknowledge Hampstead's love by at once submitting to him and effacing herself: 'To such a one as I am to sacrifice myself is all that I can do in the world' (1985: 192). When she finally does dare look her sublime lover in the eye, she does so by means of a performative gesture: she declares that she loves him. It is this that brings love into being: 'when a Trollopian heroine confesses her love for a man, she declares a truth that is of a different order than all of the rest of the novel's statements' (Jöttkandt 2006: 9). This explains why Trollope's women can only love once, which sometimes leads to tragedy, as there is nothing to prevent women from falling in love with scoundrels: Lily Dale becomes an old maid (*The Small House at Allington*), Emily Hotspur dies (*Sir Harry Hotspur of Humblethwaite*), and it is only when Ferdinand Lopez meets his Maker that Emily Wharton is released from his hold (*The Prime Minister*).[16] Trollope's girls live in a Byronic world, where 'Man's love is of man's life a thing apart, / 'Tis woman's whole existence' (Byron 1986: 71, ll. 1545–6). Marion Fay's lover may be worthy, but in her case, too, love eventually proves fatal.

The sublime theory of love can illuminate many aspects of Trollope's representation of love, but it runs up against some problems. One of Trollope's earliest comments on philosophy to have survived deals with Burke's definition of the sublime. In his copy of the *Enquiry*, which he read when he was eighteen, Trollope voices his disagreement at regular intervals. 'When Burke makes his famous connection between fear and the sublime and remarks majestically that even some small poisonous animals "are capable of raising ideas of the sublime"', for instance,

'Trollope retorts: "You cannot say a wasp has anything sublime about it"' (Humphreys 1978: 196). In his biography of Thackeray, furthermore, Trollope aligns the sublime with 'sensation' as opposed to 'real life' (1879b: 188–91). Trollope's sympathies, as a realist, were with the latter.[17] *Marion Fay* is the very opposite of a sensation novel or Gothic novel, which was a literary reworking of the Burkean sublime (Hogle 2002: 14–15), and satirises its conventions. When Lady Frances declares that she is engaged to George Roden, the Marchioness takes her to a family property in Germany, Königsgraaf, reminiscing that there 'was once a time – a very good time, as Lady Kingsbury thought now – in which a young lady could be locked up in a convent, or perhaps in a prison, or absolutely forced to marry some suitor whom her parents should find for her. But those comfortable days were past' (1985: 66). Unlike the heroines of Gothic novels, Lady Frances does not face revenants or dungeons; instead, she quietly bides her time until her father realises the absurdity of the situation.

Trollope's portrayal of love as sublime in this novel, then, is a parody, a joke. This joke reveals that the sublime is imbricated with authority and respect: 'Caricature, parody and travesty, just like their counterpart in real life, unmasking, are aimed at persons and things with a claim on authority and respect, and in some sense "*sublime*"' (Freud 2002: 195; Freud's emphasis).[18] Indeed, in Burke's view, 'while tyrants are sublime . . . only the beautiful, with its commitment to companionable resemblance between humans, disguises the disequilibrium of power so effectively that we all, like Adam' – or like Marion Fay – 'become accomplices in our own deaths' (Ferguson 1992: 53). Trollope has no truck with sublime tyrants, as his portrayal of the Marchioness indicates: the heavy-handedness of the interlingually doubled pun on the king's grave in her very name leaves perhaps too little to the imagination. If 'sublime' love is imbricated with inequality, 'tactful' love serves the interests of equality.

Equality

In 'Equality', Arnold laments that the English propensity for the power of conduct has dwarfed the other 'elements in our humanisation' (1993a: 222): beauty, intellect and science, social life and manners. This imbalance has produced a 'religion of inequality' that the Puritanism of the middle class is keeping alive (1993a: 215). The Philistines are not the only candle-bearers of inequality, though. Arnold also devotes a small part of his essay to an attack on the aristocracy. His first move, indeed, is to take 'the votes for and against equality' by comparing that mainstay of the British aristocracy, the law of bequest, to customs of other modern nations (1993a: 217). Clinging to the powers of entail and settlement, England is still in the clutches of feudalism, whereas elsewhere there is a 'diseased appetite, as we must think it, for equality' (1993a: 217–18).

At first sight, *Marion Fay* seems to side against Arnold insofar as Trollope does seem to diagnose equality as a disease. The novel gives Arnold's figure of speech a narrative elaboration, describing Hampstead's conquest of Marion Fay's heart as an infection:

> But, as it will sometimes be that a man shall in his flesh receive a fatal injury, of which he shall for a while think that only some bruise has pained him, some scratch annoyed him; that a little time, with ointment and a plaister, will give him back his body as sound as ever; but then after a short space it becomes known to him that a deadly gangrene is affecting his very life; so will it be with a girl's heart. (1985: 155)

This infection seems to spread from Hampstead's republicanism, 'the ultra virus of his political convictions' (1985: 4). Similarly, the family virus takes its toll on the Marquis's mental health. Vexed by Lady Frances's willingness to marry a Post Office man, Lord Kingsbury, too, succumbs to a depression: 'It is ill ministering to a mind diseased' (1985: 161).[19]

Actually, however, these ailments are caused by a desire for inequality, not equality. As Arnold would have it, the desire for inequality is motivated by religion. If Marion Fay's wound is understood psychologically, it is caused by a religiously ingrained sense of inferiority: 'Because he has not seen the distance, shall I be blind to it?' (1985: 192). Likewise, what ails the Marquis is not his daughter's engagement but his separation from her (Trollope 1985: 162), which is the doing of the family chaplain, whose 'presence contributes largely to the Marquis's illness' (Durey 2002: 41), and of Lady Frances's stepmother, the Marchioness, for whom 'aristocratic dogmas' are 'a religion' (Trollope 1985: 27). Lady Kingsbury's taboos, indeed, are backed up by religion. Hampstead, she writes, does not know 'how to live in that state of life to which it has pleased God to call him!' (1985: 79). Mr Greenwood sanctions her beliefs, confirming that 'the difference in rank and station which it has pleased the Lord to institute should be maintained with all their privileges and all their honours' (1985: 58).

In addition, the Marchioness exhibits what Arnold thinks of as a typically English lack of self-reflection: she considers it 'a national misfortune that [Hampstead] should outlive his father' (1985: 239) and thinks that his death 'would confer so great a benefit on the world at large' (1985: 80). Her opinion is not disinterested, however. What Lady Kingsbury really craves is to see her own son, Lord Frederic, installed as heir. This would only be possible should Hampstead die prematurely. Such a self-interested wish even she cannot articulate directly. The religion of inequality, however, smoothly channels her private desire into a public good. It allows her to think that not her son's prospects are at stake, but the glory of England itself. Why this should be so cannot be explained except by an appeal to blood as a standard for superiority:

> Think of the blood of the Traffords, of the blood of the Mountressors, of the blood of the Hautevilles – think of your own blood, [Lord Llwddythlw,] which is now to be connected with theirs, and that all this is to be defiled because [Hampstead] chooses to bring about a disreputable, disgusting marriage with the expressed purpose of degrading us all. (1985: 140)

In his depiction of the Marchioness, Trollope thus elaborates on Arnold's suggestion that we must examine the assumption that our signal inequality of classes and property is expedient for our civilisation and welfare 'of which the distinguished personages who adopt it seem so sure that they think it needless to produce grounds for it' (Arnold 1993a: 220).

Arnold argues that this lack of self-reflection is a manifestation of materialism: 'with no necessary function to fulfil, never conversant with life as it really is, tempted, flattered, and spoiled from childhood to old age, our aristocratic class is inevitably materialised' (Arnold 1993a: 234). Lady Kingsbury lives up to Arnold's image. The news that Hampstead may have died during a hunt leaves her ecstatic. Creeping into the room of her 'darlings', she

> leaned over them and kissed them all; but she knelt at that on which Lord Frederic lay, and woke him with her warm embraces . . . 'Highgate', she said, whispering to herself, as she went back to her own room, trying the sound of the title he would have to use. It had been all arranged in her own mind how it was to be, if such a thing should happen. (1985: 290–1)

Coddled and admired by his mother because of his new-found fortune, Lord Frederic is obviously flattered and spoiled. Admittedly, one could also trace Lady Kingsbury's fantasy to misspent maternal affection. But there are other symptoms of aristocratic materialism. For instance, neither Lady Kingsbury nor Lord Kingsbury seem to care about the estates that their name is supposed to stand for. In this regard, Lady Kingsbury is the exact opposite of the Marchioness of Brotherton and her children in *Is He Popenjoy?*, who forsake their own comfort in order to attend to the welfare of the community. They visit the poor, make petticoats, sit on committees for the distribution of coal and blankets, and listen to tenants' grievances. Yet in *Is He Popenjoy?*, too, aristocratic materialism is criticised. The Marchioness's two sons are both flawed. Lord George Germain is annoyingly self-important, while the Marquis of Brotherton, the elder son and head of the Germain family, is a decrepit who, having lived a life of decadence and debauchery in Italy, returns to reclaim his and his son's rightful place.

The aristocracy is not the only champion of inequality in Trollope's late novels. In *Marion Fay*, a middle-class upstart such as Crocker, too, believes that there must be some whose blood possesses a peculiar ichor. As we have seen, these plebeian characters have a wonderful preference for a nobleman for no better reason than the lord's horse and groom: 'Its splendour of station, its wealth, show, and luxury, is then what the other classes really admire in [the aristocracy]; and this is not an elevating admiration' (Arnold 1993a: 237). These characters are, in a word, vulgar.

Lord Hampstead, in contrast, represents what Arnold calls the 'lovers of man's perfection' (1993a: 218): 'He had gone through the years of his early life forming some Utopian ideas – dreaming of some perfection in politics, in philanthropy, in social reform, and the like' (Trollope 1985: 412). It is his love of perfection in politics that fuels his love for Marion Fay. Marion's first objection to Hampstead's suit is their difference in social standing, a difference that Hampstead turns upon itself: 'Let your opinion stand against mine, and neutralise it. Let mine stand against yours, and in that we shall be equal. Then after that let love be lord of all' (1985: 203). Hampstead's phrasing emphasises that such equality is created through difference, but on the same terms. *Marion Fay* thus calls into question Terry's remark that one 'principle Trollope obviously valued was that like should mate with like, particularly in regard to social level' (Terry 1977: 111). Most of Trollope's novels, in fact, take Hampstead's part. Characters who are unwilling to cross class boundaries, such as Griselda Grantley and Lord Dumbello in *Framley Parsonage*, are trapped in cold, loveless marriages. Characters who do rebel against inequality, such as Lucy Robarts and Lord Lufton in the same novel, are destined for a bright future. This idea runs throughout Trollope's oeuvre. In *The Duke's Children*, to give a later example, Lord Silverbridge falls in love with a lovely American whose grandfather worked at the quays, and Lady Mary Palliser with the second son of a commoner. In these pairs the lovers are equals in the sense that they recognise each other's right to hold opinions of their own.

In the bulk of Trollope's writings, this right is acquired by means of forgiveness. In *Is He Popenjoy?*, Lord George Germain and Mary

Lovelace fall in love only when she finds out that her husband almost had an affair. As the narrator explains,

> I do not know whether a husband's comfort is ever perfect till some family peccadilloes have been conclusively proved against him. I am sure that a wife's temper to him is sweetened by such evidence of human imperfection . . . She never feels that all the due privileges of her life have been accorded to her, till her husband shall have laid himself open to the caresses of a pardon. Then, and not till then, he is her equal; and equality is necessary for comfortable love. (1998b: 225)

Like John Henry Newman, Lady George believes in conversion (A. H. Miller 2003: 106–7). It is because she believes that her husband's sins can be expiated that he is proven to be not guilty of the crime that he is charged with. She begins to love her husband only when he opens himself to forgiveness. Many of Trollope's heroes require forgiveness at some stage: Mark Robarts (*Framley Parsonage*), Harry Clavering (*The Claverings*), Phineas Finn (*Phineas Finn*), Frank Greystock (*The Eustace Diamonds*), Paul Montague (*The Way We Live Now*), John Caldigate (*John Caldigate*), Harry Annesley (*Mr Scarborough's Family*), George Western (*Kept in the Dark*). Some of his heroines, too, go astray, the most obvious instance being Alice Vavasor. Initially, John Grey loves her 'with the perfect love of equality' (Trollope 1989a: 89), but she thinks that she can do better and breaks their engagement. Grey's efforts are successful only when George Vavasor has jilted her and she, in a way, has laid herself open to the caress of a pardon.

Marion Fay emphasises a complementary theory, depicting equality not as a product of moral imperfection but as a product of perfection in beauty and intelligence.[20] 'I have set my heart on one whom in the things of the world I regard as my equal', Hampstead pleads, to which Marion replies, 'The compliment is very sweet to me, but I have trained myself to resist sweetness' (1985: 201). As such, this novel follows the rules laid down by Newman's Oxonian successor, Matthew Arnold.[21] Arnold famously argues that to make human nature perfect on all sides, conduct must be supplemented with 'sweetness and light', or beauty and intelligence (1993b: 67). 'Sweetness and light' – a phrase that Arnold himself lifted from Swift's fable of the bee and the spider in *The Battle of the Books* (Collini 1993b: 286) – aptly describes the dual nature of Trollopian love. Hampstead is attracted by sweetness and beauty: 'To my eyes [Marion Fay] is the perfection of loveliness' (1985: 113). Marion, in contrast, is attracted by light and intelligence: Hampstead's 'smile to her was as a light specially sent from heaven' (1985: 332). Arnold's ideas provide this vocabulary with a more fitting subtext than Burke's sublime. The light that surrounds Hampstead's smile is

Arnoldian insofar as smiling signifies intelligence and wit: as we have seen, it is a joke that lights the way to love.

Death

Yet in the end Hampstead is unsuccessful. Marion's declaration of love does not end in marital and sexual fulfilment. Her wilfulness is due to the fact that her recognition of Hampstead's love also coincides with a recognition of her own mortality. Having seen her mother and sisters grow pale and spectre-thin, Marion knows that Hampstead's love has no future: 'Then there came a pang from the wound, though it was not *as yet* a pang as of death' (1985: 115, my emphasis). Trollope might seem to be invoking the mediaeval principle of passion as suffering or Plato's suggestion that 'we are wounded by our memory of a previous existence in the realm of Ideas, to which we are always longing to return' (Kirsch 2012: 28). However, Marion's renunciation has a pay-off in this world. By acknowledging Hampstead's love while denying his right to possession, she finds that the world unveils itself: 'Can you not take a joy in thinking that you have given an inexpressible brightness to your poor Marion's days; that you have thrown over her a heavenly light which would be all glorious to her if she did not see that you were covered by a cloud?' (1985: 392). Robert Musil defines this feeling as lovesickness: 'true lovesickness is not a desire for possession but the world's gentle self-unveiling, for the sake of which one willingly renounces possession of the beloved' (Musil 1997: 129).[22] Defined as such, there is a close relation between lovesickness and consumption: if Marion's experience of the present is coloured by an awareness of her mortality, then the idea of being possessed by another is vain and futile.

This elegiac sentiment is a characteristic of tact. In Arnold's work, the sentiment that Trollope calls lovesickness appears as dissatisfaction: 'culture begets a dissatisfaction which is of the highest possible value in stemming the common tide of men's thoughts in a wealthy and industrial community, and which saves the future, as one may hope, from being vulgarised, even if it cannot save the present' (Arnold 1993b: 65). One way to achieve this state is adoration. His misgivings about Puritanism notwithstanding, Arnold does not write off religion completely. Religion is a valuable example of the mode of relation that a common standard can create: 'It does not help me to think a thing more clearly that thousands of other people are thinking the same; but it does help me to worship with more emotion that thousands of other people are worshipping with me' (1993b: 158). As such, adoration stems the common tide of men's thoughts because it seeks no possessive knowledge of others.

It is here, however, that Hampstead fails. When Marion finally admits that she loves him and realises through love the meaning of tact, he loses his sense of tact, for his love then begins to fuse worship with possessiveness:

> To watch over her, to worship her, to hover round her, so that no wind should be allowed to blow too strongly on her, to teach her that she was the one treasure in the world that could be of real value to him – but at the same time to make a property of her, so that she should be altogether his own – that had been his idea of the bond which should unite him and Marion Fay together. (1985: 357–8)

It is this contradiction that might explain why Marion's death is necessary for the thematic structure of the novel. The object of adoration cannot be touched: if its aura is to remain intact, it must be kept at a distance.[23] Hampstead believes in the object of his idolatry, but he also seeks to break its spell. At times, indeed, his essential goodness is disfigured by the aggression and greediness of a spoiled child. This fusion of self-renunciation and obsession has its origin in the baroque code of *amour passion* (Luhmann 1998: 64). Up until the very end, Hampstead is deaf to Marion's warnings: 'Oh, dearest, do not kill me' (1985: 394). Hampstead and Marion thus exchange places like Chad Newsome and Lambert Strether in Henry James's *The Ambassadors* (1903), E. M. Forster's example of an hourglass-shaped plot: Marion finally finds love as tact while Hampstead loses his way. Only when Marion has died does Hampstead realise his mistake and renounce his possessiveness: 'I do think that if, while I am here, I can tame the selfishness of self, I shall reach a step upwards in that world which shall come next after this' (1985: 411). Hampstead thus gives vent to what Arnold calls dissatisfaction, albeit in terms that are undeniably religious.[24]

More precisely, one might say that Hampstead's epiphany is theological. According to Benjamin, the writings of a later and not quite so elegant Jeremiah, Karl Kraus, show that true tact takes not 'bourgeois respectability' as its standard – tact as etiquette or politeness – but rather a 'theological criterion' (Benjamin 2005: 436): it is 'the capacity to treat social relationships, though not departing from them, as natural, even paradisal, relationships, and so not only to approach the king as if he had been born with the crown on his brow, but the lackey like an Adam in livery' (2005: 436–7). This criterion eventually finds its way into Hampstead's heart. His acceptance of the fact that Marion is dying is accompanied by a resolve to regard men not as social entities but as creatures:

> He spoke to [Mrs Roden] often of his future life, always speaking of a life from which Marion would have been withdrawn by death, and did so with a cold, passionless assurance which showed her that he had almost resolved as to the future. He would see all lands that were to be seen, and converse with all people. The social condition of God's creatures at large should be his study. The task would be endless, and, as he said, an endless task hardly admits of absolute misery. (1985: 412)

Hampstead's decision to pay attention to creaturely life – his wish to explore a world that is not of our own making – is a tactful response to Marion's death. It shows that his desire for equality has acquired a deeper meaning. Initially, his advocacy of equality is still circumscribed by the existence of social differences. Wishing to break down class barriers, he takes for granted that these barriers matter. By the end of the novel, however, his intuition has ripened into contemplation. Marion Fay has made Hampstead realise that the modern practice of looking at other beings as social constructs does not reveal who, in themselves, they really are; this can only be felt.

Notes

1. Ophthalmologists enhanced observation through the measurement of the eye: 'Spectacles were routinely depicted as one of the contemporary world's most useful and necessary devices, mainly because this world was itself regularly viewed as being more ocularly demanding than previous epochs and perennially on the brink of destroying vision altogether' (Otter 2008: 40). Unlike ophthalmologists, engineers sought to preserve and enhance vision by modifying the city rather than the citizen, 'reiterating ad infinitum [the] idea that environments could themselves be instruments of improvement' (Otter 2008: 17). They achieved that aim only gradually. Bills such as the Municipal Corporations Act (1835) and Metropolitan Management Act (1855) created the conditions for easing the passage of legislation, which led to the 'appointment of municipal surveyors, engineers, and inspectors whose job it was to supervise and construct roads and buildings' (Otter 2008: 69). These new bodies did not erect panopticons, but widened thoroughfares, found ways of abating smoke, laid gas mains, positioned street lamps, and assembled electricity networks. Thus they helped to transform the public realm into a visual system that was 'bidirectional, tacit, normative, and pervasive' (Otter 2008: 50). Technology thus functioned as a governmentality: infrastructures and technicians were less visible and therefore more successful than state-imposed laws. This sheds a new light on the rise of bureaucracy in the late nineteenth century: 'The realm of legitimate intervention had increased, not so much because liberalism was being eroded, as because of a demonstrable growth in large technical systems that required organisation and regulation' (Otter 2008: 13). Lauren M. E. Goodlad offers a different reading of this phenomenon. Her understanding of a liberal

governmentality is characterised not by its deployment of nonhuman agents, but by its co-optation of individualism. This kind of governmentality did delay the rise of bureaucracy (Goodlad 2003: 23–4). Nevertheless, Otter's and Goodlad's discussions are not mutually exclusive, if only because he is describing the end of the century whereas she is focusing on the middle.

2. All his passion for the sport notwithstanding, Trollope's exploits in the hunting field were limited by his eyesight: 'My eyes are so constituted that I can never see the nature of a fence. I either follow someone or ride at it with the full conviction that I may be going into – a horsepond or a gravel pit. I have plunged into both one and the other' (1999a: 171). Spectacles apparently did not provide a remedy: 'A caller, ushered in upon him, would see a heavy figure rise from the desk, hurry to the fireplace and there fumble feverishly among the littered spectacles for the pair best able to reveal the visitor's identity' (Sadleir 1961: 337).
3. This line of thinking dates back to D. A. Miller's influential *The Novel and the Police*. Building on Michel Foucault's *Discipline and Punish*, Miller famously maintains that the novel is an instrument of disciplinary power: it 'constitutively mobilises a tactic of tact: it is the policing power that never passes for such, but is either invisible or visible only under cover of other, nobler or simply blander intentionalities (to educate, to cure, to produce, to defend)' (D. A. Miller 1988: 17). As such, the novel 'shows disciplinary power to inhere in the very resistance to it' (1988: 27). Not all critics have received this compelling account of the novel willingly. Lauren M. E. Goodlad has revised Miller's reading of *Bleak House* (Goodlad 2003: 96–101), arguing that Miller's anachronistic focus on disciplinary power leads him to ignore the novel's complex and ambivalent stance towards sanitary reform. This revision is part of her larger claim that 'the disciplinary subject of Foucault's Franco-oriented and presentist genealogy' is very different from 'the modes of character idealised by and produced in Britain's self-consciously liberal society over the course of the nineteenth century' (Goodlad 2003: x). Foucault's writings from the 1980s, however, improve 'upon genealogy's impoverished model of human subjectivity' (Goodlad 2003: 13). An essay such as 'Governmentality' does find a place for the possibility of human agency.
4. As further evidence of Trollope's capacity for sexual innuendo and hoodwinking nervous publishers, David Skilton has pointed to John Millais's illustration of Lord Lufton and Lucy Robarts's first meeting in *Framley Parsonage* (Skilton 2007).
5. Trollope's concern with oligoptic spaces is not limited to *Is He Popenjoy?* and *Marion Fay*. In *He Knew He Was Right*, a similar situation ends tragically, while Trollope's parliamentary novels repeatedly stress that space is a screen pierced by different lines of sight. In *The Way We Live Now*, Mrs Hurtle stays at a lodging-house in Islington; in *The Claverings*, Harry Clavering gives up his Cambridge fellowship for a post as engineer in a company that is building the London underground. This little-known fact is revealed quite late, in chapter 31 (Trollope 1994: 307).
6. Bodleian Library, Oxford, MSS. Don. c. 10, fol. 133. Trollope's sketches for this novel have been transcribed by R. H. Super (Trollope 1985: xxi–xxiii).

7. On the question of liberalism and anonymity, see Elaine Hadley (2010: 125–74) and Helen Small (2003).
8. Gloves present an attentive observer, such as the narrator of Trollope's 'The Turkish Bath', with a physiognomic sign that lends itself to interpretation: 'A well-to-do man may have no gloves, or may simply carry in his hands those which appertain to him rather as a thing of custom than for any use for which he requires them. But a tattered glove, worn on the hand, is to our eyes the surest sign of a futile attempt at outer respectability' (Trollope 1990–4: 4.1–2).
9. Marion Fay's clothing is not that of the average Victorian, 'conservative of dress perhaps, yet always aware of changes in fashion' (Otter 2008: 51). Until the 1860s, 'when the automatic disownment of Friends who married non-Quakers ceased' (Keen 2002: 218), the sight of an actual Quaker was uncommon: 'Their insular communities meant that a typical Victorian would be unlikely to know any of only 16,000 Friends intimately' (Keen 2002: 219). At the same time, certain Quakers had risen to public prominence. In the course of the eighteenth and nineteenth century, 'Quakers' views became better known through their activism in political and philanthropic reform' (Keen 2002: 219). The most famous Quaker activists were arguably John Bright, the Radical politician, and Elizabeth Fry, the prison reformer.
10. Trollope's promotion of tact may have had its origins in the professional work ethic that he developed as a Post Office inspector. Whereas in the 1870s the 'gaze of the inspector was never faceless or nameless, and it often did not arrive unexpectedly' (Otter 2008: 119), Trollope relied on the element of surprise: 'I have often surprised some small country postmaster, who had never seen or heard of me before, by coming down upon him at 9 in the morning with a red coat and boots and breeches, and interrogating him as to the disposal of every letter which came into his office . . . In all these visits I was in truth a beneficent angel to the public – bringing everywhere with me an earlier, cheaper, and much more regular delivery of letters. But not unfrequently the angelic nature of my mission was imperfectly understood. I was perhaps a little in a hurry to get on, and did not allow as much time as was necessary to explain to the wondering mistress of the house, or to an open-mouthed farmer, why it was that a man arrayed for hunting, asked so many questions, which might be considered impertinent as applying to his or her private affairs' (1999a: 90–1). As such, Trollope did not take advantage of the 'identifiability and politeness' with which later inspectors cultivated 'trust and cooperation' (Otter 2008: 119). One might conclude that in his professional life Trollope did not display the inspector's gift of tact. Importantly, though, this was a deliberate pose. As a stratagem in his efforts to make the Post Office mechanism run more smoothly, Trollope's alleged disregard of politeness was founded in his knowledge of what it would have meant to be polite: 'Unless I came down suddenly as a summer's storm upon them, the very people who were robbed by our messengers would not confess the robbery, fearing the ill will of the men' (1999a: 91). Trollope's trick of surprising his subordinates thus evinces a sociability that does not rely on observation but appreciation.
11. About a year before Trollope began writing his forty-fourth novel, Arnold

was at work on 'Equality', a lecture which he first delivered at the Royal Institute in February 1878 and which was published as an essay in the *Fortnightly Review* a month later. It is likely that Trollope came across Arnold's text; he still considered the *Fortnightly* to be one of his offspring. Trollope felt that E. A. Freeman's attack on foxhunting in the *Fortnightly* was 'almost as a rising of a child against the father' (Trollope 1999a: 194–5; see Freeman 1869 and chapter 4, n. 7). Furthermore, Trollope and Arnold knew one another through their shared membership of clubs such as the Athenaeum and the Garrick and organisations such as the Royal Literary Fund. They also shared friends – Sir Frederick Pollock, for instance – and participated in literary ventures such as the *Fortnightly Review*. Trollope may have been directed to 'Equality' by his good friend and Arnold's brother-in-law, W. E. Forster. Forster is a likely source for Trollope's portrayal of a Quaker family, as he was one of the few men among Trollope's close acquaintances with a Quaker past. Forster grew up as a Quaker but was excommunicated in 1850 when he married Jane Arnold, one of Matthew Arnold's sisters. In 'The Early Quakers and Quakerism', Forster presents his excommunication as inevitable in the climate of the times (Forster 1852). Better known than this little article are his advocacy of parliamentary reform and national education, and his role as Chief Secretary for Ireland.

12. Trollope's portrayal of love has yielded a variety of often conflicting interpretations. Bradford Booth, who was so instrumental in putting Trollope on the map, daringly dismisses the subject out of hand: 'the tragedy of Trollope's career is his capitulation to the stereotype of romantic love' (1958: 164). More generously, R. C. Terry maintains that love allows Trollope to create a blend of irony and illusion (1977: 102). For Shirley Letwin it is 'enchantment without illusion, a rational passion' (1982: 147), while for A. O. J. Cockshut it is 'a destroyer' (1968: 114). Juliet McMaster (1978), in turn, has shown that Trollope approaches love as an instrument of power, whereas Robert Polhemus (1982) believes that it illustrates a character's psychological needs. According to J. Hillis Miller, these critics are all off the mark. Pointing out that in Trollope's fiction falling in love can happen only once, Miller argues that for both men and women it is a permanent transformation of the self. This view of love challenges the ideological function of love as the redistribution of wealth and status, which is the view that the lovers' parents, relatives, and friends tend to take (J. H. Miller 2015: 71–7).
13. Trollope's realism uses such examples of inadequate self-interest to alienate readers from characters: 'The insistence that we should hold back is not a gesture of tact but a matter of principle with Trollope' (Small 2012: 413). On self-sacrifice and atonement in Trollope's fiction, see Blumberg (2004) and Schramm (2012).
14. In more general terms, Trollope seems to take issue with the Victorian doctrine of separate spheres. The Victorian woman, that is, was 'associated with an instinctive, well-nigh angelic devotion to the needs of others, and thus a moral "influence" which elevated and refined those around her. So complete was her selflessness that some commentators were troubled by the very idea of feminine sexual desire' (Adams 2012: 8). One thinks here of

John Ruskin's *Sesame and Lilies* (1865), a work which Trollope dismissed as 'simply rodomontade' (1865a: 635).

15. Trollope thus subtly revises Burke's own revision of the sublime: in contrast to the classical tradition, Burke maintains that women are incapable of discriminating among the beautiful and the sublime (Jöttkandt 2006). Coleridge follows this tradition in his famous anecdote of a woman who thought that a waterfall could be both. According to Jöttkandt, however, Trollope's women are capable of making this distinction. For more on the history of this gendered division, see Balfour (2006). The taboo and the sublime may not be a prominent player in Arnold's criticism, but they are in his early poetry. Arnold's call for a form of critical tact is akin to his defence of his experiment with metre in *Merope* (1858). In the preface to this poem, he argues that the poem's metrical form is an attempt to restrain the stormy agitations that it inspires: 'Powerful thought and emotion, flowing in strongly marked channels, make a stronger impression: this is the main reason why a metrical form is a more effective vehicle for them than prose: in prose there is more freedom, but, in the metrical form, the very limit gives a sense of precision and emphasis. This sense of emphatic distinctness in our impressions rises, as the thought and emotion swell higher and higher without overflowing their boundaries, to a lofty sense of the mastery of the human spirit over its own stormiest agitations; and this, again, conducts us to a state of feeling which it is the highest aim of tragedy to produce, to a *sentiment of sublime acquiescence in the course of fate and in the dispensations of human life*' (1858: xxxix–xl; Arnold's emphasis).
16. Trollope's deployment of the motif of women knowing only one true love has been explained in a number of ways. Cockshut interprets it as a convenient gesture, both narratologically and ideologically, suggesting that Trollope 'does not stress the idea that choice cannot be analysed; he simply leaves us to infer it from his silence. For him it is not mysterious, merely unknown' (1968: 112). R. C. Terry maintains that it is 'a statement on the sacredness of love, however it may seem to us to reveal perversity or masochism in the heroine' (1977: 102). One might also understand it as a symptom of male authorship. Nancy K. Miller underscores that 'in the politics of seduction, once proves generally to be enough. Thus the rule of female experience in male-authored fiction is the drama of a single misstep' (1980: x).
17. Trollope sought to distance himself from the sensation novels of Wilkie Collins and Mary Elizabeth Braddon (1999a: 228–9), which were a domesticated version of the Gothic novels of Matthew Lewis and Ann Radcliffe.
18. Freud frequently resorts to nineteenth-century physiology and idealist aesthetics: 'The sublime is something on a large scale in a metaphorical, transferred psychological sense, and I would like to make, or rather repeat, the hypothesis that this too, like that which is large somatically, is represented by an extra expenditure [of energy]' (Freud 2002: 195). Freud's footnote directs the reader to Alexander Bain's *The Emotions and the Will* (1859). Elsewhere he also refers to Herbert Spencer's 'The Physiology of Laughter' (1860) (Freud 2002: 143). Bain's and Spencer's understanding of psychical energy as a closed circuit influenced Victorian conceptions of the novel, as Nicholas Dames has shown (Dames 2007). Trollope was a close friend of

G. H. Lewes, one of the most important figures in this nexus of physiology, aesthetics, and literature.

19. In his famous Rede lecture *Literature and Science*, Arnold refers to this line from *Macbeth* (V, iii, 40) to make a point about the ability to produce a good paraphrase (1882: 228). Perhaps he was returning Trollope's compliments. Arnold's lecture took place on 14 June 1882, and was published two months later. Arnold could have read *Marion Fay* in the meantime (*Marion Fay* appeared in the *Graphic* from 3 December 1881 to 3 June 1882, and was published in book form in May 1882).
20. Christopher Herbert's claim that 'Trollope persistently highlights the imperfection and incompleteness of the love unions he praises most' (1987: 95) is not wholly accurate. Herbert only considers perfection and imperfection from a moral point of view, which leads to a contradiction: he repeatedly refers to Matthew Arnold's advocacy of perfection as an instance of the age's moral idealisation, exemplified by Puritanism and Evangelicalism, whereas Arnold is talking of perfection in beauty and intelligence and manners (e.g. Herbert 1987: 154–5). As a result of this generalisation, Herbert elides a complementary path in Victorian thinking.
21. For examinations of the presence of Newman in Arnold's writings, see DeLaura (1969) as well as de Graef and Gilleir (2010).
22. Musil's definition of lovesickness and Trollope's portrayal turn the standard Victorian conceptualisation of lovesickness on its head. From antiquity up to the early modern period, physicians analysed lovesickness, 'the emotional despair entailed in unrequited love' (Altbauer-Rudnik 2012: 86), as a form of melancholy. One way to cure this illness was by addressing its social origins: 'Robert Burton (1577–1640), an English divine with an amateur interest in medicine, criticised parents, teachers and guardians who withheld their consent to a match because of the limitations imposed by law and custom, especially on account of an inequality of status between the lovers' (Altbauer-Rudnik 2012: 84). In the course of the seventeenth and eighteenth century, however, while the humoral model was being replaced by a mechanistic one, the diagnosis shifted from aetiological to symptomatic explanations. By the beginning of the nineteenth century, lovesickness had been redefined as erotomania, 'a delusional disorder, characterised by the patients' fantasy that their desire for their love object was reciprocated' (Altbauer-Rudnik 2012: 87). This condition, better known as the de Clérambault syndrome after Gaëtan de Clérambault's ground-breaking analysis in *Les Psychoses Passionelles* (1921), has been represented more recently in Ian McEwan's *Enduring Love* (1997). Marion Fay, however, does not suffer from delusion, but melancholia. Like the melancholia that Robert Burton describes, Marion's illness seems to have been induced by a difference in social status. There is an additional and more compelling cause for melancholia at work as well, that is, the awareness of our mortality.
23. While the powerful concept of the aura has come to be associated with the work of Walter Benjamin, it had a pre-history in Ludwig Klages's vitalist philosophy and Gershom Scholem's Jewish mysticism. Benjamin's deployment of it was ambivalent, 'torn between the extremes of revolutionary avant-gardism and elegiac mourning for beautiful semblance' (M. B. Hansen 2008: 338).

24. Surprisingly, perhaps, the topic of Trollope and religion has been graced with only one full-length study (Durey 2002). In general, one is led to agree with Geoffrey Harvey that Trollope was attached to ritualism: 'his instincts were high church. He was sympathetic to the influential Oxford Movement . . . He admired the fact that Roman Catholicism so directly addressed human nature' (1999: 455). Evangelicalism he seems to have detested. Above all, he despised its hypocrisy and cant; see, for instance, his critique of Sabbatarianism (1866). He was tolerant of other faiths, though he held fast to his own. One anecdote can tell more than these generalities. When Trollope was engaged in establishing what would become the *Fortnightly Review*, he and his collaborators agreed on freedom of speech, but only to a certain extent. When John Morley was asked to replace G. H. Lewes as editor in 1866, Trollope questioned his credentials: '"Now do you", he asked, glaring as if in fury through his spectacles, and roaring like a bull of Bashan, "do you believe in the divinity of our blessed Lord and Saviour Jesus Christ?" He had not a perfect sense of the shades and delicacies of things, nor had he exactly the spirit of urbanity' (Morley and Ward 1883: 56). In his *Autobiography*, however, Trollope tells us that he knows that he was being irrational (which is a kind of rationality in itself) and turns this into a joke: 'We would be neither conservative nor liberal, neither religious nor free-thinking, neither popular nor exclusive – but we would let any man who had a thing to say and knew how to say it speak freely. But he should always speak with the responsibility of his name attached. In the very beginning I militated against this impossible negation of principles – and did so most irrationally, seeing that I had agreed to the negation of principles – by declaring that nothing should appear denying or questioning the divinity of Christ. It was a most preposterous claim to make for such a publication as we proposed, and it at once drove from us one or two who had proposed to join us' (1999a: 189–90). Trollope here paints a picture of the *Fortnightly* as the kind of middle space that Russell associates with the essay. Given the fact that the periodical was founded upon the principles espoused in Arnold's 'The Function of Criticism at the Present Time' (1864), this fits. In Trollope's novels, religion seems to function as a social setting rather than a genuine concern, similar to his depiction of politics. For an overview, see Letwin (1982: 216–17). At times, Trollope does engage specific topics, such as Irish Church disestablishment in *Phineas Redux* (Frank 2008). Particularly suggestive, though perhaps a bit rushed, is J. Russell Perkin's comparison of Arnold's writings on religion and Trollope's *The Bertrams* (parts of which are set in the Holy Land), which concludes that the 'difference between Arnold and Trollope lies in Trollope's notion of reserve. It was best, he thought, not to talk of such things very much and allow the changes to occur beneath the cover of the old forms; that way their effect could be minimised . . . Trollope too may have believed in the *Zeitgeist*, but unlike Arnold he had no interest in speculating about it' (Perkin 2009: 123).

Chapter 9

'Affectionate Reserve': Tact as Comedy

> No doubt the cause of that fear which did exist as to novels arose from an idea that this matter of love would be treated in an inflammatory and generally unwholesome manner. 'Madam', says Sir Anthony in the play, 'a circulating library in a town is an evergreen tree of diabolical knowledge. It blossoms through the year; and, depend on it, Mrs Malaprop, that they who are so fond of handling the leaves, will long for the fruit at last'. (Trollope 1999a: 225)

Trollope's narratives, this final chapter suggests, attain a measure of reserve by embedding the depiction of love within the framework of comedy. Trollope hints at the imbrication of these two concerns when, after having proposed that to teach wholesome lessons novelists must know how to handle love, he backs up this theory with an allusion to *The Rivals* (I, ii, 235–9), a comedy by the eighteenth-century Anglo-Irish playwright Richard Brinsley Sheridan (1775). This passage can be read as a spun-out metaphor: handling love is like handling pages. Love has morphed into a book, the novelist has morphed into 'they'. At first sight, this comparison may seem nothing more than the logic of courtship fiction: it is a cultural orthodoxy that novels are the means with which men and (especially) women are to be taught the meaning of love – wholesome lessons, in short. Although this theory is one of Trollope's hobby-horses in his non-fiction, in his fiction novels serve a more sinister purpose: Leah Price has argued that in 'coding the handling of books as authentic and the reading of texts as a front Trollope's comedies of manners upstage textually occasioned absorption by bibliographically assisted repulsion' (2012: 71). She illustrates this argument with a notorious scene from *The Small House at Allington*, Adolphus Crosbie and Lady Alexandrina's train ride towards their not-so-romantic honeymoon destination, Folkestone. Crosbie has with a small bribe secured a railway carriage for the two of them. When the train comes to a tunnel, Crosbie 'had half intended to put out his hand again, under some mistaken idea that the tunnel afforded him an opportunity. The whole journey was one long opportunity, had he desired it; but his wife hated tunnels, and so he drew his hand back again' (2005: 497). Instead of making love, Crosbie reaches for *The Times*, at which point Lady Alexandrina withdraws her novel. This comic scene suggests not just that a book can be a sad substitute for sex. Crosbie and Lady Alexandrina pretend to read in order to ignore: handling the leaves allows them to carve out a private space in which they cannot be touched. What, then, is the function of the comedy of manners in Trollope's argument about tact?[1]

Like the experience of love as depicted by Trollope, the comedy of manners provides a pattern for a tactful mode of sociability. By insisting 'on a gap between the stage and audience', between fiction and reality, the comedy of manners forms an 'artificial middle ground that enables a playful interaction' (Russell 2012: 188). As Charles Lamb notes in the *Essays of Elia* (1823), characters in Restoration comedies 'have got out of Christendom into the land – what shall I call it ? – of cuckoldry – the Utopia of gallantry, where pleasure is duty, and the manners perfect freedom. It is altogether a speculative scene of things, which has no reference whatever to the world that is' (Lamb 1912: 163). George Meredith elaborates on this premise in his essay 'On the Idea of Comedy', delivered as a lecture and published in 1877. Pure comedy, Meredith argues, rests on a 'clear Hellenic perception of facts' and originates in the 'play of the intellect', thus giving voice to a laughter that 'is impersonal and of unrivalled politeness, nearer a smile' (1877: 26, 33). Matthew Arnold's language shimmers through in this conception of comedy. Just as Arnold locates culture in France and Greece, so Meredith believes that it is in those parts of the world that the comic spirit reigns: 'Menander and Molière stand alone specially as comic poets of the feelings and the idea' (1877: 19). Arnold, indeed, admired Menander, the most important representative of the Athenian New Comedy.[2] He opens his essay on 'Equality' (1878) by citing one of Menander's dicta:

> the Jerusalemite Paul, exhorting his converts, enforces what he is saying by a verse of Athenian comedy – a verse, probably, from the great master of that comedy, a man unsurpassed for fine and just observation of human life, Menander: φθείρουσιν ἤθη χρησθ' ὁμιλίαι κακαί – 'Evil communications corrupt good manners'. (Arnold 1993a: 212)

To fully understand Meredith's Arnoldian definition of comedy, however, it is more helpful to turn to Arnold's essay on Heinrich Heine. Heine is so effective a writer, Arnold writes, 'because he unites so much wit with so much pathos' (1863: 238). Many of Heine's poems, that is, rely on the pattern of caustic disenchantment or *Stimmungsbrechung*.

This creates distance between the reader and the characters that he or she is invited to identify with.[3] One might compare this procedure to that of bathos, that is, an 'anti-climax . . . by an unintentional lapse in mood from the sublime to the trivial or ridiculous' (Stevenson 2010: 139).[4]

Although Trollope often aligns himself with one of Lamb's staunchest opponents, Thomas Babington Macaulay, in his artistic practice he does defer to the comedy of manners.[5] Like Lamb, Meredith, and Arnold, Trollope appreciates comedy because it creates a neutral ground within which the subject's identity is broken up. For Trollope, comic pleasure is

> nothing but the euphoria of momentarily being allowed to shed our oppressive judgmental responsibility – in other words, of being able actually to shed our habitual selves for the duration of the play. Comedy's radical impulse is thus to show how burdensome our habitual selves really are. (Herbert 1987: 22)

Contemporary critics did not fail to notice Trollope's penchant for this radical impulse, nor did they hesitate to voice their disapproval. Throughout his career, but especially from *The Eustace Diamonds* onwards, Trollope was charged with 'a supposed moral irresponsibility in the choice and treatment of his subject-matter' (Skilton 1996: 58). Nothing less could have been expected, of course, from a critical tradition that took sympathy as its artistic criterion. The first person to comment upon Trollope's approach in a more appreciative way was a contemporary French essayist, Émile Montégut, who reviewed the first three Barchester novels for the prestigious *Revue des Deux Mondes*:

> His novels are written in a very radical spirit [*un esprit très radical*], and yet it is almost touching to see with what affectionate reserve [*quelle affectueuse réserve*] he speaks of those very people he seems to like least. He feels inclined to excuse each of the faults which he wishes to condemn, and he ends by forgiving [*il arrive à pardonner*], by means of all kinds of ingenious reasonings, the errors which in his heart he reprobates . . . He talks about his characters as one would talk about one's relatives and parents to an intimate friend, with a liberty full of reserve [*une liberté pleine de réserve*]. A smiling scepticism and a sly benevolence [*un scepticisme souriant et une bienveillance sournoise*] are the soul of these tales and inspire the writer's judgement of English society. Even if his opinions are radical, they are not bitter. His indulgence is lukewarm and without charity, yet his railleries are not malicious. (Montégut 1858: 759–60)[6]

Montégut appreciates Trollope's criticism of the establishment. At the same time, he indicates that Trollope was careful not to cause too much offence. Trollope finds a middle ground: he is radical without being bitter, led to forgive what he wants to condemn. Montégut's very phrasing – 'affectionate reserve' and 'a liberty full of reserve' – emphasises that Trollope's comic stance falls within the remit of tact.

Towards the end of his career, in particular, Trollope developed an interest in both Restoration drama and the world of Molière.[7] Many of his late novels feature characters who seem to have been born on the French stage. Colonel John Stubbs in *Ayala's Angel* is one whose irreverent wit makes him the most sociable of companions. Ayala 'would go anywhere with Colonel Stubbs, and feel herself to be quite safe. She hoped she might meet him again very often. He was, as it were, the Genius of Comedy, without a touch of which life would be very dull' (1989b: 127). Trollope labours the point by alluding to a line from Thomas Moore's *The Fudge Family in Paris* (5.98), a comedy, in his mocking description of the Angel of Light as a 'Sallow, sublime, sort of Werther-faced man' (1989b: 127). *Marion Fay*, which was written in the wake of Meredith's essay, like *Ayala's Angel*, is a comedy of manners. Satirising the manners and affectations of contemporary society, three of the novel's four plotlines use the conventions of this genre in a relatively straightforward fashion. Their protagonists are all to some extent caricatures, types who cannot – or do not attempt to – think beyond the limits of their own self. As such, the novel closely resembles its seventeenth-century predecessors, in which there was a 'neutral ground of character, which stood between vice and virtue; or which in fact was indifferent to neither, where neither properly was called in question' (Lamb 1912: 162). The novel's most obvious figures of fun are plebeian. Adept at saying the wrong thing at the wrong time, Samuel Crocker and Clara Demijohn represent a stock character in the comedy of manners: the buffoon. More important in this regard is the story of Lord Llwddythlw's and Lady Amaldina's engagement which, set in an aristocratic milieu whose inhabitants bear the most wonderful names, faithfully follows the conventions of the genre. When Llwddythlw is taxed for having a 'terrible Welsh name', Lady Amaldina declares that when 'you once know how to pronounce it it is the prettiest word that poetry ever produced' (1985: 86). Being the daughter of Lord Persiflage, she bears the same cross. Lord Persiflage himself is only a minor character, but the Secretary of State for Foreign Affairs, who 'liked to treat everything as a joke' (1985: 83), adds more to the scenery than just his name. He is a parody of Lord Palmerston, of whom Trollope writes in his biography that, as Home Secretary, Palmerston 'passed on from the light courteous *persiflage* of the Foreign Minister to the common John Bull fun of an English magistrate, without an apparent effort, but with an evident intention' (2003: 148, Trollope's italics). Trollope may be echoing Arnold: 'When there is need, as now, for any large forecast of the course of human affairs, for an acquaintance with the ideas which in the end sway mankind, and for an estimate of their power, aristocracies are out of their element' (Arnold 1993a: 234).

The real comedy lies in the story's action, however. Lord Llwddythlw, stiff and bald, yet intelligent and diligent, is constantly engaged in business on behalf of the Conservative interest. He therefore feels compelled to put his courtship with Lady Amaldina on the back burner: though his love is genuine, he cannot find a suitable day in his busy schedule. Nevertheless, Lady Amaldina craftily badgers him into fixing a date. A victim to circumstances and guided by wills other than his own, Lord Llwddythlw is a variation on the typical dupe. Lady Amaldina, in contrast, is a trickster. Good-natured though she may be, she wears a mask, though not always successfully. Her enthusiasm is abundant, for instance, when she congratulates Lady Frances, her cousin, on the fact that her lover turns out to have the blood of the Bourbons flowing in his veins. Writing to Llwddythlw, however, her praise is more guarded:

> I have written to Fanny Trafford to congratulate her; because you know it is after all better than being *a mere Post Office clerk*. That was terrible – so bad that one hardly knew how to mention her name in society! When people talked about it, I really *did feel* that I blushed all over. One can mention her name now because people are not *supposed* to know that he has got nothing. Nevertheless, it is very dreadful. *What on earth are they to live on?* (1985: 327)

The fact that these two letters are presented consecutively creates humour, highlighting that the writer seems to hold two different opinions at the same time.[8] Yet she is not a hypocrite. It would be a mistake to think that Lady Amaldina is being candid. What she writes to Llwddythlw is said in the belief that her words will please the man she loves. In this, she is mistaken: 'I should think him quite as respectable, earning his bread as a clerk in a public office' (1985: 328). It is in the exposure of her failed attempts at gauging the feelings of others, then, that Lady Amaldina reveals herself as a character in a comedy of manners.

George Roden and Lady Frances, finally, find themselves caught up in a comedy that has spiralled out of control, that is, a farce. When Roden turns out to be the eldest son of the Duca di Crinola and is told that 'there was very little of the best blood which Europe had produced in the last dozen centuries of which some small proportion was not running in his veins' (1985: 306), no obstacles to their union remain. The resolution of this plot resonates with Meredith's description of Restoration drama:

> When [the Comedy of Manners] has frolicked through her five Acts to surprise you with the information that Mr Aimwell is converted by a sudden

> death in the world outside the scenes into Lord Aimwell, and can marry the lady in the light of day, it is to the credit of her vivacious nature that she does not anticipate your calling her Farce. (1877: 4)

This plot has been read as a conservative attempt to defuse or sidestep the challenge that Roden represents:

> since it is the disclosure of the secret that puts an end to George and Lady Frances's worries, not anything that they themselves say or do, all the preceding argument about the responsibilities of rank and the sanctity of class distinctions is suddenly made superfluous and inconsequential. (P. D. Edwards 1978: 133–4)

Indeed, although Roden refuses to use his title, he does accept a job at the Foreign Office, the most feudal of government departments. Nevertheless, it is hardly believable that Roden had never inquired more deeply into his own past. Twice the novel mentions that he obeys his mother's wish 'with a spirit of reticence which was peculiar with him' (1985: 251, 310). Such an exaggerated sense of tact, not unlike Miranda's in *The Tempest* or Daniel Deronda's, confirms the impression that the 'discovery that Roden is in fact an Italian nobleman is not a device to evade the issue; it is quite simply a superb piece of burlesque' (Super 1985: ix). We must not take Roden's rank seriously, then. His aristocratic rebirth does not function as a way to smooth over class differences, but to mock those for whom these differences are all and everything, such as Mr Greenwood, the family chaplain, and Lady Kingsbury, his proposed stepmother-in-law.

The novel's central plot, however, seems to be devoid of comedy. Hampstead and Marion Fay's story is essentially tragic. Showing signs of the onset of consumption, Marion nobly refuses Hampstead's advances: 'as Marion's death approaches, pathos becomes so overpowering that we almost forget the difference in rank between the two lovers' (P. D. Edwards 1978: 134).[9] As in the poetry of Heine, however, Hampstead's exalted feelings are often undercut. When Hampstead has bid Marion a final farewell and has returned home, for instance, he

> walked straight into the drawing-room, and having carefully closed the door, he took the poker in his hand and held it clasped there as something precious. 'It is the only thing of mine', he said, 'that she has touched. Even then I swore to myself that this hearth should be her hearth; that here we would sit together, and be one flesh and one bone'. Then surreptitiously he took the bit of iron away with him, and hid it among his treasures – to the subsequent dismay of the housemaid. (1985: 433)

Reading about Hampstead's suffering, one is tempted to feel pity and sympathy. *In cauda*, however, Trollope reminds us that the poker is, for others, just a poker. Through this reference to the commonplace, we abruptly descend from the exalted to the banal. Many of Hampstead's encounters with Marion involve such a moment, often as a punchline at the end of a paragraph or chapter. In this novel, the 'line between the comic and the serious is sometimes a fine one, a matter of emphasis perhaps and of a sense of proportion' (Super 1985: x). Fainting after her heroic avowal not to marry Hampstead in spite of her love, Marion causes Hampstead to be transported from the realm of emotions into a medical emergency. Not knowing what to do, he is forced to call in her maid, who urges him to retreat with dignity: 'I can't do nothing, my lord, while you stand over her that way' (1985: 277). Hampstead is thus made to realise that his world is not necessarily shared by others. Told to bear his plight with courage, for instance, he escapes the room, only to find himself in a plight of a much more mundane nature: 'He had come out without his hat, and he could not stand there in the sun to be stared at' (1985: 415). Earlier in the novel, pacing to and fro while brooding over his troubles, Hampstead is similarly 'ashamed of himself, as he felt rather than heard that he had absolutely shouted her name aloud' (1985: 360). These comic unions of wit and pathos create a form of bathos and, as such, the kind of reserve that is characteristic of tact.

The principle of bathos also operates on a higher level. The novel's three other heroes find themselves in similar predicaments; their stories, like Hampstead's, reflect on the powerlessness of individuals in the face of forces they cannot control. George Roden's desire to see his beloved is persistently thwarted, just as Lord Llwddythlw's marriage is continually postponed, and Samuel Crocker's sanction for destroying Post Office documents is repeatedly adjourned. These narratives end happily, however: Roden turns out to be a son of the Duca di Crinola ('Duke of Horsehair'), Llwddythlw is badgered into marriage, and Crocker gets off with a reprimand. If they resemble Hampstead, they do so with a difference: 'The comic paralysis revealed in these sub-plots throws Hampstead's tragic frustration into sharper relief' (Nardin 1999: 349). This contrast between tragic frustration and comic paralysis on the level of the plot is similar to the contrast between the exalted and the commonplace on the level of the sentence. It certainly creates a kind of friction that leaves the reader shifting uncomfortably, which is the mark of pure comedy. As Meredith notes, the conception of the comic in Menander and Molière often 'refines even to pain', for 'keen-edged intelligence . . . is by nature merciless' (1877: 19, 26).

It is by means of comedy, then, that Trollope elaborates on the level of genre his understanding of perfect love. Comedy yields the 'wholesome' effect that is folded within Trollope's conceptualisation of love: believing that love should be guided by chance and intuition may be joyful, but embracing the knowledge that we will never fully know our beloved is painful. When love is approached as a form of tact, it may stave off divorce, but not dissatisfaction. Implying that the future is never closed off, this awareness nevertheless gives the reader a comic sense of relief: Trollope's comedies teach us that regarding the present with tact can extend it into the kind of future we might love.

Notes

1. James Kincaid's seminal study (1978) provides the most sustained analysis of Trollope's novels against the history of the comedy of manners.
2. Although none of Menander's works were known in their entirety until the 1950s, he had a profound influence on Western literature, in no small part thanks to the Latin adaptations by Plautus and Terence. This current peaked in the work of Molière and kept up its strength throughout the eighteenth century, as the work of Richard Brinsley Sheridan illustrates. A text of Menander's Δύσκολος (*The Grouch*) was discovered in the mid-1950s, written on papyrus. This is, so far, the only complete copy of a Greek New Comedy that we possess. Δύσκολος illustrates Menander's indirect influence: its portrayal of a skinflint may have inspired Plautus's characterisation of Euclio in his *Aulularia* (*The Pot of Gold*), which was in turn adapted by Molière in *L'Avare* (*The Miser*). This figure appears in Trollope's novels as well. Consider, for instance, Squire Prosper in *Mr Scarborough's Family*. On the furtive operations of influence in the nineteenth century, see Douglas-Fairhurst (2004).
3. Consider, for instance, Heine's 'Allnächtlich im Traume':

   Allnächtlich im Traume seh' ich dich,
   Und sehe dich freundlich grüßen,
   Und lautaufweinend stürz' ich mich
   Zu deinen süßen Füßen.

   Du siehst mich an wehmütiglich,
   Und schüttelst das blonde Köpfchen;
   Aus deinen Augen schleichen sich
   Die Perlentränentröpfchen.

   Du sagst mir heimlich ein leises Wort,
   Und gibst mir den Strauß von Zypressen –
   Ich wache auf, und der Strauß ist fort,
   Und's Wort hab' ich vergessen. (Heine 1975: 189)

   Each night in dreams thou com'st to me,
   I hear thee gently calling,
   And then, loud weeping leap to thee,
   At thy dear feet down falling.

Thou look'st on me so mournfully,
Thy fair blonde tresses shaking;
Then from thine eyes all tremblingly
The pearly tears come breaking.

Thou breathes a word in under-tone,
And givest me cypress braided:
I wake – and the cypress-wreath is gone,
And the word from my memory faded. (Leland 1864: 100–1)

Heine's poem ends ironically: the speaker is about to reach the moment of truth, only to awaken and have it cut off. This anti-climax is an element of bathos, as is the poem's contrast between its genre – the lover's lament – and its diction: 'The blatantly unpoetic 'süßen Füßen' is Heine's way of showing that the poet's despair is not tragic but ridiculous' (Brauner 1981: 264). The poem is a bit of a joke, the speaker a bit of a prankster. As such, he resembles the skilled comedian, who 'keeps up a tacit understanding' with his listeners or readers and 'makes them, unconsciously to themselves, a party in the scene' (Lamb 1931: 229). Just as Elia envisages a bond between actor and audience, so does Heine's poem create an understanding between speaker and reader. Audience and reader are reminded that the speaker is mocking himself, yet they cannot but feel with him.

4. This term itself goes back to Alexander Pope's essay '*Peri Bathous*, or the Art of Sinking in Poetry' (1727). Pope's essay is a parody of Longinus's treatise *On the Sublime* (Περὶ ὕψους). It is a manual on how to write poetry badly, illustrated with pedestrian verses crafted by his literary adversaries, the Dunces. These verses are unintended failures. While they attempt to evoke pathos and sympathy, they overreach their mark, and thus tumble into jocularity. Pope's poetry is one example, but one could just as well refer to Hoffmann's *Lebens-Ansichten des Katers Murr* (1819–21) or John Kennedy Toole's *A Confederacy of Dunces* (1980).
5. When Leigh Hunt published an edition of Restoration comedies in which he maintained, like his friend Lamb, that there is no ground for the charge of immorality, Thomas Babington Macaulay begged to disagree: 'this part of our literature is a disgrace to our language and our national character' (Macaulay 1841: 493). In the course of his review, Macaulay singles out Lamb's argument as 'altogether sophistical' (1841: 495) and refutes it on two counts. First, Restoration plays do represent real life: 'Here the costume, the manners, the topics of conversation are those of the real town, and of the passing day. The hero is in all superficial accomplishments exactly the fine gentleman, whom every youth in the pit would gladly resemble . . . A hundred little touches are employed to make the fictitious world appear like the actual world' (1841: 496). This is in itself not a sin. Second, however, this actual world is not amoral, but immoral. Macaulay believes that we must read the plays of Wycherley and Congreve in their historical context, that is, as a backlash against two decades of Puritan suppression: wickedness is the stuff that they are made of. There is, as a result, nothing 'conventional' about the plays' lack of decency: 'the immorality is of a sort which never can be out of date, and which all the force of religion, law, and public opinion united can but imperfectly

restrain' (1841: 496). This combination of realism and immorality is to be deplored. The Restoration comedy, in Macaulay's view, uses the capacity of the theatre to generate sympathy with characters who are fundamentally unsound. Macaulay is one of Trollope's personal heroes, both as a stylist and a historian. In Trollope's 1867 copy of Macaulay's *Critical and Historical Essays*, he records that the essay on Hunt met with his approval (Landow and Chew 2001: 155). In his literary criticism, moreover, Trollope repeatedly declares that his work was written with Macaulay's standards of moralism and realism in mind (1879b: 200; 1983: 791; 1999a: 106, 78, 235).

6. This review was not included in Smalley's *Trollope: The Critical Heritage*. Credit is due to Hugh Sykes Davies, who reads this little-known piece with a slightly different focus and translates the first half of the passage quoted here (Davies 1960: 82–5). This was not the only review of Trollope's novels to appear in the *Revue des Deux Mondes*. E. D. Forgues reviewed *The Bertrams* and *Castle Richmond* (15 September 1860), praising 'Trollope's almost scientific detachment in presenting his characters and their moral dilemmas' (Trollope 1983: 121, n. 8).
7. It is likely that Trollope had a hand in helping his son Henry write an article on the subject, announcing the fruits of Henry's efforts in a letter to John Blackwood with more bravado than the occasion warranted: 'Harry is coming out in the family line, having an article in February's Macmillan on the French Stage [under Louis XIV], which of course I regard as the best thing ever written on that subject' (see H. Trollope 1875; A. Trollope 1983: 642). Perhaps Trollope's interest in the world of Molière was kindled by his reading of Meredith, whose judgement Trollope set great store by, and whom he knew through his work for Chapman and Hall (Trollope 1983: 583, 636). In any case, Trollope's works bear the traces of this interest. His instinct for generous tolerance 'found in comedy, its historical "smuttiness" notwithstanding, his most natural medium of expression' (Herbert 1987: 21).
8. Freud believes that we should distinguish between the joke, the comic, and humour. Comedy and humour differ from the joke in that they originate in the preconscious, whereas the joke originates in the interaction between the preconscious and the unconscious. In turn, comedy and the joke differ from humour in that they rely on the difference between two ways of apprehending things, whereas humour does not: 'The condition required for comedy to arise is that we should be prompted to use two different ways of imagining for the same idea *simultaneously or in rapid succession*; it is between these that the "comparing" then takes place, producing the comic difference' (Freud 2002: 227). One could also look at Lady Amaldina's way of thinking from a more historical perspective. In *Hypocrisy and the Politics of Politeness*, Jenny Davidson 'demonstrates that thinking one thing and doing another was a perfectly acceptable and often powerfully pedagogical way of living in the world of the eighteenth century' (Davidson 2004; Hadley 2010: 52, n. 24).
9. Trollope was familiar with the horrors of consumption, horrors that were clearly on his mind while he was thinking about the novel. The setting of the novel alludes to the death of Trollope's brothers and sisters (Arthur,

Henry, Emily, and Cecilia): 'Hendon, the home of Lord Hampstead, is close to Hadley Cross, where Emily was buried, and Castle Hautboy, where Persiflage live[s], [is] close to Penrith, the first home of Cecilia Trollope and John Tilley' (Super 1990: 403, footnote).

Bibliography

Adams, James Eli (2012), *A History of Victorian Literature*, Oxford and Malden, MA: Wiley-Blackwell.
Adorno, Theodor (2005), *Beethoven: The Philosophy of Music*, ed. Rolf Tiedemann, trans. Edmund Jephcott, Cambridge: Polity Press.
Adorno, Theodor, and Max Horkheimer (1972), *Dialectic of Enlightenment*, trans. John Cumming, New York: Herder and Herder.
Aguirre, Robert D. (2005), *Informal Empire: Mexico and Central America in Victorian Culture*, Minneapolis: University of Minnesota Press.
Alessio, Dominic (2004), 'A Conservative Utopia? Anthony Trollope's *The Fixed Period* (1882)', *Journal of New Zealand Literature*, 22, 73–94.
Altbauer-Rudnik, Michal (2012), 'The Changing Faces of Love Torments: Continuity and Rupture in the Medical Diagnosis of Lovesickness in the Modern West', in Leona Toker (ed.), *Knowledge and Pain*, Amsterdam: Rodopi, pp. 81–99.
Ammar, Jean (2010), 'Saints and Sinners: The Physiognomy of Trollope's "Good" and "Bad" Girls', *Trollopiana*, 87, 10–17.
Anderson, Amanda (2001), *The Powers of Distance: Cosmopolitanism and the Cultivation of Detachment*, Princeton: Princeton University Press.
—(2005), 'Victorian Studies and the Two Modernities', *Victorian Studies*, 47.2, 195–203.
—(2007), 'Trollope's Modernity', *ELH*, 74.3, 509–34.
Anderson, Benedict (2006), *Imagined Communities: Reflections on the Origin and Spread of Nationalism*, London: Verso.
apRoberts, Ruth (1969), '*Cousin Henry*: Trollope's Note from Antiquity', *Nineteenth-Century Fiction*, 24.1, 93–8.
—(1971), *The Moral Trollope*, Athens: Ohio University Press.
Arendt, Hannah (2004), *The Origins of Totalitarianism*, New York: Schocken.
Arnold, Matthew (1858), *Merope: A Tragedy*, London: Longman.
—(1863), 'Heinrich Heine', *The Cornhill Magazine*, 8.44, 233–49.
—(1882), 'Literature and Science', *The Nineteenth Century*, 12.66, 216–30.
—(1960), 'On Translating Homer', in *On the Classical Tradition*, ed. R. H. Super, in *The Complete Prose Works of Matthew Arnold*, Ann Arbor: University of Michigan Press, vol. 1, pp. 97–216.
—(1993a), 'Equality', in Stefan Collini (ed.), *Culture and Anarchy and Other Writings*, Cambridge: Cambridge University Press, pp. 212–39.
—(1993b), 'Culture and Anarchy', in Stefan Collini (ed.), *Culture and Anarchy and Other Writings*, Cambridge: Cambridge University Press, pp. 53–211.

—(1996–2001), *The Letters of Matthew Arnold*, ed. Cecil Y. Lang, 6 vols, Charlottesville and London: University Press of Virginia.

Arrighi, Giovanni (1994), *The Long Twentieth Century: Money, Power and the Origins of Our Times*, London: Verso.

Auden, Wystan Hugh (1973), 'A Poet of the Actual', in Edward Mendelson (ed.), *Forewords and Afterwords*, London: Faber and Faber, pp. 262–7.

Bagehot, Walter (1995), 'A Later Judgment: Caesarism after Thirteen Years', in Forrest Morgan (ed.), *The Works of Walter Bagehot*, London: Routledge and Thoemmes, vol. 2, pp. 440–7.

—(2001), *The English Constitution*, ed. Paul Smith, Cambridge: Cambridge University Press.

Bakhtin, Mikhail (1968), *Rabelais and His World*, trans. Hélène Iswolsky, Cambridge, MA: MIT Press.

Balfour, Ian (2006), 'Torso: (The) Sublime Sex, Beautiful Bodies, and the Matter of the Text', *Eighteenth-Century Studies*, 39.3, 323–36.

Banville, John (1998), *The Untouchable*, London: Picador.

Bartlett, Thomas (2010), *Ireland: A History*, Cambridge: Cambridge University Press.

Baucom, Ian (2005), *Specters of the Atlantic*, Durham, NC, and London: Duke University Press.

Beard, Mary (2012), 'Highway Codes', *Times Literary Supplement*, 5693, 3.

Beckman, Ericka (2012), 'An Oil Well Named Macondo: Latin American Literature in the Time of Global Capital', *PMLA*, 127.1, 145–51.

Beesly, E. S. (1865), 'Catiline as a Party Leader', *The Fortnightly Review*, 1, 167–84.

—(1866), 'Cicero and Clodius', *The Fortnightly Review*, 5.28, 421–41.

Bell, Duncan (2006), 'From Ancient to Modern in Victorian Imperial Thought', *The Historical Journal*, 49.3, 735–59.

Ben-Yishai, Ayelet (2010), 'Trollope and the Law', in Carolyn Dever and Lisa Niles (eds), *The Cambridge Companion to Anthony Trollope*, Cambridge: Cambridge University Press, pp. 155–67.

Benjamin, Walter (2003a), 'The Work of Art in the Age of Its Technological Reproducibility', in *Selected Writings: Volume 4, 1938–1940*, ed. Howard Eiland and Michael Jennings, Cambridge, MA: Harvard University Press, pp. 251–83.

—(2003b), 'The Paris of the Second Empire in Baudelaire', in *Selected Writings: Volume 4, 1938–1940*, ed. Howard Eiland and Michael Jennings, Cambridge, MA: Harvard University Press, pp. 3–92.

—(2004a), 'On the Program of the Coming Philosophy', in *Selected Writings: Volume 1, 1913–1926*, ed. Howard Eiland and Michael Jennings, Cambridge, MA: Harvard University Press, pp. 100–10.

—(2004b), 'Critique of Violence', in *Selected Writings: Volume 1, 1913–1926*, ed. Howard Eiland and Michael Jennings, Cambridge, MA: Harvard University Press, pp. 236–52.

—(2004c), 'The Task of the Translator', in *Selected Writings: Volume 1, 1913–1926*, ed. Howard Eiland and Michael Jennings, Cambridge, MA: Harvard University Press, pp. 253–63.

—(2004d), 'Fate and Character', in *Selected Writings: Volume 1, 1913–1926*, ed. Howard Eiland and Michael Jennings, Cambridge, MA: Harvard University Press, pp. 201–6.

—(2005), 'Karl Kraus', in *Selected Writings: Volume 2, Part 2, 1931–1934*,

ed. Howard Eiland, Michael Jennings, and Gary Smith, Cambridge, MA: Harvard University Press, pp. 433–58.
—(2009), *The Origin of German Tragic Drama*, trans. John Osborne, London and New York: Verso.
Biagini, Eugenio F. (1996), 'Liberalism and Direct Democracy: J. S. Mill and the Model of Ancient Athens', in E. F. Biagini (ed.), *Citizenship and Community: Liberals, Radicals and Collective Identites in the British Isles, 1865–1931*, Cambridge: Cambridge University Press, pp. 21–44.
—(2003), 'Neo-Roman Liberalism: "Republican" Values and British Liberalism, ca. 1860–1875', *History of European Ideas*, 29.1, 55–72.
Bigelow, Gordon (2003), *Fiction, Famine, and the Rise of Economics in Victorian Britain and Ireland*, Cambridge: Cambridge University Press.
Blumberg, Ilana M. (2004), '"Unnatural Self-Sacrifice": Trollope's Ethic of Mutual Benefit', *Nineteenth-Century Literature*, 58.4, 506–46.
Blumenthal-Barby, Martin (2009), 'Pernicious Bastardizations: Benjamin's Ethics of Pure Violence', *MLN*, 124.3, 728–51.
Blythe, Helen Lucy (2014), *The Victorian Colonial Romance with the Antipodes*, New York: Palgrave Macmillan.
Boddice, Rob (2008), '"Manliness and the Morality of Field Sports": E. A. Freeman and Anthony Trollope', *Historian*, 70.1, 1–29.
Bollas, Christopher (1989), *The Shadow of the Object: Psychoanalysis of the Unthought Known*, New York: Columbia University Press.
Booth, Bradford A. (1946), 'Trollope on Froude's *Caesar*', *Trollopian*, 1.2, 33–47.
—(1958), *Anthony Trollope: Aspects of His Life and Art*, London: Edward Hulton.
Booth, Wayne Clayson (1974), *A Rhetoric of Irony*, Chicago and London: University of Chicago Press.
Bowen, John (2011), 'Introduction', in Anthony Trollope, *Phineas Redux*, ed. John Bowen, Oxford: Oxford University Press, pp. xi–xxix.
Brand, Dana (1991), *The Spectator and the City in Nineteenth-Century American Literature*, Cambridge: Cambridge University Press.
Brauner, Charles S. (1981), 'Irony in the Heine Lieder of Schubert and Schumann', *The Musical Quarterly*, 67.2, 261–81.
Briggs, Asa (1970), *Victorian People: A Reassessment of Persons and Themes 1851–67*, Chicago: University of Chicago Press.
Bronk, Richard (2009), *The Romantic Economist: Imagination in Economics*, Cambridge: Cambridge University Press.
Brooks, Cleanth (1947), *The Well Wrought Urn: Studies in the Structure of Poetry*, New York: Reynal & Hitchcock.
Bruns, Gerald L. (1979), 'Allegory and Satire: A Rhetorical Meditation', *New Literary History*, 11.1, 121–32.
Burgess, Miranda (2006), 'The National Tale and Allied Genres, 1770s–1840s', in John Wilson Foster (ed.), *The Cambridge Companion to the Irish Novel*, Cambridge: Cambridge University Press, pp. 39–59.
Burke, Edmund (1834), *Works*, 2 vols, London: Holdsworth and Ball.
Buzard, James (2010), 'Trollope and Travel', in Carolyn Dever and Lisa Niles (eds), *The Cambridge Companion to Anthony Trollope*, Cambridge: Cambridge University Press, pp. 168–80.
Byler, Lauren (2009), 'If the Shoe Fits . . . Trollope and the Girl', *Novel: A Forum on Fiction*, 42.2, 268–77.

Byron, George Gordon (1986), *Don Juan*, ed. Jerome J. McGann, in *The Complete Poetical Works*, vol. 5, Oxford: Clarendon Press.

Cain, P. J., and A. G. Hopkins (1993), *British Imperialism: Innovation and Expansion, 1688–1914*, London and New York: Longman.

Cheah, Pheng (1999), 'Grounds of Comparison', *Diacritics*, 29.4, 2–18.

Cicéron (1962), *Correspondance*, ed. L.-A. Constans, *Collection des universités de France publiée sous le patronage de l'association Guillaume Budé*, Paris: Société d'Édition «Les Belles Lettres».

Clarke, John W. (1975), *The Language and Style of Anthony Trollope*, London: André Deutsch.

Cockshut, A. O. J. (1968), *Anthony Trollope*, London: Methuen.

Colebrook, Claire (2004), *Irony*, London: Routledge.

Colella, Silvana (2006), 'Sweet Money: Cultural and Economic Value in Trollope's *Autobiography*', *Nineteenth-Century Contexts*, 28.1, 5–20.

Coleridge, Samuel Taylor (1954), *Biographia Literaria*, ed. J. Shawcross, 2 vols, Oxford: Oxford University Press.

Collini, Stefan (1993a), *Public Moralists: Political Thought and Intellectual Life in Britain*, Oxford: Clarendon Press.

—(1993b), 'Arnold', in A. Laurence Le Quesne (ed.), *Victorian Thinkers: Carlyle, Ruskin, Arnold, Morris*, Oxford and New York: Oxford University Press, pp. 191–326.

—(1999), *English Pasts: Essays in History and Culture*, Oxford: Oxford University Press.

Collins, W. Lucas (1883), 'Autobiography of Anthony Trollope', *Blackwood's Magazine*, 134.817, 577–96.

Conrad, Joseph (2007), *The Collected Letters of Joseph Conrad: 1923–1924*, ed. Laurence Davies and Gene M. Moore, vol. 8, Cambridge: Cambridge University Press.

Copeland, Rita, and Peter T. Struck (2010), *The Cambridge Companion to Allegory*, Cambridge: Cambridge University Press.

Corbett, Mary Jean (2000), *Allegories of Union in Irish and English Writing, 1790–1870: Politics, History, and the Family from Edgeworth to Arnold*, Cambridge: Cambridge University Press.

Craig, David M. (2010), 'Advanced Conservative Liberalism: Party and Principle in Trollope's Parliamentary Novels', *Victorian Literature and Culture*, 38.2, 355–71.

Cronin, John (1980), 'Trollope and the Matter of Ireland', in Tony Bareham (ed.), *Anthony Trollope*, London: Vision, pp. 13–35.

Culler, Jonathan (1999), 'Anderson and the Novel', *Diacritics*, 29.4, 19–39.

Curthoys, M. C. (2011), 'Collins, William Lucas (1815–1887)', *Oxford Dictionary of National Biography*, <http://www.oxforddnb.com/view/article/5960>, accessed 2 January 2013.

Dames, Nicholas (2003), 'Trollope and the Career: Vocational Trajectories and the Management of Ambition', *Victorian Studies*, 45.2, 247–78.

—(2007), *The Physiology of the Novel: Reading, Neural Science, and the Form of Victorian Fiction*, Oxford: Oxford University Press.

Davidoff, Lenore (1973), *The Best Circles: Women and Society in Victorian England*, Totowa, NJ: Rowman & Littlefield.

Davidson, Jenny (2004), *Hypocrisy and the Politics of Politeness: Manners and Morals from Locke to Austen*, New York: Cambridge University Press.

Davies, Hugh Sykes (1960), 'Trollope and His Style', *A Review of English Literature*, 1.4, 73–85.

Davis, Tracy C. (2000), *The Economics of the British Stage*, Cambridge and New York: Cambridge University Press.

de Graef, Ortwin, and Anke Gilleir (2010), '"The Stigma of Its Present Name": Matthew Arnold's Scripts of State', *Occasion: Interdisciplinary Studies in the Humanities*, 2, 22 pages, <http://occasion.stanford.edu/node/48>, accessed 21 July 2013.

De Quincey, Thomas (2001), 'Cicero', in *Works of De Quincey*, ed. Grevel Lindop and John Whale, London: Pickering and Chatto, vol. 13, pp. 159–88.

Delany, Paul (2002), *Literature, Money and the Market: From Trollope to Amis*, New York: Palgrave.

DeLaura, David J. (1969), *Hebrew and Hellene in Victorian England: Newman, Arnold, and Pater*, Austin: University of Texas Press.

Denenholz Morse, Deborah (1987), *Women in Trollope's Palliser Novels*, Ann Arbor: UMI Research Press.

—(2013), *Reforming Trollope: Race, Gender, and Englishness in the Novels of Anthony Trollope*, Aldershot: Ashgate.

Dickens, Charles (2005), *The Mystery of Edwin Drood and Other Stories*, ed. Peter Preston, Ware: Wordsworth Editions.

Dolin, Kieran (1999), *Fiction and the Law: Legal Discourse in Victorian and Modernist Literature*, Cambridge: Cambridge University Press.

Douglas-Fairhurst, Robert (2004), *Victorian Afterlives: The Shaping of Influence in Nineteenth-Century Literature*, Oxford: Oxford University Press.

—(2011), *Becoming Dickens: The Invention of a Novelist*, Cambridge, MA, and London: The Belknap Press of Harvard University Press.

Dowling, Linda (1994), *Hellenism and Homosexuality in Victorian Oxford*, Ithaca, NY: Cornell University Press.

Duckenfield, Mark, Stefan Altorfer, and Benedikt Koehler (eds) (2006), *The History of Financial Disasters, 1763–1995*, 3 vols, London: Pickering and Chatto.

Duguid, Paul (2002), 'Getting and Spending', *Times Literary Supplement*, 5203, 22–1.

Durey, Jill Felicity (2002), *Trollope and the Church of England*, Basingstoke: Palgrave.

Earle, Bo (2006), 'Policing and Performing Liberal Individuality in Anthony Trollope's *The Warden*', *Nineteenth-Century Literature*, 61.1, 1–31.

Edwards, Owen Dudley (1983), 'Anthony Trollope, the Irish Writer', *Nineteenth-Century Fiction*, 38.1, 1–42.

Edwards, Peter David (1978), *Anthony Trollope, His Art and Scope*, Brighton: Harvester Press.

Elias, Norbert (2000), *The Civilizing Process: Sociogenetic and Psychogenetic Investigations*, trans. Edmund Jephcott, Oxford: Blackwell.

Elliott, Robert C. (1960), *The Power of Satire: Magic, Ritual, Art*, Princeton: Princeton University Press.

Evangelista, Stefano (2009a), 'Vernon Lee in the Vatican: The Uneasy Alliance of Aestheticism and Archaelogy', *Victorian Studies*, 52.1, 31–41.

—(2009b), *British Aestheticism and Ancient Greece: Hellenism, Reception, Gods in Exile*, Basingstoke: Palgrave Macmillan.

Farrar, Frederic William (1867), *Essays on a Liberal Education*, London: Macmillan.

—(1868), 'Public School Education', *The Fortnightly Review*, 3.15, 233–49.
Felber, Lynette (2010), 'The Advanced Conservative Liberal: Victorian Liberalism and the Aesthetics of Anthony Trollope's Palliser Novels', *Modern Philology*, 107.3, 355–71.
Felluga, Dino (2015), *Critical Theory: The Key Concepts*, New York: Routledge.
Ferguson, Frances (1992), *Solitude and the Sublime: Romanticism and the Aesthetics of Individuation*, New York and London: Routledge.
Fessenbecker, Patrick (2014), 'Anthony Trollope on Akrasia, Self-Deception, and Ethical Confusion', *Victorian Studies*, 56.4, 649–74.
Finn, Margot (2002), 'Victorian Law, Literature and History: Three Ships Passing in the Night', *Journal of Victorian Culture*, 7.1, 134–46.
Ford, Trowbridge H. (1973), 'Dicey's Conversion to Unionism', *Irish Historical Studies*, 18.72, 552–82.
Forster, W. E. (1852), 'The Early Quakers and Quakerism', *Westminster Review*, 57.112, 593–624.
Foster, R. F. (1976), *Charles Stewart Parnell: The Man and His Family*, Hassocks: Harvester Press.
—(2002), 'Stopping the Hunt: Trollope and the Memory of Ireland', in *The Irish Story: Telling Tales and Making It Up in Ireland*, Harmondsworth: Penguin, pp. 127–47.
—(2011), *Paddy and Mr Punch: Connections in Irish and English History*, London: Faber and Faber.
Foucault, Michel (1977), *Discipline and Punish: The Birth of the Prison*, trans. Alan Sheridan, New York: Vintage.
—(1997), *'Society Must Be Defended': Lectures at the Collège de France 1975–76*, ed. Mauro Bertani and Allessandro Fontano, trans. David Macey, New York: Picador.
—(2008), *The Birth of Biopolitics. Lectures at the Collège de France 1978–79*, ed. Michel Senellart, trans. Graham Burchell, Basingstoke: Palgrave Macmillan.
Frank, Cathrine O. (2008), 'Trial Separations: Divorce, Disestablishment, and Home Rule in *Phineas Redux*', *College Literature*, 35.3, 30–56.
Franklin, J. Jeffrey (2003), 'Anthony Trollope Meets Pierre Bourdieu: The Conversion of Capital as Plot in the Mid-Victorian British Novel', *Victorian Literature and Culture*, 31.2, 501–21.
Frederickson, Kathleen (2007), 'Liberalism and the Time of Instinct', *Victorian Studies*, 49.2, 302–12.
Freeman, Edward Augustus (1869), 'The Morality of Field Sports', *The Fortnightly Review*, 6.34, 353–85.
—(1883), 'Anthony Trollope', *Macmillan's Magazine*, 47.279, 236–40.
Freud, Sigmund (1961), *Totem and Taboo: Some Points of Agreement between the Mental Lives of Savages and Neurotics*, trans. James Strachey, London: Routledge and Kegan Paul.
—(2002), *The Joke and Its Relation to the Unconscious*, ed. Adam Phillips, trans. Joyce Crick, Harmondsworth: Penguin.
Friedman, Norman (1955), 'Point of View in Fiction: The Development of a Critical Concept', *PMLA*, 70.5, 1160–84.
Froude, James Anthony (1879), *Caesar: A Sketch*, London: Longmans and Green.
Frye, Northrop (1957), *Anatomy of Criticism*, Princeton: Princeton University Press.

Fuchs, Catherine (1982), *La Paraphrase*, Paris: Presses Universitaires de France.

Gagnier, Regenia (2000), *The Insatiability of Human Wants: Economics and Aesthetics in Market Society*, Chicago: University of Chicago Press.

—(2009), 'Gender, Liberalism, and Resentment', in Margaret Markwick, Deborah Denenholz Morse, and Regenia Gagnier (eds), *The Politics of Gender in Anthony Trollope's Novels: New Readings for the Twenty-First Century*, Aldershot: Ashgate, pp. 235–48.

Gallagher, Catherine (2006), 'The Rise of Fictionality', in Franco Moretti (ed.), *The Novel, 1: History, Geography, and Culture*, Princeton: Princeton University Press, pp. 337–63.

Garratt, Peter K. (2012), 'Moving Worlds: Fictionality and Illusion after Coleridge', *Literature Compass*, 9.11, 752–63.

Gasché, Rodolphe (1994), 'Objective Diversions: On Some Kantian Themes in Benjamin's "The Work of Art in the Age of Mechanical Reproduction"', in Andrew Benjamin and Peter Osborne (eds), *Walter Benjamin's Philosophy: Destruction and Experience*, New York: Routledge, pp. 183–204.

Genette, Gérard (1980), *Narrative Discourse: An Essay in Method*, trans. Jane E. Lewin, Ithaca, NY: Cornell University Press.

Giles, Paul (2008), 'Antipodean American Literature: Franklin, Twain, and the Sphere of Subalternity', *American Literary History*, 20.1–2, 22–50.

Gill, James E. (1995), *Cutting Edges: Postmodern Critical Essays on Eighteenth-Century Satire*, Knoxville: University of Tennessee Press.

Glendinning, Victoria (1994), *Anthony Trollope*, Harmondsworth: Penguin.

—(2010), 'Trollope as Autobiographer and Biographer', in Carolyn Dever and Lisa Niles (eds), *The Cambridge Companion to Anthony Trollope*, Cambridge: Cambridge University Press, pp. 17–30.

Goethe, Johann Wolfgang von (2007), *The Man of Fifty*, trans. Andrew Piper, London: Hesperus.

Goldhill, Simon (2010), review of *British Aestheticism and Ancient Greece: Hellenism, Reception, Gods in Exile* by Stefano Evangelista, *Victorian Studies*, 52.3, 474–6.

—(2011), *Victorian Culture and Classical Antiquity: Art, Opera, Fiction, and the Proclamation of Modernity*, Princeton and Oxford: Princeton University Press.

Goodlad, Lauren M. E. (2003), *Victorian Literature and the Victorian State: Character and Governance in a Liberal Society*, Baltimore: Johns Hopkins University Press.

—(2008), '"Character Worth Speaking Of": Individuality, John Stuart Mill, and the Critique of Liberalism', *Victorians Institute Journal*, 36, 7–46.

—(2009), 'Trollopian "Foreign Policy": Rootedness and Cosmopolitanism in the Mid-Victorian Global Imaginary', *PMLA*, 124.2, 437–54.

—(2010a), 'The Trollopian Geopolitical Aesthetic', *Literature Compass*, 7.9, 867–75.

—(2010b), 'Cosmopolitanism's Actually Existing Beyond: Toward a Victorian Geopolitical Aesthetic', *Victorian Literature and Culture*, 38.2, 399–411.

Goodlad, Lauren M. E., and Julia Wright (2007), 'Introduction and Keywords', *Romanticism and Victorianism on the Net*, 48, 38 pages, <http://www.erudit.org/revue/ravon/2007/v/n48/017435ar.html>, accessed 24 May 2015.

Gray, Peter (2002), 'The Peculiarities of Irish Land Tenure 1800–1914: From Agent of Impoverishment to Agent of Pacification', in Donald Winch and

Patrick Karl O'Brien (eds), *The Political Economy of British Historical Experience, 1688–1914*, Oxford: Oxford University Press, pp. 139–62.

Gray, Richard T. (2012), 'Accounting for Pleasure: Sigmund Freud, Carl Menger, and the Economically Minded Human Being', *PMLA*, 127.1, 122–30.

Griffin, Dustin H. (1994), *Satire: A Critical Reintroduction*, Lexington: University Press of Kentucky.

Grote, George (1880), *History of Greece*, New York: Harper and Brothers.

Habermas, Jürgen (1989), *The Structural Transformation of the Public Sphere: An Inquiry into a Category of Bourgeois Society*, trans. Thomas Burger, Cambridge, MA: MIT Press.

Hadley, Elaine (2005), 'On a Darkling Plain: Victorian Liberalism and the Fantasy of Agency', *Victorian Studies*, 48.1, 92–102.

—(2010), *Living Liberalism: Practical Citizenship in Victorian Britain*, Chicago: University of Chicago Press.

Hall, N. John (1991), *Trollope: A Biography*, Oxford: Clarendon Press.

Halperin, John (1999), 'Introduction', in Anthony Trollope, *The American Senator*, ed. John Halperin, Oxford: Oxford University Press, pp. vii–xiv.

Halpern, Richard (1997), *Shakespeare among the Moderns*, Ithaca, NY, and London: Cornell University Press.

Hamer, Mary (1993), 'Introduction and Notes', in Anthony Trollope, *The Landleaguers*, ed. Mary Hamer, Oxford: Oxford University Press, pp. ix–xxii, 413–44.

Hansen, Jim (2005), 'Formalism and Its Malcontents: Benjamin and De Man on the Function of Allegory', *New Literary History*, 35.4, 663–83.

Hansen, Miriam Bratu (2008), 'Benjamin's Aura', *Critical Inquiry*, 34.2, 336–75.

Harootunian, Harry (2007), 'Remembering the Historical Present', *Critical Inquiry*, 33.3, 471–94.

Harrison, Frederic (1878a), 'The English School of Jurisprudence: Part I.—Austin and Maine on Sovereignty', *The Fortnightly Review*, 24.142, 475–92.

—(1878b), 'The English School of Jurisprudence: Part II.—Bentham's and Austin's Analysis of Law', *The Fortnightly Review*, 24.143, 682–703.

—(1879), 'The English School of Jurisprudence: Part III.—the Historical Method', *The Fortnightly Review*, 25.145, 114–30.

Hartley, Lucy (2001), *Physiognomy and the Meaning of Expression in Nineteenth-Century Culture*, Cambridge: Cambridge University Press.

Harvey, Geoffrey (1980), *The Art of Anthony Trollope*, London: Weidenfeld and Nicolson.

—(1999), 'Religious Faith and Worship', in R. C. Terry (ed.), *Oxford Reader's Companion to Trollope*, Oxford: Oxford University Press, pp. 454–5.

Hawes, Derek (1999), 'Was Trollope a Freemason?', *Trollopiana*, 47, 14–22.

Heath, Kay (2006), 'In the Eye of the Beholder: Victorian Age Construction and the Specular Self', *Victorian Literature and Culture*, 34.1, 27–45.

Heine, Heinrich (1975), *Buch der Lieder*, ed. Pierre Grappin, Hamburg: Hoffmann und Campe.

Hensley, Nathan K. (2009), '*Armadale* and the Logic of Liberalism', *Victorian Studies*, 51.4, 607–32.

Herbert, Christopher (1987), *Trollope and Comic Pleasure*, Chicago: University of Chicago Press.

—(1991), 'The Novel of Cultural Symbolism: *Doctor Thorne*', in *Culture and*

Anomie: Ethnographic Imagination in the Nineteenth Century, Chicago: University of Chicago Press, pp. 253–99.

Hogle, Jerrold E. (2002), 'Introduction', in Jerrold E. Hogle (ed.), *The Cambridge Companion to Gothic Fiction*, Cambridge: Cambridge University Press, pp. 1–20.

Humphreys, Susan L. (1978), 'Trollope on the Sublime and Beautiful', *Nineteenth-Century Fiction*, 33.2, 194–214.

Hurst, Isobel (2006), *Victorian Women Writers and the Classics: The Feminine of Homer*, Oxford: Oxford University Press.

—(2009), 'Ancient and Modern Women in the *Woman's World*', *Victorian Studies*, 52.1, 42–51.

—(2010), 'Victorian Literature and the Reception of Greece and Rome', *Literature Compass*, 7.6, 484–95.

Hynes, John G. (1988), 'The American Senator: Anthony Trollope's Critical "Chronicle of a Winter at Dillsborough"', *English Studies*, 69.1, 48–54.

Ingelbien, Raphaël (2010), 'Elizabeth Gaskell's "The Poor Clare" and the Irish Famine', *Irish University Review*, 40.2, 1–19.

James, Henry (1883), 'Trollope', *The Century*, 26.3, 385–95.

—(1971), 'Our Mutual Friend', in Philip Collins (ed.), *Dickens: The Critical Heritage*, London: Routledge and Kegan Paul, pp. 479–82.

Jameson, Fredric (1991), *Postmodernism, or, the Cultural Logic of Late Capitalism*, London: Verso.

—(1992), *The Geopolitical Aesthetic: Cinema and Space in the World System*, Bloomington: Indiana University Press.

Jay, Martin (1998), 'Experience without a Subject: Walter Benjamin and the Novel', in *Cultural Semantics: Keywords of Our Time*, Amherst: University of Massachusetts Press, pp. 47–61.

Jenkins, Anthony (1999), 'Drama, Elizabethan and Jacobean', in R. C. Terry (ed.), *Oxford Reader's Companion to Trollope*, Oxford: Oxford University Press, pp. 161–2.

Jenkyns, Richard (1980), *The Victorians and Ancient Greece*, Oxford: Blackwell.

Jöttkandt, Sigi (2006), 'Truths of Beauty, Truths of Love in Trollope's Novels of Beautiful Men', paper presented at the 'Trollope and Gender' conference at the University of Exeter, 17–19 July 2006.

Juergensmeyer, Mark (2000), *Terror in the Mind of God: The Global Rise of Religious Violence*, Berkeley, Los Angeles, and London: University of California Press.

Kahn, Paul (2005), *Putting Liberalism in Its Place*, Princeton: Princeton University Press.

Keen, Suzanne (2002), 'Quaker Dress, Sexuality, and the Domestication of Reform in the Victorian Novel', *Victorian Literature and Culture*, 30.1, 211–36.

Kendrick, Walter (1980), *The Novel-Machine: The Theory and Fiction of Anthony Trollope*, Baltimore: Johns Hopkins University Press.

Kernan, Alvin Bernard (1959), *The Cankered Muse: Satire of the English Renaissance*, New Haven, CT: Yale University Press.

Kincaid, James (1978), *The Novels of Anthony Trollope*, Oxford: Clarendon Press.

Kindleberger, Charles Poor (1990), *Historical Economics: Art or Science?*, Berkeley and Los Angeles: University of California Press.

Kirsch, Adam (2012), 'At Home in the World of Nobjects', *Times Literary Supplement*, 5702, 28.

Lamb, Charles (1912), 'On the Artificial Comedy of the Last Century', in *Elia and the Last Essays of Elia*, ed. E. V. Lucas, *The Works of Charles and Mary Lamb*, London: Methuen, vol. 2, pp. 161–8.

—(1931), 'Stage Illusion', in *The Essays of Elia and the Last Essays of Elia*, Oxford: Oxford University Press, pp. 229–32.

Landow, George P., and Ernest Chew (2001), 'Anthony Trollope's Marginalia in Macaulay's Critical and Historical Essays', *Notes and Queries*, 48.2, 152–5.

Langbauer, Laurie (1999), *Novels of Everyday Life: The Series in English Fiction, 1850–1930*, Ithaca, NY: Cornell University Press.

Lansbury, Coral (1981), *The Reasonable Man: Trollope's Legal Fiction*, Princeton: Princeton University Press.

Leacock, Nina K. (2002), 'Character, Silence, and the Novel: Walter Benjamin on Goethe's *Elective Affinities*', *Narrative*, 10.3, 277–306.

Leland, Charles G. (1864), *Heine's Book of Songs*, Philadelphia: Frederik Leypoldt.

Letwin, Shirley (1982), *The Gentleman in Trollope: Individuality and Moral Conduct*, Cambridge, MA: Harvard University Press.

Luhmann, Niklas (1998), *Love as Passion: The Codification of Intimacy*, ed. Mieke Bal and Hent de Vries, trans. Jeremy Gaines and Doris L. Jones, Stanford: Stanford University Press.

Macaulay, Thomas Babington (1841), 'Comic Dramatists of the Restoration', *Edinburgh Review*, 72.146, 490–528.

McCann, Andrew Lachlan (2004), *Marcus Clarke's Bohemia. Literature and Modernity in Colonial Melbourne*, Melbourne: Melbourne University Press.

McCormack, W. J. (1994), *From Burke to Beckett: Ascendancy, Tradition and Betrayal in Literary History*, Cork: Cork University Press.

McCourt, John (2015), *Writing the Frontier: Anthony Trollope between Britain and Ireland*, Oxford: Oxford University Press.

McDonald, Russ (2009), *Shakespeare's Late Style*, Cambridge: Cambridge University Press.

McGann, Tara (2008), 'Literary Realism in the Wake of Business Cycle Theory', in Francis O'Gorman (ed.), *Victorian Literature and Finance*, Oxford: Oxford University Press, pp. 133–56.

Machosky, Brenda (2010), *Thinking Allegory Otherwise*, Stanford: Stanford University Press.

McKeon, Michael (2002), *The Origins of the English Novel, 1600–1740*, Baltimore: Johns Hopkins University Press.

McLaughlin, Kevin (2008), 'Culture and Messianism: Disinterestedness in Arnold', *Victorian Studies*, 50.4, 615–39.

McMaster, Juliet (1978), *Trollope's Palliser Novels*, New York: Oxford University Press.

McMaster, R. D. (1986), *Trollope and the Law*, New York: St. Martin's Press.

McWilliam, Rohan (2007), *The Tichborne Claimant: A Victorian Sensation*, London: Hambledon Continuum.

Maine, Henry Sumner (1861), *Ancient Law: Its Connection with the Early History of Society, and Its Relation to Modern Ideas*, London: John Murray.

Malachuk, Daniel S. (2005), *Perfection, the State, and Victorian Liberalism*, Basingstoke: Palgrave Macmillan.

Markwick, Margaret (1997), *Trollope and Women*, London: Hambledon Press.

—(2007), *New Men in Trollope's Novels: Rewriting the Victorian Male*, Aldershot: Ashgate.

Matz, Aaron (2010), *Satire in an Age of Realism*, Cambridge: Cambridge University Press.

Meredith, George (1877), 'On the Idea of Comedy, and of the Uses of the Comic Spirit', *New Quarterly Magazine*, 8, 1–40.

—(1912), *Letters, Collected and Edited by His Son. Volume 1, 1844–1881, The Works of George Meredith*, 28 vols, New York: Charles Scribner's Sons.

Michie, Elsie (2006), 'The Odd Couple: Anthony Trollope and Henry James', *The Henry James Review*, 27.1, 10–23.

Mieszkowski, Jan (2004), 'Art Forms', in David S. Ferris (ed.), *The Cambridge Companion to Walter Benjamin*, Cambridge: Cambridge University Press, pp. 35–53.

Mill, John Stuart (1967a), 'The Quarterly Review on Political Economy', in *Essays on Economics and Society*, ed. J. M. Robson, *Collected Works of John Stuart Mill*, London: University of Toronto Press/Routledge and Kegan Paul, vol. 4, pp. 25–43.

—(1967b), 'The Currency Question', in *Essays on Economics and Society*, ed. J. M. Robson, *Collected Works of John Stuart Mill*, London: University of Toronto Press/Routledge and Kegan Paul, vol. 4, pp. 343–61.

—(1978), 'Grote's History of Greece II', in *Essays on Philosophy and the Classics*, ed. J. M. Robson, *Collected Works of John Stuart Mill*, London: University of Toronto Press/Routledge and Kegan Paul, vol. 11, pp. 307–38.

—(1981a), *Autobiography*, in *Autobiography and Literary Essays*, ed. J. M. Robson and Jack Stillinger, *Collected Works of John Stuart Mill*, London: University of Toronto Press/Routledge and Kegan Paul, vol. 1, pp. 1–290.

—(1981b), 'Macaulay's *Lays of Ancient Rome*', in *Autobiography and Literary Essays*, ed. J. M. Robson and Jack Stillinger, *Collected Works of John Stuart Mill*, London: University of Toronto Press/Routledge and Kegan Paul, vol. 1, pp. 523–32.

—(2008a), *Considerations on Representative Government*, in *On Liberty and Other Essays*, ed. John Gray, Oxford: Oxford University Press, pp. 205–467.

—(2008b), *On Liberty*, in *On Liberty and Other Essays*, ed. John Gray, Oxford: Oxford University Press, pp. 5–128.

Miller, Andrew H. (1995), *Novels Behind Glass: Commodity Culture and Victorian Narrative*, Cambridge: Cambridge University Press.

—(2003), 'John Henry Newman, Knowingness, and Victorian Perfectionism', *Texas Studies in Literature and Language*, 45.1, 92–113.

Miller, D. A. (1988), *The Novel and the Police*, Berkeley: University of California Press.

Miller, Dale E. (2000), 'John Stuart Mill's Civic Liberalism', *History of Political Thought*, 21.1, 88–113.

Miller, J. Hillis (1968), *The Form of Victorian Fiction: Thackeray, Dickens, Trollope, George Eliot, Meredith, and Hardy*, Notre Dame: University of Notre Dame Press.

—(2001), 'Anthony Trollope: Ideology as Other in *Marion Fay*', in *Others*, Princeton: Princeton University Press, pp. 83–103.

—(2005), 'Henry James and "Focalisation", or Why James Loves Gyp', in James Phelan and Peter J. Rabinowitz (eds), *A Companion to Narrative Theory*, Oxford: Blackwell, pp. 124–35.

—(2015), *Communities in Fiction*, New York: Fordham University Press.
Miller, J. Hillis, and Manuel Asensi (1999), *Black Holes: J. Hillis Miller or Boustrophedonic Reading*, Stanford: Stanford University Press.
Miller, Nancy K. (1980), *The Heroine's Text: Readings in the French and English Novel*, New York: Columbia University Press.
Milnes, Richard Monckton (1867), 'On the Present Social Results of Classical Education', in Frederic William Farrar (ed.), *Essays on a Liberal Education*, London: Macmillan, pp. 365–84.
Milton, John (2007), *Paradise Lost*, ed. Alastair Fowler, London: Longman.
Mohamed, Feisal G. (2010), 'Poignancy as Human Rights Aesthetic', *Journal of Human Rights*, 9.2, 143–60.
Montégut, Émile (1858), 'Le Roman de Mœurs en Angleterre', *Revue des Deux Mondes*, 756–88.
Morley, John, and Mrs Humphry Ward (1883), 'Anthony Trollope', *Macmillan's Magazine*, 49.289, 47–56.
Mullen, Richard (1990), *Anthony Trollope: A Victorian in His World*, London: Duckworth.
Murphy, James H. (2011), 'Frenzied Form: The Land-War Novel', in *Irish Novelists and the Victorian Age*, Oxford: Oxford University Press, pp. 167–92.
Musil, Robert (1997), *The Man without Qualities*, trans. Sophie Wilkins and Burton Pike, London: Picador.
Myers, Janet C. (2009), *Antipodal England: Emigration and Portable Domesticity in the Victorian Imagination*, ed. Pamela K. Gilbert, Albany, NY: SUNY Press.
Nardin, Jane (1989), *He Knew She Was Right: The Independent Woman in the Novels of Anthony Trollope*, Carbondale and Edwardsville: Southern Illinois University Press.
—(1990), 'The Social Critic in Anthony Trollope's Novels', *Studies in English Literature*, 30.4, 679–96.
—(1996), *Trollope & Victorian Moral Philosophy*, Athens: Ohio University Press.
—(1999), 'Marion Fay', in R. C. Terry (ed.), *Oxford Reader's Companion to Trollope*, Oxford: Oxford University Press, pp. 347–9.
Newman, John Henry (1961), *The Letters and Diaries of John Henry Newman*, ed. Charles Stephen Dessain and Thomas Gornall, 32 vols, Oxford: Clarendon Press.
Northcote, Sir Stafford, and Charles Trevelyan (1855), *Papers on the Re-Organisation of the Civil Service. Presented to Both Houses of Parliament by Command of Her Majesty*, London: George E. Eyre and William Spottiswoode.
Ó Gráda, Cormac (1994), *Ireland: A New Economic History, 1780–1939*, Oxford: Clarendon Press.
O'Sullivan, Timothy M. (2011), *Walking in Roman Culture*, Cambridge: Cambridge University Press.
Olsen, Erik J. (2006), *Civic Republicanism and the Properties of Democracy: A Case Study of Post-Socialist Political Theory*, Lanham, MD: Lexington Books.
Osborne, Hugh (2001), 'Hooked on Classics: Discourses of Allusion in the Mid-Victorian Novel', in Roger Ellis and Liz Oakley-Brown (eds), *Translation and a Nation: Towards a Cultural Politics of Englishness*, Clevedon: Multilingual Matters, pp. 120–66.

Østermark-Johansen, Lene (2009), 'Frieze: Getting beneath the Surface of the Past in Aestheticist Painting and Writing', *Victorian Studies*, 52.1, 20–30.
Otter, Chris (2008), *The Victorian Eye: A Political History of Light and Vision in Britain, 1800–1910*, Chicago: University of Chicago Press.
Overton, Bill (1982), *The Unofficial Trollope*, Brighton: Harvester Press.
Parry, Jonathan (1993), *The Rise and Fall of Liberal Government in Victorian Britain*, New Haven, CT: Yale University Press.
—(2006), *The Politics of Patriotism: English Liberalism, National Identity and Europe, 1830–1886*, Cambridge: Cambridge University Press.
Paulson, Ronald (1967), *The Fictions of Satire*, Baltimore: Johns Hopkins University Press.
Perkin, J. Russell (2009), *Theology and the Victorian Novel*, Montreal and Kingston: McGill-Queen's University Press.
Petch, Simon (1997), 'Law, Equity, and Conscience in Victorian England', *Victorian Literature and Culture*, 25.1, 123–39.
—(2007), 'Law, Literature, and Victorian Studies', *Victorian Literature and Culture*, 35.1, 361–84.
Peters, Julie Stone (2005), 'Law, Literature, and the Vanishing Real: On the Future of an Interdisciplinary Illusion', *PMLA*, 120.2, 442–53.
Pettitt, Clare (2005), 'Legal Subjects, Legal Objects: The Law and Victorian Fiction', in Francis O'Gorman (ed.), *A Concise Companion to the Victorian Novel*, Malden, MA: Blackwell, pp. 71–90.
Piggott, Gillian (2012), *Dickens and Benjamin: Moments of Revelation, Fragments of Modernity*, Aldershot: Ashgate.
Piper, Andrew (2010), 'Paraphrasis: Goethe, the Novella, and Forms of Translational Knowledge', *Goethe Yearbook*, 17, 179–201.
Plotz, John (2011), 'Provincial Semi-Detachment', *Victorian Studies*, 53.3, 405–16.
Polhemus, Robert M. (1968), *The Changing World of Anthony Trollope*, Berkeley and Los Angeles: University of California Press.
—(1982), 'Being in Love in *Phineas Finn/Phineas Redux*: Desire, Devotion, Consolation', *Nineteenth-Century Fiction*, 37.3, 383–95.
Poovey, Mary (1995), *Making a Social Body: British Cultural Formation, 1830–1864*, Chicago: University of Chicago Press.
Pope-Hennessy, James (1971), *Anthony Trollope*, London: Jonathan Cape.
Price, Leah (2012), *How to Do Things with Books in Victorian Britain*, Princeton: Princeton University Press.
Prins, Yopie (1999), *Victorian Sappho*, Princeton: Princeton University Press.
Rae, John (1989), 'Introduction', in Anthony Trollope, *Dr Wortle's School*, ed. David Skilton, London: The Trollope Society, pp. vii–xiv.
Redfield, Marc (1999), 'Imagi-Nation: The Imagined Community and the Aesthetics of Mourning', *Diacritics*, 29.4, 58–83.
Reeve, A. J. H. (2011), 'Arnold, Thomas (1795–1842)', *Oxford Dictionary of National Biography*, <http://www.oxforddnb.com/view/article/5960>, accessed 2 January 2013.
Remer, Gary (2010), 'The Classical Orator as Political Representative: Cicero and the Modern Concept of Representation', *The Journal of Politics*, 72.4, 1063–82.
Robbins, Bruce (2007), *Upward Mobility and the Common Good: Toward a Literary History of the Welfare State*, Princeton: Princeton University Press.

Rodensky, Lisa (2003), *The Crime in Mind: Criminal Responsibility and the Victorian Novel*, New York: Oxford University Press.

Rosa, Richard (2012), 'Finance and Literature in Nineteenth-Century Spanish America', *PMLA*, 127.1, 137–44.

Rosenheim, Edward W. (1963), *Swift and the Satirist's Art*, Chicago: University of Chicago Press.

Rosner, Mary (1986), 'Reflections on Cicero in Nineteenth-Century England and America', *Rhetorica*, 4.2, 153–82.

Rubery, Matthew (2009), *The Novelty of Newspapers: Victorian Fiction after the Invention of the News*, New York: Oxford University Press.

Russell, David James (2012), '"Our Debt to Lamb": The Romantic Essay and the Emergence of Tact', *ELH*, 79.1, 179–209.

—(2013), 'Aesthetic Liberalism: John Stuart Mill as Essayist', *Victorian Studies*, 56.1, 7–30.

Sachs, Jonathan (2009), 'Greece or Rome? The Uses of Antiquity in Late Eighteenth- and Early Nineteenth-Century British Literature', *Literature Compass*, 6.2, 314–31.

Sadleir, Michael (1961), *Trollope: A Commentary*, London: Oxford University Press.

Said, Edward W. (2007), *On Late Style: Music and Literature against the Grain*, New York: Vintage Books.

Savage, Robert (2010), 'The Polemic of the Late Work', in Gerhard Richter (ed.), *Language without Soil*, New York: Fordham University Press, pp. 172–94.

Schama, Chloe (2010), *Wild Romance: The True Story of a Victorian Scandal*, London: Bloomsbury.

Schiller, Friedrich (1861), 'On the Pathetic', in *Schiller's Complete Works*, ed. Charles J. Hempel, Philadelphia: Kohler, vol. 2, pp. 478–86.

Schmitt, Cannon (2009), 'Rumor, Shares, and Novelistic Form: Joseph Conrad's *Nostromo*', in Nancy Henry and Cannon Schmitt (eds), *Victorian Investments: New Perspectives on Finance and Culture*, Bloomington and Indianapolis: Indiana University Press, pp. 182–201.

Schramm, Jan-Melissa (2000), *Testimony and Advocacy in Victorian Law, Literature, and Theology*, Cambridge: Cambridge University Press.

—(2012), *Atonement and Self-Sacrifice in Nineteenth-Century Narrative*, Cambridge: Cambridge University Press.

Sennett, Richard (1976), *The Fall of Public Man*, New York: Norton.

Shuman, Cathy (2000), *Pedagogical Economies: The Examination and the Victorian Literary Man*, Stanford: Stanford University Press.

Siddle, Yvonne (2004), 'Anthony Trollope's Representation of the Great Famine', in Peter Gray (ed.), *Victoria's Ireland? Irishness and Britishness, 1837–1901*, Dublin: Four Courts Press, pp. 141–50.

Skilton, David (1973), '*The Fixed Period*: Anthony Trollope's Novel of 1980', *Studies in the Literary Imagination*, 6.2, 39–50.

—(1988), 'Schoolboy Latin and the Mid-Victorian Novelist: A Study in Reader Competence', *Browning Institute Studies*, 16, 39–55.

—(1993), 'Introduction', in Anthony Trollope, *The Fixed Period*, ed. David Skilton, Oxford: Oxford University Press, pp. vii–xix.

—(1996), *Anthony Trollope and His Contemporaries: A Study in the Theory and Conventions of Mid-Victorian Fiction*, Basingstoke: Macmillan.

—(1998), 'Introduction', in Anthony Trollope, *An Old Man's Love*, ed. David Skilton, London: The Trollope Society, pp. vii–xv.

—(2007), 'The Centrality of Literary Illustration in Victorian Visual Culture: The Example of Millais and Trollope from 1860 to 1864', *Journal of Illustration Studies*, <http://jois.uia.no/articles.php?article=30>, accessed 24 April 2015.

—(2010), 'The Construction of Masculinities', in Carolyn Dever and Lisa Niles (eds), *The Cambridge Companion to Anthony Trollope*, Cambridge: Cambridge University Press, pp. 128–41.

Skinner, Quentin (1998), *Liberty before Liberalism*, Oxford: Oxford University Press.

Small, Helen (2003), 'Liberal Editing in the *Fortnightly Review* and the *Nineteenth Century*', *Publishing History*, 53, 74–96.

—(2007), *The Long Life*, Oxford: Oxford University Press.

—(2011), 'The Forms of Liberalism', *Victorian Studies*, 53.2, 287–302.

—(2012), 'Against Self-Interest: Trollope and Realism', *Essays in Criticism*, 62.4, 396–416.

Smalley, Donald (ed.) (1969), *Trollope: The Critical Heritage*, London: Routledge.

Smith, Josiah (1845), *A Manual of Equity Jurisprudence*, London: Stevens and Norton.

Snyder, John (1991), *Prospects of Power: Tragedy, Satire, the Essay, and the Theory of Genre*, Lexington: University Press of Kentucky.

Spitzer, Michael (2006), *Music as Philosophy: Adorno and Beethoven's Late Style*, Bloomington: Indiana University Press.

Starck, Nigel (2014), *The First Celebrity: Anthony Trollope's Australasian Odyssey*, Bath: Landsdown Media.

Stephen, James Fitzjames (1861), *Edinburgh Review*, 114.232, 456–86.

Stevenson, Angus (ed.) (2010), *Oxford English Dictionary: Third Edition*, Oxford: Oxford University Press.

Stewart, Garrett (2000), 'The Foreign Offices of British Fiction', *Modern Language Quarterly*, 61.1, 181–206.

Stryker, David (1950), 'The Significance of Trollope's "American Senator"', *Nineteenth-Century Fiction*, 5.2, 141–9.

Super, R. H. (1985), 'Introduction', in Anthony Trollope, *Marion Fay*, ed. R. H. Super, Ann Arbor: University of Michigan Press, pp. v–xx.

—(1990), *The Chronicler of Barsetshire: A Life of Anthony Trollope*, Ann Arbor: University of Michigan Press.

—(1992a), 'Introduction', in Anthony Trollope, *The Landleaguers*, ed. R. H. Super, Ann Arbor: University of Michigan Press, pp. v–xii.

—(1992b), 'Explanatory Notes', in Anthony Trollope, *The Landleaguers*, ed. R. H. Super, Ann Arbor: University of Michigan Press, pp. 335–41.

Sussman, Matthew (2013), 'Trollope's Honesty', *SEL*, 53.4, 877–95.

Sutherland, John (1982), 'Trollope at Work on *The Way We Live Now*', *Nineteenth-Century Fiction*, 37.3, 472–93.

Swingle, L. J. (1991), *Romanticism and Anthony Trollope: A Study in the Continuities of Nineteenth-Century Literary Thought*, Ann Arbor: University of Michigan Press.

Taylor, George (1828), *The Eton Latin Grammar: In the Order and Arrangement of Which, an Attempt Is Made to Engage the Attention, Quicken the Research, and Assist the Memory of the Learner*, London: Longman, Rees, Orme, Brown, Green, Whittaker, and Swinborne and Walter.

Taylor, Jenny Bourne (2009), 'Bastards to the Time: Legitimacy as Legal

Fiction in Trollope's Novels of the 1870s', in Margaret Markwick, Deborah Denenholz Morse, and Regenia Gagnier (eds), *The Politics of Gender in Anthony Trollope's Novels: New Readings for the Twenty-First Century*, Aldershot: Ashgate, pp. 45–59.

Taylor, Rober H. (1947), 'The Manuscript of Trollope's *The American Senator*. Collated with the First Edition', *Bibliographical Society of America Papers*, 41, 123–9.

Terry, R. C. (1977), *Anthony Trollope: The Artist in Hiding*, Totowa, NJ: Rowman & Littlefield.

—(1987), *Anthony Trollope: Interviews and Recollections*, Basingstoke: Macmillan.

Test, George A. (1991), *Satire: Spirit and Art*, Tampa: University of South Florida Press.

Thackeray, William Makepeace (1904), *Works*, 20 vols, New York: Charles Scribner's Sons.

Thomas, David Wayne (2004), *Cultivating Victorians: Liberal Culture and the Aesthetic*, Philadelphia: University of Pennsylvania Press.

Tracy, Robert (1978), *Trollope's Later Novels*, Berkeley: University of California Press.

—(1981), 'Introduction', in Anthony Trollope, *The Landleaguers*, New York: Arno, n. pag.

Trevelyan, Charles (1848), *The Irish Crisis*, London: Longman, Brown, Green & Longmans.

Trollope, Anthony (1856), review of Charles Merivale, *The History of the Romans under the Empire*, *Dublin University Magazine*, 30–47.

—(1865a), review of John Ruskin, *Sesame and Lilies. Two Lectures delivered at Manchester in 1864*, *The Fortnightly Review*, 1, 633–5.

—(1865b), 'Public Schools', *The Fortnightly Review*, 2, 476–87.

—(1865c), 'The Zulu in London', *Pall Mall Gazette*, 10 May, 3–4.

—(1866), 'The Fourth Commandment', *The Fortnightly Review*, 3.17, 529–38.

—(1868), 'On Hunting', in *British Sports and Pastimes*, London: Virtue, pp. 70–129.

—(1869), 'Mr Freeman on the Morality of Hunting', *The Fortnightly Review*, 6.36, 616–25.

—(1870a), review of *Ancient Classics for English Readers*, *Saint Paul's Magazine*, 5, 664–8.

—(1870b), *The Commentaries of Caesar*, in *Ancient Classics for English Readers*, ed. W. Lucas Collins, Edinburgh and London: William Blackwood and Sons.

—(1877a), 'Cicero as a Politician', *The Fortnightly Review*, 21.124, 495–515.

—(1877b), 'Cicero as a Man of Letters', *The Fortnightly Review*, 22.129, 401–22.

—(1878), *How the 'Mastiffs' Went to Iceland*, London: Virtue.

—(1879a), 'A Walk in a Wood', *Good Words*, 20, 595–600.

—(1879b), *Thackeray*, in *English Men of Letters*, ed. John Morley, London: Macmillan.

—(1880), *The Life of Cicero*, 2 vols, London: Chapman and Hall.

—(1938), 'The Higher Education of Women', in *Four Lectures*, ed. Morris Longstreth Parrish, London: Constable, pp. 67–88.

—(1951), *North America*, New York: Knopf.

—(1983), *The Letters of Anthony Trollope*, ed. N. John Hall, Stanford: Stanford University Press.
—(1985), *Marion Fay: A Novel*, ed. R. H. Super, Ann Arbor: University of Michigan Press.
—(1987), *The Irish Famine: Six Letters to the Examiner 1849/1850*, ed. Lance O. Tingay, London: Silverbridge Press.
—(1989a), *Can You Forgive Her?*, ed. David Skilton, London: The Trollope Society.
—(1989b), *Ayala's Angel*, London: The Trollope Society.
—(1989c), *Dr Wortle's School*, ed. David Skilton, London: The Trollope Society.
—(1990–4), *The Complete Short Stories*, ed. Betty Breyer, 5 vols, London: The Trollope Society.
—(1992), *The Way We Live Now*, ed. David Skilton, London: The Trollope Society.
—(1993a), *The Bertrams*, ed. David Skilton, London: The Trollope Society.
—(1993b), *Cousin Henry*, ed. David Skilton, London: The Trollope Society.
—(1994), *The Claverings*, ed. David Skilton, London: The Trollope Society.
—(1995a), *The Landleaguers*, ed. David Skilton, London: The Trollope Society.
—(1995b), *John Caldigate*, ed. David Skilton, London: The Trollope Society.
—(1997), *The Fixed Period*, ed. David Skilton, London: The Trollope Society.
—(1998a), *An Old Man's Love*, ed. David Skilton, London: The Trollope Society.
—(1998b), *Is He Popenjoy?*, ed. David Skilton, London: The Trollope Society.
—(1998c), *Mr Scarborough's Family*, ed. David Skilton, London: The Trollope Society.
—(1999a), *An Autobiography*, ed. Michael Sadleir and Frederick Page, Oxford: Oxford University Press.
—(1999b), *The American Senator*, ed. John Halperin, Oxford: Oxford University Press.
—(2002), *Australia and New Zealand*, 2 vols, London: The Trollope Society.
—(2003), *Lord Palmerston*, London: The Trollope Society.
—(2004), *Framley Parsonage*, ed. Peter Miles and David Skilton, Harmondsworth: Penguin.
—(2005), *The Small House at Allington*, ed. Julian Thompson, Harmondsworth: Penguin.
—(2011), *The Duke's Children*, Oxford: Oxford University Press.
Trollope, Henry (1875), 'The French Theatre under Louis XIV', *Macmillan's Magazine*, 31, 522–32.
Trotter, Jackson (1992), 'Foxhunting and the English Social Order in Trollope's *the American Senator*', *Studies in the Novel*, 24.3, 227–41.
Tucker, Irene (2000), *A Probable State: The Novel, the Contract, and the Jews*, Chicago: University of Chicago Press.
Turner, Frank M. (1981), *The Greek Heritage in Victorian Britain*, New Haven, CT: Yale University Press.
—(1982), 'Antiquity in Victorian Contexts', *Browning Institute Studies*, 10, 1–14.
—(1986), 'British Politics and the Demise of the Roman Republic: 1700–1939', *The Historical Journal*, 29.3, 577–99.
—(1989), 'Why the Greeks and Not the Romans in Victorian Britain?', in

G. W. Clarke (ed.), *Rediscovering Hellenism: The Hellenic Inheritance and the English Imagination*, Cambridge: Cambridge University Press, pp. 61–81.
Van, Annette (2005), 'Ambivalent Speculations: America as England's Future in *The Way We Live Now*', *Novel: A Forum on Fiction*, 39.1, 75–96.
Van Dam, Frederik (2015), 'Allegorical Landscapes: The Psychology of Seeing in Anthony Trollope's Later Novels', in Laurence Grove and Simon Grennan (eds), *Transforming Anthony Trollope: Dispossession, Victorianism and Nineteenth-Century Word and Image*, Leuven: Leuven University Press, pp. 71–87.
Vance, Norman (1997), *The Victorians and Ancient Rome*, Oxford: Blackwell.
—(2004), 'Farrar, Frederic William (1831–1903)', *Oxford Dictionary of National Biography*, <http://www.oxforddnb.com/view/article/33088>, accessed 6 December 2012.
—(2011), 'Anxieties of Empire and the Moral Tradition: Rome and Britain', *International Journal of the Classical Tradition*, 18.2, 246–61.
Vasunia, Phiroze (2003), *The Classics and Colonial India*, Oxford: Oxford University Press.
—(2005), 'Greater Rome and Greater Britain', in Barbara E. Goff (ed.), *Classics and Colonialism*, London: Duckworth, pp. 38–64.
Vermeulen, Pieter (2009), 'Community and Literary Experience in (between) Benedict Anderson and Jean-Luc Nancy', *Mosaic*, 42.4, 96–112.
Wall, Stephen (1988), *Trollope and Character*, London: Faber and Faber.
Warner, Michael (2002), *Publics and Counterpublics*, New York: Zone Books.
Watson, George (1973), 'Trollope's Forms of Address', *Critical Quarterly*, 15.3, 219–30.
Weber, Samuel (2008), 'God and the Devil – in Detail', in *Benjamin's -abilities*, Cambridge, MA: Harvard University Press, pp. 240–9.
Willey, Basil (1969), *More Nineteenth Century Studies: A Group of Honest Doubters*, New York: Columbia University Press.
Williams, Carolyn (2011), *Gilbert and Sullivan: Gender, Genre, Parody*, New York: Columbia University Press.
Wolf, Werner (2004), 'Aesthetic Illusion as an Effect of Fiction', *Style*, 38.3, 325–51.
Wolfreys, Julian (2012), *Dickens's London: Perception, Subjectivity and Phenomenal Urban Multiplicity*, Edinburgh: Edinburgh University Press.
Wolfreys, Julian, Ruth Robbins, and Kenneth Womack (2006), *Key Concepts in Literary Theory*, Edinburgh: Edinburgh University Press.
Woolf, Virginia (1966a), 'On Not Knowing Greek', in *Collected Essays*, ed. Leonard Woolf, London: The Hogarth Press, vol. 1, pp. 1–13.
—(1966b), 'Phases of Fiction', in *Collected Essays*, ed. Leonard Woolf, London: The Hogarth Press, vol. 4, pp. 56–102.
Wordsworth, William (1990), *Poems, in Two Volumes, and Other Poems, 1800–1807*, ed. Jared Curtis, Ithaca, NY: Cornell University Press.

Index